THIRD EDITION

WEB-BASED INSTRUCTION

A GUIDE FOR LIBRARIES

SUSAN SHARPLESS SMITH

AMERICAN LIBRARY ASSOCIATION
CHICAGO   2010

*ALA Editions purchases fund advocacy,
awareness, and accreditation programs for
library professionals worldwide.*

Susan Sharpless Smith is director of research, instruction, and technology services for Z. Smith Reynolds Library, Wake Forest University, in Winston-Salem, North Carolina. Her long-term interests have been in exploring the potential the Web offers for the provision of library services and instruction. In her current position, she has had the opportunity to experiment with the use of Web 2.0 technologies to enhance the educational experience by focusing on approaching instruction from the online social networking skills that students bring to class. She received the 2008 Association of College and Research Libraries' Instruction Section Innovation Award for her work as an embedded librarian in a two-week sociology course that traveled by bus through the Deep South. Smith received a master's degree in library and information studies from the University of North Carolina–Greensboro and a master's degree in educational technology leadership from George Washington University.

While extensive effort has gone into ensuring the reliability of the information in this book, the publisher makes no warranty, express or implied, with respect to the material contained herein.

Library of Congress Cataloging-in-Publication Data
Smith, Susan Sharpless.
   Web-based instruction : a guide for libraries / Susan Sharpless Smith. -- 3rd ed.
      p. cm.
   Includes bibliographical references and index.
   ISBN 978-0-8389-1056-6 (alk. paper)
   1. Library orientation—Computer-assisted instruction. 2. Web sites—Design. 3. Library Web sites—Design. 4. Web-based instruction. 5. Libraries and the Internet. I. Title.
   Z711.2.S59 2010
   025.5'60785--dc22

                                                                    2010006452

ISBN-13: 978-0-8389-1056-6

Printed in the United States of America
14 13 12 11 10   5 4 3 2 1

Book design in Melior and Museo Sans by Casey Bayer

♾ This paper meets the requirements of ANSI/NISO Z39.48-1992 (Permanence of Paper).

ALA Editions also publishes its books in a variety of electronic formats. For more information, visit the ALA Store at www.alastore.ala.org and select eEditions.

CONTENTS

Additional material can be found on this book's website, at www.ala.org/editions/extras/smith10566.

ABBREVIATIONS

ADC	analog-to-digital converter
AIFF	Audio Interchange File Format
AJAX	asynchronous JavaScript + XML
API	application program interface
ASP	Active Server Page
AU	Audio File Format
AVI	Audio-Video Interleave
BMP	bitmap
CBI	computer-based instruction
CCD	charge-coupled device
CD-ROM	compact disc—read-only memory
CD-RW	compact disc—rewritable
CGI	Common Gateway Interface
CIS	contact image sensor
CMS	course management system
CMS	content management software (or system)
codec	compressor/decompressor
COM	Component Object Model
CPU	central processing unit
CRT	cathode-ray tube
CSS	Cascading Style Sheets
CSS-P	Cascading Style Sheets positioning
DAC	digital-to-analog converter
dHTML	Dynamic HTML
DOM	Document Object Model
dpi	dots per inch

DSL	digital subscriber line
DV	digital video
DVD	digital video disc
FTP	File Transfer Protocol
GB	gigabyte
GHz	gigahertz
GIF	Graphics Interchange Format
HCI	human-computer interaction
HTML	Hypertext Markup Language
IE	Internet Explorer
IIS	Internet Information Server
IM	instant messaging
ISD	Instructional Systems Design
ISP	Internet service provider
IT	information technology
JPEG, JPG	Joint Photographic Experts Group
JSP	JavaServer Page
LAMP	Linux, Apache, MySQL, PHP (or Perl, or Python)
LCD	liquid crystal display
LED	light emitting diode
LiOn	lithium ion
LMS	learning management system
MB	megabyte
MHz	megahertz
MIDI	Musical Instrument Digital Interface
MNG	Multiple-Image Network Graphics
MOO	Multiuser Domain, Object Oriented
MPEG	Moving Pictures Expert Group
MP3	MPEG-1 Audio Layer-3
NIC	network interface card
NiCad	nickel cadmium
NiMH	nickel metal hydride
OCR	optical character recognition
OPL	Open Publication License
OS	operating system
PC	personal computer (IBM compatible)
PCI	Peripheral Component Interconnect
PCMCIA	Personal Computer Memory Card International Association
PDA	personal digital assistant
PDF	Portable Document Format
Perl	Practical Extraction and Report Language
PFR	Portable Font Resource
PHP	(Personal Home Page) PHP Hypertext Processor

PNG	Portable Network Graphics
ppi	pixels per inch
RAM	random access memory
RSS	Really Simple Syndication/Rich Site Summary
SCORM	Shareable Content Object Reference Model
SCSI	Small Computer System Interface
SD	Secure Digital
SDHC	Secure Digital High Capacity
SGML	Standard Generalized Markup Language
SMIL	Synchronized Multimedia Integration Language
SVG	Scalable Vector Graphics
SVGA	Super Video Graphics Array
SXGA	Super Extended Graphics Array
Tcl	Tool Command Language
TIFF	Tagged Image File Format
Tk	Tool Kit
3-D	three dimensional
UID	user interface design
URL	uniform resource locator
USB	Universal Serial Bus
UXGA	Ultra Extended Graphics Array
VGA	Video Graphics Array
VHS	Video Home System
VHS-C	Compact VHS
VoIP	Voice over Internet Protocol
VRML	Virtual Reality Modeling Language
W3C	World Wide Web Consortium
WAV	Waveform Audio File Format
WBI	web-based instruction
WMA	Windows Media Audio
WWW	World Wide Web
WYSIWYG	what you see is what you get
X3D	Extensible 3-D Graphics
XGA	Extended Graphics Array
XHTML	Extensible Hypertext Markup Language
XML	Extensible Markup Language
XP	Extreme Programming
XSL	Extensible Stylesheet Language
XSL-FO	Extensible Stylesheet Language-Formatting Objects
XSLT	Extensible Stylesheet Language Transformation

ACKNOWLEDGMENTS

SINCE THE SECOND edition of this book was published, significant changes have occurred not only in Web instruction technology but in the publishing world as well. These changes ensured that the third edition of *Web Based Instruction: A Guide for Libraries* would benefit from a different approach, so readers will find changes not only in subject coverage but also in the addition of a Web component to facilitate a closer connection to the Web content discussed. Thanks go to ALA Acquisitions Editor Christopher Rhodes for his assistance in helping me establish a framework for these changes. Copyeditor Katherine Faydash has done a wonderful job shaping my words into better expression and meaning.

My long-distance bicycle training rides are where I worked through idea development and writer's block. Thanks to my colleague and training partner, Erik Mitchell, for listening as we rode those long miles and for providing valuable input on a wide range of technology topics as well as helping to shape ideas into words.

The bulk of my writing took place over almost a year of nights and weekends. As before, I continue to depend on my family members, Ron, Sarah, Josh, and Nancy for moral and domestic support. Since the last edition, we have a new family member, four-year-old Meredith, who offers a special type of motivation that only comes from a granddaughter!

INTRODUCTION

WELCOME TO THE third edition of *Web-Based Instruction: A Guide for Libraries.* When the first edition was published in 2001, the Web was still in its infancy. In the four years since the second edition was published, the Web has become a key avenue for the delivery of services by all types of libraries and is leading to major changes in teaching and learning. This introduction to the third edition reviews why web-based instruction has reached the mainstream in education and why it is now a given in designing library instruction—and why a revision of this book is in order.

TRADITIONAL LIBRARY INSTRUCTION IS NO LONGER ENOUGH

There are common themes that appear in discussions about traditional library instruction, originally referred to as bibliographic instruction. Historically, library instruction was designed to teach library users how to use the library and its resources effectively. For years, however, the goals of library instruction have expanded to a more comprehensive concept—information literacy—which the Association of College and Resource Libraries (ACRL 2000) defines as the "set of abilities requiring individuals to 'recognize when information is needed and have the ability to locate, evaluate, and use effectively the needed information.'" Today's information environment has become complex, and libraries recognize this. It's not enough to teach students about finding and evaluating traditional print library resources, electronic databases and journals, and web resources. The explosion of information on the Web, coupled with technological advances taking place at the speed of light, presents a critical need to teach learners other skills necessary to be successful members of the information society. Although ACRL standards served library instruction adequately, other metaliteracy models have been developed that address the need more broadly. One example of such a model is the Shapiro and Hughes (1996) prototype in which they define literacy as consisting of seven distinct areas:

1. *Tool literacy:* the ability to understand and use the practical and conceptual tools of current information technology, including software, hardware, and multimedia, which are relevant to education and professional life.

2. *Resource literacy:* the ability to understand the form, format, location, and methods of accessing information resources.

3. *Social-structural literacy:* the knowledge that information is socially situated and produced, including how it fits into the life of groups (e.g., institutions and social networks).

4. *Research literacy:* the ability to understand and use the IT-based tools relevant to the work of today's scholars and their research.

5. *Publishing literacy:* the ability to format and publish research and ideas electronically and in electronic communities.

6. *Emerging technology literacy:* the ability to adapt to, understand, evaluate, and make use of the continually emerging innovations in information technology.

7. *Critical literacy:* the ability to evaluate critically the intellectual, human, and social strengths and weaknesses, potentials and limits, and benefits and costs of information technologies. This literacy includes different perspectives: historical, philosophical, sociopolitical, and cultural.

These multiple literacies are all ones that are natural fits for library instruction and appropriate goals of a comprehensive instruction program. Other factors should also be considered when designing an instruction program:

- Today's students have grown up as digital natives, and as such, their understanding of the world has come primarily from digital sources. This fact has enormous implications for how these learners acquire and process information and for the best methods to teach them (Mabrito and Medley 2008).
- Demographics change, and libraries are finding that their constituencies have transformed. In a 2007 survey by the American

Library Association, 78 percent of public libraries reported Spanish as the number-one language for which they develop services and programs, with Asian languages ranked second, at 29 percent (ALA Office for Research and Statistics 2007). Students who are not native English speakers may find it especially difficult to retain all that is taught in a face-to-face class.

- Many libraries now support distance-education programs and must design instruction to reach out to those students, who may be dispersed globally and of diverse cultures.

These situations present challenges to providing effective library instruction and opportunities to find creative solutions.

WHY USE THE WEB FOR LIBRARY INSTRUCTION?

Today, we live in a web world. The Web is no longer a medium limited to a certain population or use. It has become part of our daily lives. The advent of Web 2.0, or the read-write Web (meaning the Web that allows users to interact and collaborate), has changed our lives so that we all can be participants in conversations that are taking place all over the world. The capabilities of the Web are changing the fabric of our everyday lives and are doing the same in the world of education. The positive aspects of delivering library instruction through the use of web technologies that have existed since the Web's early days are still true: library skills can be taught to a large number of students, the web can be interactive, there are no limitations of time or space, and it is available 24/7. Web technologies have evolved past the early tutorial model, which was a self-contained, static, instructional website that required that the author have programming skills to add interactivity. There is no longer a question of instructors having to choose between face-to-face versus online instruction. Research has shown that there is no significant difference in learning between face-to-face and online instruction. And instruction librarians have many options for blended learning that combine both methods.

WHICH TYPES OF WEB-BASED INSTRUCTION ARE APPROPRIATE?

Unless you and your users are in an environment that does not have Internet connectivity, there are viable options and good reasons for incorporating some level of web-based library instruction. Chapter 1 presents some of those reasons. It's important to understand your institution's mission to decide what type of web-based instruction supports that mission. For example, if your institution places a high value on classroom instruction, not only in the library but also throughout the campus, then instruction conducted solely online may be inappropriate for that environment. Basic roadblocks such as inadequate infrastructure at your institution may be a legitimate reason to consider other ways to incorporate web-based instruction, perhaps by turning to the cloud (web-based services). The availability of free web-based services such as Google Docs, Blogger, and Wikispaces has expanded web-based instruction possibilities considerably for those who do not have a good institutional infrastructure in place.

THE EFFECTIVENESS OF WEB-BASED INSTRUCTION

Before embarking into the realm of designing web-based instruction, you may well ask about the effectiveness of such instruction. A review of the literature on the effectiveness of computer-based instruction (CBI) in general and its value in delivering library instruction specifically is reassuring. In almost every study reviewed, neither the face-to-face nor the CBI delivery method was found to be significantly different from the other.

An interesting resource to consult is Thomas Russell's (1999) annotated bibliography on distance-education technology *The No Significant Difference Phenomenon*. Russell decided more than a decade ago to document the fact that technology improved instruction. Instead, he found that, in most studies, no statistically significant difference could be claimed to support that technology improved or caused a decline in effective instruction. In this compilation of results from studies on whether technology improves instruction, Russell cites 355 studies that support his finding of no significant difference. He concludes that technology doesn't denigrate instruction, which, in essence, opens up our choices for selecting the type of instruction that works best for our institutions and missions. Russell's website presents citations of studies done after the publication of the book (www.nosignificantdifference.org).

WHAT'S NEW AND DIFFERENT SINCE THE SECOND EDITION?

The second edition of *Web-Based Instruction: A Guide for Libraries* was published in 2006. At that writing, glimpses of the Web 2.0 phenomenon that has now changed the landscape of the Internet were just starting to emerge. Prior to the availability of social networking with collaborative or participatory capabilities and the advent of easy-to-create user content, web instruction was more commonly a method to deliver instruction, unless you possessed the programming skills to build in interaction. Web 2.0 has made web instruction authoring much more mainstream, and in 2010, Web 2.0 skills can almost be considered a core competency for new librarians entering the profession. This puts web-based instruction in the hands of the practitioner, who no longer must depend totally on the technologist.

In this edition, chapters are still ordered in the process that a web project would unfold. Rather than isolating old-technology tutorial information from new-technology Web 2.0 information, both are interwoven throughout the various chapters. There is a place in web-based instruction for both approaches. For instance, the sort of web project that would have produced a stand-alone instructional tutorial still is seen extensively in reusable-learning-object repositories. Many of the communication interactions are now easily implemented using Web 2.0 tools, and multimedia production has become approachable for the average person. Both ends of the spectrum have their place in the discussions that take place in this third edition of the book.

Because the Web is fluid, it is difficult to write a technology-centric print book that doesn't become dated before it is released. Technologies change, as do URLs, resulting in inaccuracies for readers. Two changes have been made in this edition to try to minimize this. Screenshots of examples to illustrate topics discussed have been eliminated. Screenshots show just a snapshot in time, and often the interface has changed or the site has been removed by the time of publication. Details are difficult to discern in a small grayscale facsimile of a web page. Instead, a web component has been added to supplement the print version of this book. Located at www.ala .org/editions/extras/smith10566, the site includes links to cited products, technologies, websites, and resources.

Each chapter has been updated as appropriate to reflect new technologies and ideas in web-based instruction. It is gratifying to realize that many of the topics discussed in the first two editions of the book have had staying power and are still relevant today.

In the previous edition, an effort was made to be more inclusive of nonacademic libraries. Although library instruction remains a larger focus for academic libraries because of the nature of their mission, it has a solid place in other types of libraries, as well. However, in this edition, the treatment of topics is more generic, primarily because screenshots are no longer included. I believe that the technologies, pedagogies, processes, and techniques are applicable across the spectrum of library types and that each library best knows what its users require in the way of instruction. All of the material in this edition can be adapted for different instructional needs.

I continue to be in a PC environment and not a Macintosh one. However, with the move of many services to the cloud, platform is becoming less of an issue. Today there are options for development tools that are not client based, and therefore not PC or Mac based. So don't be surprised not to see as much cross-platform discussion, although it is still mentioned when appropriate.

WHAT CAN YOU EXPECT FROM THIS BOOK?

The goal for the third edition of *Web-Based Instruction: A Guide for Libraries* is to help you explore *how* you would like to implement web-based instruction and to guide you through the process. It is still aimed toward the library instruction practitioner who has some basic knowledge of and experience with web-authoring procedures, but it is also aimed at those who are comfortable using Web 2.0 technologies but have not done traditional web authoring and prefer to design instruction using newer technologies. It is important to understand that this is a guidebook, so you will be disappointed if you expect to see in-depth treatment of any of the topics covered. The book is meant to introduce you to a wide range of topics, ideas, and technologies, and it includes an appendix with additional resources and a web supplement that can lead you to more in-depth information on most topics.

This book is organized in the order that planning and executing a web project takes place; therefore, you may encounter an early mention of some technical terms that are fully explained in later chapters, in the sequence of those topics as they would normally take place during a project. Chapter 1 is an overview of concepts relating to web-based learning and pedagogy. Chapter 2 presents best practices and explores the different types of web-based instruction that institutions are creating. Chapter 3 is geared to help you organize a project from start to finish. Chapter 4 presents considerations for selecting development tools for a web project and identifies and assesses potential hardware and software authoring tools. Chapter 5 covers the design of the user experience. We look in detail at the use of multimedia and the importance of interactivity in chapters 6 and 7, which also discuss tools that will help accomplish that use. Chapter 8 focuses on an overview of evaluation, testing, and assessment methods for your project and how to measure student progress. Each chapter includes practical information to ensure that a library instruction web project is a manageable, enriching experience.

CHAPTER ONE

SETTING THE STAGE

CONVERSATIONS ABOUT THE use of educational technology in the classroom and instructive environment take place with regularity. It would be easy for me to take for granted that readers are already well acquainted with the terms and meanings associated with web-based learning. Rather than making that assumption, this chapter introduces and discusses some of the basic concepts that are involved in web-based learning. This chapter is meant to provide not comprehensive coverage of the various topics but a brief introduction. The resources section in the appendix points readers to more in-depth coverage of topics.

HISTORY OF WEB-BASED INSTRUCTION

In the years since the introduction of the World Wide Web in 1993, the use of the Web to deliver instruction has increased immensely. In 1997, Khan first defined web-based instruction (WBI) as "a hypermedia-based instructional program which utilizes the attributes and resources of the World Wide Web to create a meaningful learning environment where learning is fostered and supported" (Khan 1997, 6). However, it may be useful to review where WBI came from in relation to other concepts that preceded it.

When many people first think about web-based instruction, they immediately picture instruction that takes place without the restrictions of time and place. They visualize that, in such instruction, an instructor makes materials available so that students can access them from anywhere and at any time. This model has its beginning in what is traditionally thought of as distance education. Distance education, in some form, has been around for a long time, although it has become known by that name only recently. As it has evolved, so have the factors that define it. Zvacek (2004) specifies the components of distance education:

- physical distance that separates teachers and learners
- use of mechanical or electronic means to deliver content
- interaction between teachers and learners
- the influence of a formal educational organization that outlines the roles of the participants, expectations, and expected outcomes

Using these criteria, it is easy to see the variety of instructional methods that distance education includes: correspondence courses, videotaped classes, and audio classes in which students and instructors communicate by telephone are just a few examples. As technology has advanced and come to be used to deliver distance instruction, improvements in interaction and delivery have followed. Interaction between an instructor and students is much harder to maintain via a print-based correspondence course than it is via Internet technologies. Zvacek (2004) also identifies three guiding principles that frame the purpose of distance education:

1. To provide educational opportunities for unserved or underserved populations

2. To save money (particularly in corporate training)

3. To offer a wider variety of courses to students than would be possible in one physical location

TEACHING WITH WEB-BASED TECHNOLOGY

There are a number of different broad categories that can be considered in discussions of web-based instruction approaches. And the choice of approaches certainly isn't between just face-to-face and distance learning. The common thread among the categories is that computer-based technologies play a central role. The three broad categories to consider are augmented, blended (distributed, hybrid), and online (distance) (Siemens and Tittenberger 2009).

Augmented

In the "augmented" category, web-based instruction is used to extend the physical classroom in order to supplement face-to-face instruction. The online component may be incorporated into activities during class time or used to accomplish assignments outside of scheduled class periods. In this model, students meet with instructors in classrooms on a regular schedule. Some common tools used in this category are online discussion forums, WebQuests, blogs, group work in wikis, and online quizzes.

Blended Learning

You will hear different terms for the second category: *blended, distributed*, and *hybrid learning* are used interchangeably. Blended learning is a method of instructional delivery that includes a mix of web-based instruction, streaming video conferencing, face-to-face classroom time, distance learning through television or video, or other combinations of electronic and traditional educational models. Although blended learning can be implemented in a combination of ways, it always accommodates a separation of geographical locations for part (or all) of the instruction and focuses on learner-to-learner as well as instructor-to-learner interaction. A typical model for blended learning might involve an initial face-to-face orientation followed by a period of online classes and then a face-to-face wrap-up class.

Online Learning

In the "online" or "distance" category, all instruction takes place remotely, either synchronously or asynchronously. Distance learning is often associated with adult learning because it is a model that has the flexibility to fit into busy lives better than traditional models of instruction. For those people with full-time careers and families, there are real benefits to educational opportunities that they can adapt to daily responsibilities. Adults also tend to adapt more readily to the independent structure of distance education and the self-motivation it requires.

THE INTERNET AND THE WEB

The pervasiveness of the Internet has provided the opportunity to expand the capabilities of conducting instruction outside the classroom. According to Internet World Stat's usage statistics (www.internetworldstats.com/stats .htm), as of fall 2009, there were 1.7 billion Internet users worldwide. A 2003 analysis of Internet use by children three years old through grade 12 concluded that 59 percent used the Internet, and for grade 9–12 students only, that figure was 79 percent (DeBell and Chapman 2006). The Educare Center for Applied Research's 2009 Study of Undergraduate Students and Information Technology reported that nine of ten respondents used the

Internet for at least some academic work, and 79.5 percent chose to learn by running Internet searches (Smith, Salaway, and Caruso 2009).

These types of statistics illustrate why the incorporation of web-based instruction is an attractive option. Today's learners are adept at using the Web to discover and learn. The Web holds a number of implications for learning environments and students (Oblinger, Barone, and Hawkins 2001):

Exploration: Today's students use the Web as an exploratory tool to find information and resources.

Experience: The Web offers wide-ranging learning experiences, from synchronous learning to threaded discussions to self-paced study.

Engagement: The Web captivates learners by enabling creative approaches to learning that foster collaboration and sense of community.

Ease of use: The Web is easy to use for both learners and learning providers. Content is platform independent.

Empowerment: The Web allows for tools that enable learners to personalize content and choose the way they learn best.

Effectiveness: A growing body of evidence shows that blended learning can be more effective than classroom lectures.

WHAT IS INCLUDED IN WEB-BASED INSTRUCTION?

Web-based instruction "encompasses the integrated design and delivery of instructional resources via the World Wide Web and promotes student engagement with text-based, hypermedia, multimedia, and collaborative resources for the purposes of teaching and learning" (Bannan-Ritland 2004, 638). As Web technologies have evolved, the possible approaches to design and delivery have expanded considerably. For example, WBI can be used to perform basic support functions, such as the provision of a repository of student resources, including a course syllabus, assignments, and instructor notes. But that repository can be much more with the incorporation of multimedia, which can engage students with streaming video, audio, and simulations and animations.

MEDIA

Many types of media can be used in the delivery of educational content, ranging from printed text to analog audio or video and digital multimedia. In this book, discussions revolve around the use of digital media as it can be deployed over the Web. However, it is important to understand the main characteristics of transmitting multimedia. Bates and Poole (2003) identify major distinctions in the technologies used to transmit digital multimedia:

Broadcast versus communication technologies: A broadcast is a one-way technology that moves information from the producer to the receiver but doesn't include a mechanism for two-way interaction. In contrast, communication technologies facilitate equal communication back and forth among all participants.

Synchronous versus asynchronous technologies: Synchronous technologies operate in real time; all parties must participate simultaneously. Asynchronous technologies allow participants to choose a time and place convenient to them.

Figure 1.1 shows how different digital multimedia technologies fall into the two frameworks of broadcast versus communication and synchronous versus asynchronous.

Figure 1.1
DIGITAL MEDIA AND TRANSMISSION TECHNOLOGIES

	TECHNOLOGIES			
	Broadcast (One-Way) Applications		**Communication (Two-Way) Applications**	
	Synchronous	Asynchronous	Synchronous	Asynchronous
Digital media	webcast audio streaming video streaming	text learning objects multimedia clips images podcasting	chat web conferencing voice over IP (VoIP) virtual worlds games	e-mail discussion forums blogs wikis simulations

Source: Adapted from Bates and Poole (2003, 55).

PEDAGOGY

The basic definition of *pedagogy* is "the art of teaching." It is important to understand that effective web-based instruction starts with instructional strategies based on theories of learning and transforms them to work in the web environment. Reeves and Reeves (1997) present a model of ten pedagogical dimensions of interactive learning that illustrate important values to be analyzed when creating instruction. Each dimension reflects a spectrum:

> *Pedagogical philosophy—Instructivist ↔ constructivist.* The instructivist approach assigns the learner to the role of passive recipient of instruction. The constructivist approach focuses on the learner who constructs knowledge on the basis of previous knowledge and experience.

> *Learning theory—Behavioral ↔ cognitive.* Behavioral psychology is a learning theory in which the use of stimuli, feedback, and reinforcement shape behavior. There are many examples of this approach found in today's WBI. A tutorial contains instructional material in a presentation, followed by a short quiz with feedback provided depending on the student's responses. The cognitive end of this spectrum places emphasis on internal mental states and incorporates a variety of learning strategies, including memorization, direct instruction, deduction, drill and practice, and induction, depending on the type of knowledge that the learner is constructing.

> *Goal orientation—Sharply focused ↔ general.* The goals for any given educational experience can vary from sharply focused, such as learning a specific medical procedure, to more general, higher-ordered ones, such as motivation of employees. Different goals call for different tactics.

> *Task orientation—Academic ↔ authentic.* Historically, instruction has occurred via academic exercises that do not necessarily offer any context or relevance for learners. A basic tenet of adult learning theory is that context is highly important to learners. With respect to orientation, an academic exercise might be to diagram sentences to learn proper sentence structure, whereas in an authentic learning experience, students would learn through a more practical activity, such as writing a résumé.

Source of motivation—Extrinsic ↔ intrinsic. Motivation plays a role in all learning theories. Extrinsic motivation draws from external sources to motivate—such as working to receive a passing grade. Intrinsic motivation depends heavily on individual learners and what they want to take from the educational experience. It is easier to offer extrinsic than intrinsic motivation. Presenting a way for learners to determine their own outcomes from the instruction is one way to try to intrinsically motivate learners.

Teacher role—Didactic ↔ facilitative. The traditional didactic teacher role is that of sage on the stage—instructors are the possessors of the knowledge that they are to impart to students. The facilitative role is one of being the guide on the side. This approach puts the responsibility for learning with the student; the teacher functions more as a mentor.

Metacognitive support—Unsupported ↔ integrated. Metacognition refers to learners' awareness of objectives, ability to plan and evaluate learning strategies, and ability to monitor progress and adjust their behaviors according to need. Unlike an unsupported system, which offers no feedback, an integrated system provides a means for students to reflect on their progress, assess their needs, and adjust their learning processes.

Collaborative learning strategies—Unsupported ↔ integral. Web-based instruction can be constructed to disregard or promote collaborative learning opportunities. Using synchronous or asynchronous technologies to allow students to work collaboratively in small groups is one example of integrating this dimension into a learning experience.

Cultural insensitivity—Insensitive ↔ respectful. Because the Web is far reaching, it is important to consider cultural implications when designing web-based instruction. Accommodating diverse cultural and ethnic backgrounds should be a WBI goal.

Structural flexibility—Fixed ↔ open. A fixed system is fixed in time and place, for instance, a traditional class held in a specific room at a specific time. An open system accommodates asynchronous learning, thus permitting greater flexibility in the learning experience.

LEARNING STYLES

People have different preferences for acquiring and processing new information. Some are visual learners and learn best through seeing the material, whether text, charts, or other graphics. Some are auditory learners and prefer to gain knowledge by hearing information first. Still others are kinesthetic learners and do best through experience. There are numerous learning-style classification systems. For instance, Kolb's (1984) Learning Style Inventory focuses on concrete experience versus abstract conceptualization, reflective observation, and active experimentation. In another example, Gardner (1999) takes a different path and puts forth a theory of multiple intelligences. He proposes that each person has a different biological composition made up of the following intelligences: linguistic (sensitivity to spoken and written language), mathematical-logical (ability to analyze problems logically, calculate mathematics, and investigate scientifically), musical (skill in the performance, composition, and appreciation of musical patterns), spatial (potential to recognize and manipulate patterns of wide space), bodily-kinesthetic (potential to use one's body to solve problems or fashion products), interpersonal (ability to understand the intentions, motivations, and desires of other people), intrapersonal (ability to understand oneself), naturalist (ability to recognize and classify species), and existential (ability to handle profound questions about existence). Figure 1.2 shows an example of Gardner's multiple intelligences and potential online teaching strategies to address each type.

No matter what learning style one subscribes to, the Web can accommodate the various types within it.

Figure 1.2
ONLINE TECHNOLOGIES AND MULTIPLE INTELLIGENCES

INTELLIGENCE	DESCRIPTION	ONLINE TEACHING STRATEGY
Verbal-linguistic	Preference for reading, writing, and speaking	Web-based research, computer-mediated communication
Mathematical-logical	Aptitude for numbers, reasoning skills	Problem solving, data analysis
Musical	Ability to produce and appreciate pitch, rhythms, learns well through song	Music and composition software, multimedia
Visual-spatial	Visual and spatial stimulation; learners enjoy charts, maps, and puzzles	Web-based presentations, object and document analysis, 3-D modeling
Bodily-kinesthetic	Good sense of balance and hand-eye coordination; handles objects skillfully	Virtual reality, interactive simulations, whiteboard
Interpersonal	Ability to detect and respond to moods and motivations of others tries to see things from another's point of view	Collaborative learning, WebQuests
Intrapersonal	Uses self-reflection to remain aware of one's inner feelings	Online journaling, reflective assessment
Naturalist	Enjoyment of outdoors; ability to detect subtle differences in meaning	WebQuests, case studies, virtual field trips
Existential	Capacity to handle profound questions about existence	Computer-mediated communication, online journaling, authentic learning

From Jennifer Gramling, "Learning Styles," in *Education and Technology: An Encyclopedia*, ed. Ann Kovalchick and Kara Dawson (Santa Barbara, CA: ABC-CLIO, 2004), 420.

CHAPTER TWO

LIBRARY INSTRUCTION ON THE WEB

CHARACTERISTICS OF GOOD LIBRARY INSTRUCTION

One of your primary goals as you start to think about how to develop a web-based library instruction project will be to incorporate the characteristics of good library instruction. What constitutes the best practices? Much research has been done over the years to identify best practices and their characteristics. The Association of College and Research Libraries' (2006) Best Practices Initiative produced a best-practices guideline for information literacy programs that details specific recommendations in nine categories, which address broad areas including goals, support, and pedagogy. Core characteristics that can be applied at the course level include the following:

- Reflect the desired outcomes of preparing students for their academic pursuits and for effective lifelong learning.
- Establish measurable outcomes.
- Support diverse approaches to teaching.
- Incorporate appropriate information technology and other media resources.
- Include active and collaborative activities.
- Encompass critical thinking and reflection.
- Respond to multiple learning styles.
- Support student-centered learning.
- Build on students' existing knowledge.
- Link information literacy to ongoing coursework and real-life experiences appropriate to program and course level.

- Recognize and encourage collaboration among disciplinary faculty, librarians, and other program staff.
- Fuse information literacy concepts and disciplinary content.
- Establish a process for course and student assessment.

Is it possible to incorporate these criteria into web-based instruction? Does it make a difference if the instruction is totally online rather than a supplement to face-to-face instruction? As you start to consider how to transfer these characteristics to a new medium, you will find that there are comparable techniques in web instruction that demonstrate the use of best practices. This chapter and subsequent ones identify those techniques and provide examples that illustrate the incorporation of good instruction criteria, including active learning, collaborative learning, and the use of multiple mediums. A main goal of this book is to teach you how to integrate active learning and collaboration into your web-based instruction through the use of social, interactive technologies and how to use graphics, sound, and/or animation to deliver information through more than one medium.

Delivering course-related content, establishing objectives, teaching concepts, and providing ongoing assistance are pedagogical issues that you and your team must build into the instructional design of your instruction. No matter what format it takes, these are issues that every good instructor addresses when developing a class or course.

DEVELOPING EFFECTIVE WEB-BASED LIBRARY INSTRUCTION

The ACRL's Instruction Section Instructional Technologies Committee (2007) has assembled several tips on the pedagogy of web instruction:

- Outline the objectives and outcomes clearly to establish purpose and realistic expectations.

  Outcomes address the larger overall goal(s) of student learning.

  Keeping this tip in mind helps to avoid the use of technology for technology's sake.

- Provide a clear, intuitive structure that:

  Reflects the objectives of the instruction

  Allows for different learning styles

  Permits the student to self-pace and remediate

- Include active learning techniques to foster student-computer, student-student, and/or student-instructor interaction. Some techniques to consider incorporating include:

  Promoting user-created content

  Developing tools to aid in student self-assessment and feedback

  Providing occasion for discussion

  Creating collaborative opportunities to enhance comprehension of concepts being taught

  Giving attention to information literacy concepts rather than the mechanics of a particular technology so that skills learned will be more transferable to future use.

- Incorporate contemporary language and topics, be as succinct as possible, and don't be afraid to entertain. This strategy will:

  Establish relevance to students' lives

  Not overwhelm them with verbiage

  Help to keep their interest

- Provide multiple ways for students to communicate with the instructor and subject experts such as librarians.

- Whenever possible, make instruction course related so that it:

  Provides context for the concepts being taught

  Makes the material more relevant to the student

WHAT TYPES OF LIBRARIES ENGAGE IN WEB-BASED INSTRUCTION?

Academic libraries come to mind most often when the subject of library instruction is discussed simply because the concept originated in academia more than a century ago. It was in the academic environment that it developed and matured. Undoubtedly, most of the literature available on the subject focuses on the academic library's research into and experiences with the subject. However, in today's complex world of information overload, it is not practical (or prudent) to expect students to wait until their college years to learn information literacy skills. Nor should adults without postsecondary education have to struggle to understand how to find, evaluate, and use information in the most effective manner possible. So, unsurprisingly, other types of libraries are turning to the Web to meet the needs of their constituents.

As is true with the academic library, the school library media center plays an important role in educating students about information literacy. Library media specialists and teachers collaborate to integrate information literacy skills into the school curriculum.

Public libraries have become the place where people expect to be able to find online access. As of 2007, 98.9 percent of public libraries provided that service. As might be expected, patrons also turn to public library staff for instruction on how to use technology and the Internet. A study by the National Commission on Libraries and Information Science also showed that 74 percent of public libraries provide technology-training services of some form, which includes the 48 percent of libraries that teach information literacy skills and the 43 percent that offer online instruction courses (Bertot et al. 2008).

You will find that there are many examples of uses of the Web by school and public libraries to assist their patrons in learning a wide range of subjects. Topics covered include those that are typical of academic library instruction plus different approaches to engage students and lifelong learners by zeroing in on specific target audiences, such as children, teens, and seniors.

Special libraries cover a wide variety of potential students and educational needs, including special academic (e.g., business, law, medical), art, museum, corporate, government agencies, newspapers, and film, to name just a few. The educational needs of the users of special libraries are wide ranging also. But the importance of offering library instruction spans all types of special libraries. In an era of limited financial resources, many special libraries have been forced to justify their budget and their existence. A good library education program can keep a special library visible and valuable (Haverkamp and Coffey 1999). Many special libraries have patrons who are geographically dispersed and are busy adults who need to become proficient with computer technologies and the Internet to perform their jobs in today's global economy. Web-based instruction can be one cost-effective avenue to reach each targeted audience. Driscoll (2002) cites tactical advantages of the use of web-based training:

- reduced travel and related costs
- learning that can occur any time and any place
- the provision of just-in-time learning
- the leveraging of existing infrastructure

- platform-independent delivery
- easy updates

TYPES AND EXAMPLES OF WEB-BASED LIBRARY INSTRUCTION

What kind of library instruction can you deliver via the Web? An examination of current web technologies coupled with the range of library instruction content shows that you are limited only by your imagination. This section introduces some of the major topics and examples of their use.

The Changing Information Landscape

In recent years, attention has focused on the change in the information landscape. Ten years ago, information was primarily prepackaged in a book, a newscast, or a magazine; today it is acquired in myriad ways that learners often completely control. As Siemens and Tittenberger (2009) note, "Our learning and information acquisition is a mashup." Helping learners understand this new paradigm and the changes in the information cycle has become a basic goal of library instruction.

The creation of information is now largely in the hands of individuals. User-generated content has introduced new facets to the origin of information:

The packaging of information has been altered: Instead of being prepackaged, information can be packaged according to the needs and interests of each individual learner, which requires a new skill set of the student.

Validation of information: No longer can you assume that only experts create reliable information. Wikipedia and other resources like it rely on the wisdom of crowds to discuss and validate information.

Dissemination of information: Although peer review and critical discussion are still prominent parts of the dissemination of scholarly information, changes are under way in the process to disseminate information at an accelerated rate. Ideas such as postpublication review and new models of scholarship are areas for instruction.

Sharing and publication of information: This portion of the information cycle is one that libraries typically address in their instruction.

General Research or Reference Skills

One common type of web-based library tutorial deals with how to undertake research in general. Although at first it might appear that this type of instruction will not meet the criteria of having a course-based focus, it can be integrated into many different disciplines as a supplement (or learning object) because the research process follows a similar path in many subject areas. Furthermore, as mentioned earlier, web-based tutorials can be the primary method of instruction for distance-education students who will not have an opportunity to receive face-to-face course instruction. Typical topics covered in this type of tutorial include planning research, identifying and refining a topic, using available research tools (e.g., online catalog, periodical indexes), evaluating information, citing resources, and differentiating among types of resources.

Online Catalog Skills

A library's online catalog is its main tool for finding materials in its collection. A tutorial that instructs library users in searching that specific system can be helpful to all concerned. Online systems today are sophisticated enough to permit complex search strategies. If a tutorial is developed to teach users how to search in one system, users can then transfer the strategies learned to other online systems. Concepts that an online catalog tutorial can convey include searching by keyword versus subject, the meaning of call numbers and how they are structured, when to try different access points to find materials (e.g., author, title, subject, keyword), and how to search different fields simultaneously with Boolean logic. Students can learn about different types of information available in the library and how to interpret and refine the results they retrieve from the catalog.

Database- or Software-Specific Search Skills

A tutorial on database- or software-specific search skills teaches users to use specific databases or to master particular search-software interfaces. Because there are so many database interfaces, it is necessary to help users learn how to navigate them. Some search software, such as EBSCOhost or ProQuest, provides one interface to search multiple databases. Instruction designed to teach how to search specific interfaces can be integrated into subject-specific and course-related instruction by focusing on an appropriate database for a particular field. Mastery of the search software can translate into knowledge of how to use the program in another discipline.

Discipline- or Course-Specific Research Skills

Instruction in discipline- or course-specific research skills zeros in on teaching students to conduct research in a certain discipline. A humanities student approaches a research project in a much different manner than a physics student does. Usually a discipline-specific tutorial supports a particular course, often a survey course with multiple sections. This type of tutorial is quite focused and provides students with in-depth instruction on how to do research in a particular field, as well as information about appropriate sources and research processes unique to that discipline.

Assignment-Specific Instruction

Instruction can also be developed to guide a student through a specific assignment for a course. This is a perfect opportunity for a librarian to collaborate with a professor to create an interactive web research project.

Internet Instruction

In many libraries, teaching Internet-related topics has become a standard part of the instruction mission. This type of instruction can range from teaching the mechanics of navigating the Internet to how to use the Web for research. Different libraries have included a vast assortment of instruction topics about the Internet in their lessons. The following potential Internet topics will give you an idea of the possibilities.

Introduction to the Internet
Even though the Internet may seem ubiquitous to many people, there are still many others who seek instruction on how to access and use it. For instance, 56 percent of seniors between the ages of sixty-four and seventy-two and 31 percent of those older than seventy-two are online (Pew Internet 2009), and many turn to their public libraries to learn about the basics of the Internet.

History of the Internet
Tutorials that cover the history of the Internet and the World Wide Web can help students understand that it is not a single entity but rather a non-centralized global network of networks.

Internet Skills
There are many different skills that new Internet users need to learn to function efficiently on the Web.

Web Browser Navigation. As with any software application, people who are new to the Internet often find it helpful to receive instruction on how to use web browsers. The interfaces in the various available browsers are not always user friendly. Highlighting the available features and functions will assist new users.

Communication on the Internet. One of the top uses of the Internet for many people is to communicate with others. There are asynchronous and synchronous methods to engage in online communication, including e-mail, discussion groups, blogging, microblogging, instant messaging and chat, and texting.

Netiquette. Unique sets of social conventions surround appropriate behavior on the Internet. These come into play in most online environments and may be completely different depending on individual settings. For instance, proper English may be appropriate in a blog posting, whereas texting encourages abbreviated language and slang because of limitations on message length. Although new users may think such things are common sense once they are introduced, they will appreciate a vehicle for learning them before they make an online faux pas!

Research on the Web

Use of Web Search Tools. New search engines, directories, and indexes are introduced regularly. There will continue to be a need to instruct people to use them as they are introduced.

Web Search Strategies. Without a solid understanding of the most efficient techniques to conduct searches, the amount of information a web search returns easily overwhelms users.

Evaluation of Web Resources. Because anyone can publish to the Web, it has never been so important to teach students the criteria required to assess the quality of information retrieved from the Internet. Wikipedia, a collaboratively written encyclopedia, is one of the popular choices to use in a discussion of evaluation.

WebQuests. The term *WebQuests*, coined in 1995, describes an "inquiry-oriented lesson format in which most or all the information that learners work with comes from the web" (www.webquest.org). The lesson's objective is to promote learning outcomes, which are achieved through the reading, analysis, and synthesis of Web-based information (Dodge, 2007).

WebQuests have become a popular tool for educators who want to use the Internet while teaching their students to use critical-thinking skills. The technology of a WebQuest is straightforward, but it is more than a series of pages with hyperlinks. An effective WebQuest

- is centered on a doable and interesting task that is ideally a scaled-down version of things that adults do as citizens or workers
- requires higher-level thinking, not simply summarizing, including synthesis, analysis, problem solving, creativity, and judgment
- makes good use of the Web

Deep Web. The deep Web (also called the invisible Web or hidden Web) is that content which is not easily discoverable through standard search engines. It includes dynamically generated content (i.e., content that is contained in databases and retrieved through queries), as well as unlinked, password-protected, contextual, and scripted content.

Making and Publishing Web Pages and Sites

There are a wide variety of topics included under making and publishing web pages and websites: the creation of basic web pages, the use of specific web editors, Cascading Style Sheets language, the creation of accessible web pages, the control of access to pages and sites, the creation of web graphics, design and layout principles, writing for the Web, and more. In fact, online instruction could be created for almost every subject you will encounter in this book!

File Sharing

Electronic files (most often audio and video files) are made available for download via the Internet. They are most often stored on individual users' computers and shared using a peer-to-peer model. The sharing of such files has been a major issue in campuses across the nation over the past several years. However, file sharing is not restricted to academia, as evidenced by Pew's report that 15 percent of adult Internet users participate in file sharing (Pew Internet and American Life Project 2009). The difficulty arises when downloaded material is copyrighted and is therefore illegal to share without permission. Educating people about the legal and moral aspects of file sharing has become, by necessity, an important topic.

Internet and Digital Safety

Internet safety is an important topic, especially with regard to children using the Web. Topics that have become important as preteens' Internet access expands include such serious issues as cyberbullying, identity protection, and sexual predators. Digital safety includes protection from such things as identity theft by ploys such as phishing, spam, and spyware.

Phishing. Phishing describes hackers creating a replica of an existing legitimate web page (often a commercial site such as a bank) to fool a user into submitting personal, financial, or password data. It is a scam that has become prevalent and that users need to be educated about.

Spam. Spam is unwanted, unsolicited, junk e-mail addressed to a large number of recipients. It has become so prevalent in the past few years that it has become more than just an annoyance. Learning how to minimize one's chances for attracting spam, how to filter it, and what to do with it when it is received are necessary skills in today's electronic world.

Spyware. Spyware is a technology that surreptitiously collects information about a person without his or her knowledge. A software program is installed on the user's computer, often when the user is downloading another program. Also known as adware, spyware gathers information and shares it with third parties, often advertisers who use the information to target their marketing. Besides raising serious concerns over user privacy, this software can affect the performance of the computer on which it is installed, sometimes going as far as to hijack the web browser and slow performance considerably.

Internet Telephony

Voice-over-Internet protocol (VoIP) is a technology for transmitting ordinary telephone calls over the Internet. It takes analog audio signals, like the kind you hear when you talk on the phone, and turns them into digital data for transmission over the Internet. Because it bypasses the regular phone system, long distance calls are often free, and costs are restricted to the cost of your network subscription. As this technology has become more widely available, there is increased interest in learning about how it works.

Web 2.0

The second-generation read-write web has exploded into popular culture and is a topic of widespread interest. The various social networking technologies and applications that comprise Web 2.0 are timely fodder for instructional opportunities. Topics such as user-generated content, tags, mashups, cloud computing, the long tail, and remix culture are just a few of the newer concepts that you could easily incorporate into instruction.

Social Networking. Web 2.0 is built around the concept of social network-ing, or building communities of people who have shared interests and activities. There are many directions that have developed in addition to connecting to friends. It is now simple to join online conversations that take place on blogs, to provide recommendations on merchandise such as videos and books, and to share your network for business purposes.

Blog. The blog (from *weblog*) is a concept that has been around since the mid-1990s. Originally, blogs were personal communication tools operated by individuals (bloggers) who compiled lists of links to sites of interest to them and intermingled this with information and editorials. As the idea caught on, their purpose has expanded to more serious uses including politics, corporate communication with customers, and collaborative space. Over the past five years, educators, including librarians, have discovered the value of blogs. Teaching students about blogs—their history, purpose, and potential—is now a standard component of information literacy instruction (chapter 7 discusses blogs in greater detail).

Wiki. A wiki is a collaborative website comprising the perpetual collective work of many authors. It is similar to a blog in structure and logic. However, it allows anyone to edit, delete, or modify content, including the work of previous authors. The collaborative nature of a wiki has great potential in educational settings and for group projects (chapter 7 discusses wikis in more detail).

User-generated content. A basic tenet of Web 2.0 is user-generated content, which includes all the types of media content that end users produce. Some of the most commonly known types of user-generated content include discussion boards, blogs, customer review sites, social networking sites, digital video, image sharing, podcasting, and wikis. Wikipedia is one of the best-known examples of collaborative user-created content and is ripe for inclusion in instruction on accuracy of sources.

Tags. Tags are user-generated terms assigned to information to describe it. Tagging is the opposite of expert-created descriptions like Library of Congress subject headings. Because tagging is an informal system, educa-tion on its history, meaning, and advantages can help users understand its potential and limitations.

Cloud Computing. The term *cloud computing* is used to describe when vir-tualized resources are provided as a service by using Internet technologies.

Users don't need to know or understand the technology infrastructure or location of the "cloud" that supports them. There is no need for local expenditures for hardware (servers) and application. Examples of popular cloud computing services are Google Apps and web-based e-mail services. According to the research firm Gartner (2009) and its report *Hype Cycle for Cloud Computing, 2009*, the move toward cloud computing is predicted to become a transformational change within two to five years..

RSS. The acronym RSS originally stood for RDF (Resource Description Framework) Site Summary, which was soon simplified to Rich Site Summary. More commonly known as Really Simple Syndication or web feed, RSS is an XML format for distributing news headlines and new content on the Web. This technology can be set up to help users stay abreast of new information by having it delivered to and constantly updated via a news aggregator, a piece of software freely available on the Web. Tutorials on RSS can be valuable in helping users set up their own feeds or to instruct information providers in setting up an RSS feed for their content.

Podcasts. Podcasts have become an effective method for delivering instruction over the Web. A podcast is an audio or video file that users download through web syndication. Because the process of creating podcasts is different from other ways of accessing media over the Internet, teaching students or educators how to create a podcast is a pertinent topic (chapter 6 discusses podcasts in more detail).

Wi-Fi. The term *wi-fi* is short for *wireless fidelity* and is used commonly when referring to the IEEE 802.11 wireless networking specification. This is the technology that allows computers and personal digital assistants (PDAs) to share a high-speed Internet connection over a distance of about three hundred feet and to connect to a local network without wires. Many libraries are moving toward incorporating this technology into their buildings because it can be more cost effective than a wired network (especially when retrofitting an existing building) and can provide patrons with both mobility to connect throughout the building and access to the Internet in difficult-to-reach areas. As more people become interested in having a wireless network in their homes, they will seek instruction on how the technology works.

General Library Orientation

Most academic libraries hold library orientation tours each semester when new students arrive on campus. Any library can be an intimidating structure to new patrons. Helping students learn where departments, services, and materials are located in the library is the first step in transforming them into independent information seekers. A virtual library tour can serve the same purpose. It provides patrons with a map they can use to become acquainted with the library building and its services. This can also be beneficial in special and public libraries to help orient patrons.

Information Literacy Courses

As the world of information becomes more complex, information literacy instruction has become an increasingly important part of the education process. Many higher education institutions include an information literacy class as a required part of the curriculum, often during a student's first year. The class may be offered as a separate class for credit or incorporated into a survey course, such as freshman English. These courses allow concepts to be covered in an in-depth manner because they remove the time constraints of a one-shot class. In this type of forum, there are many opportunities to incorporate active learning, collaborative learning, multimedia to present information, and other characteristics of good library instruction. The recognition of the need to educate people to be information literate is not limited to academia by any means. A survey of information literature over a thirty-year period indicates that school librarians and school media specialists have had to address this need to teach information skills from kindergarten through high school. It also found that, although user instruction generally was minimal in public libraries, current demands for distance-education support and from K–12 students have grown and need to be tackled by public librarians (Rader 2002).

A typical approach to online information literacy instruction can be found in the modules developed by the University of Hawaii system libraries in their tutorial "Learning Information Literacy Online" (LILO; www.hawaii.edu/lilo/). Broad topics in the LILO tutorial include the research process, assignments, research strategies, conducting searches, evaluation, and synthesis.

Other researchers are addressing broader views of literacies that are important for today's students and tomorrow's citizens (Mitchell and Smith 2009) (for an introduction to some of those expanded models, see chapter 1). Literacies that are prime candidates for instruction include Shapiro and Hughes' (1996) tool, social-structural, and emerging technology literacies. Other pertinent literacies include current information issues literacy, data management literacy, and document modeling literacy (the inherent structure of a document).

Academic Integrity and Intellectual Property

Although most information literacy courses include information about academic integrity and intellectual property, because those are hot issues in education today, instructional units focusing strictly on this area are common. The two issues permeate all areas of the academic experience, but in many cases, libraries are taking the lead in getting out information to educate students about what is acceptable and unacceptable behavior.

The Internet has made it easy for users to access others' work and advances in technology have made it easy to manipulate those works. A major facet of academic inquiry is the concept of building on others' work and then synthesizing the previous knowledge into something new. The ease of this in the electronic world makes it more important than ever to teach the ethics of properly acknowledging prior knowledge. Because many students today are very connected into electronic media, including music, mashups, and remix culture, those areas can offer concrete parallels for the concept of building on others' work.

The word *mashup* has different meanings. It refers to digital media that comprises pieces drawn from preexisting sources to create a new derivative work. It also refers to music that is created by blending two or more songs, typically by overlaying the vocal track of one song over the music track of a different song. Finally, in web development, *mashup* refers to an application that combines data or functionality from multiple sources to create a new service (for examples, see the ProgrammableWeb Mashup Matrix, at www.programmableweb.com/mashups/). In all cases, however, the resulting product (music or application) has been altered from preexisting creative work.

The term *remix culture* describes a society that encourages the creation of new derivative works by making changes and/or improvements to works held under copyright. Copyright activists look to this type of culture as preferable to a permission culture in which copyright restrictions are pervasive. Proponents believe that a remix culture promotes creativity and the birth of essentially new works. These concepts can be integrated into meaningful instruction on fair use and copyright. They can become springboards for introducing new models of permission such as Creative Commons (creativecommons.org), which allows creators to determine the ranges of protection for use of their works.

Productivity Software Applications

As the need for computing skills has evolved, many libraries—public ones in particular—have become the providers of training for productivity software applications. Instruction has been developed to teach the use of applications, such as word processing, spreadsheets, web editing, multimedia, graphics creation, and bibliographic management software such as EndNote and Zotero.

CHAPTER THREE

PROJECT FRAMEWORK

A S WITH ANY undertaking, setting up a systematic process that will guide you as a project proceeds is important. In the software industry, this is known as the design and development cycle. The cycle incorporates the planning, development, production, and evaluation of a product from start to finish, and it is a circular process rather than a linear one. By the time one version of a product is released, the next one is already being worked on. In education, this same process is called instructional systems design. This chapter identifies several models of development (see figure 3.1) and discusses the common components of typical design and development systems. You will find that components don't always surface in the same place, and they often overlap. In fact, the process is best when fluid.

No matter what size project you are embarking on, it is important to understand the different components and to incorporate them into your process. Establishing a system will allow you to develop the project within a specified time and evaluate it according to objective criteria. A system will also allow you to execute the project efficiently, thereby saving you time overall.

MODELS
Software Development Models

Waterfall

The waterfall development model was originally developed in the manufacturing industry. It is a sequential development process that is seen as flowing downward like a waterfall. The steps, in order, are as follows: requirement specification, design, construction (implementation), integration, verification (testing and debugging), installation, and maintenance. The waterfall model is commonly viewed as flawed because of the belief that it is impossible to perfect any one stage before moving to the next.

Iterative or Incremental Development
The model of iterative or incremental development addresses the perceived weaknesses of the waterfall model because its premise is to develop a software system incrementally, thus allowing for redesigns along the way as developers and users identify problems and improvements.

Agile
The agile model is based on iterative development. Its focus is on a leadership philosophy that leverages teamwork, self-organization, and accountability that facilitates rapid development of high-quality software. This model is people oriented rather than process oriented. Core values of the approach are described in the Agile Manifesto (Beck et al. 2001):

- individuals and interactions over processes and tools
- working software over comprehensive documentation
- customer collaboration over contract negotiation
- responding to change over following a plan

Within each short-term iteration, a team addresses a full software development cycle, including planning, requirements analysis, design, coding, and testing.

Extreme Programming
The extreme programming (XP) model extends agile software development by advocating frequent small releases in short development cycles. This is intended to be a rapid response to customer requirements with the expectation that those requirements will change over time. There are some basic tenets of XP: short release cycles, simple designs, writing tests before code, pair programming (two programmers work at one computer, and one codes while the other reviews), collective code ownership, continuous integration, and strict coding standards. The four basic steps in this model are planning, design, coding, and testing.

Instructional Design Models

ADDIE
The generic instructional systems design (ISD) model acronym ADDIE stands for five sequential phases: analysis, design, development, imple-

mentation, and evaluation. This linear model serves as the basis for most of the subsequent ISD models:

Analysis phase: The instructional problem is clarified; the goals and objectives are established; the learning environment and learner's existing knowledge are identified.

Design phase: A systematic instructional strategy is developed; the format and visual design is determined.

Development phase: The instruction is produced.

Implementation phase: The plan is put into action; materials are delivered.

Evaluation phase: Consists of both formative and summative evaluation.

Rapid Prototyping

Originally associated with software development, the rapid prototyping modification to the ADDIE model merges steps to streamline the process, with formative evaluation throughout for feedback and reactions. Early in the process, a small-scale prototype is developed to allow for testing of key features of the design. The goal is to catch problems at a point where they are easier to fix. Typical steps in this model are

- concept definition
- implementation of a skeletal system
- user evaluation and concept refinement
- implementation of refined requirements
- user evaluation and concept refinement
- implementation of refined requirements

Dick and Carey

The Dick and Carey (2009) model was introduced by Walter Dick and Lou Carey, and it follows the basic linear design of ADDIE with more detail:

- Identify instructional goals.
- Conduct instructional analysis.
- Analyze learners and contexts.
- Write performance objectives.
- Develop assessment instruments.
- Develop instructional strategy.
- Develop and select instructional materials.
- Design and conduct formative evaluation of instruction.
- Revise instruction design and conduct summative evaluation.

Figure 3.1
MODELS

Steps compared by model	SOFTWARE DEVELOPMENT MODELS				INSTRUCTIONAL DESIGN MODELS			
	Waterfall	Iterative/ Incremental	Agile	Extreme	ADDIE	Rapid Prototyping	Dick & Carey	Morrison, Ross, Kemp
	Requirement specification	Planning	Planning	Planning		Concept definition	Identify instructional goals	Identify instructional problems; set goals
						Implementation of skeletal system		
		Requirements analysis	Requirements analysis		Analysis	User evaluation and concept refinement	Conduct instructional analysis	Examine learner characteristics
							Analyze learners and contexts	Identify subject content; analyze tasks
	Design	Analysis and design	Design	Design	Design		Write performance objectives	State instruction objectives
							Develop assessment instruments	Sequence content

Construction	Implementation			Development		Develop instructional strategy	Design instructional strategies
Integration	Deployment			Implementation	Implementation of refined requirements	Develop and select instructional materials	Plan instructional message and delivery
Verification	Testing	Coding	Coding		User evaluation and concept refinement	Design and conduct formative evaluation of instruction	Develop evaluation instruments
Installation		Testing	Testing			Revise instruction design and conduct summative evaluation	Select resources to support instruction and learning activities
Maintenance	Evaluation			Evaluation	Implementation of refined requirements		
Key points Sequential and one time	Cyclic modification and integration	Short-term iteration, people focused	Simplicity and communication, pair programming	Linear and basis for most ISD models	Skeletal working model developed to test key features	Adds detail to the basic ADDIE model	Designed for flexibility

Morrison, Ross, Kemp

The Morrison, Ross, and Kemp (2004) model includes nine interrelated steps that are designed to be flexible in that any of the elements can be addressed at any time in the process, making it possible for the designer to modify instruction as necessary:

1. Identify instructional problems, and specify goals for designing an instructional program.

2. Examine learner characteristics that should receive attention during planning.

3. Identify subject content, and analyze task components related to stated goals and purposes.

4. State instructional objectives for the learner.

5. Sequence content within each instructional unit for logical learning.

6. Design instructional strategies so that each learner can master the objectives.

7. Plan the instructional message and delivery.

8. Develop evaluation instruments to assess objectives.

9. Select resources to support instruction and learning activities.

These models, even with their unique aspects, share themes that are important to include when setting up the structure for your web-based instruction project. Figure 3.1 illustrates the commonalities and overlap among the software and instructional design model.

Typical Design and Development Activities

The models include some broad areas that comprise typical design and development activities: preproduction (planning and design), production, publication, and postproduction. In addition, two facets appear in all stages: project management and evaluation. Figure 3.2 illustrates the design and development cycle for web-based instruction.

PREPRODUCTION

No matter how simple a project appears at first consideration, if you jump right in and start authoring immediately, it will end up taking much longer than if you take the time up front to carefully plan each aspect of the project. This planning step is called the preproduction phase and normally encompasses about two-thirds of the entire project timeline.

Needs Analyses

Preproduction starts with an idea. Maybe you and your colleagues have decided that an online tutorial is a good objective, or perhaps a faculty member who would like web instruction for a specific class has approached you. Whatever the origin of the idea, it has been formed in response to some perceived need. You must develop a good understanding of what that need is. Thus, the first step is to perform needs analyses of the client, audience, stakeholders, information, and resources.

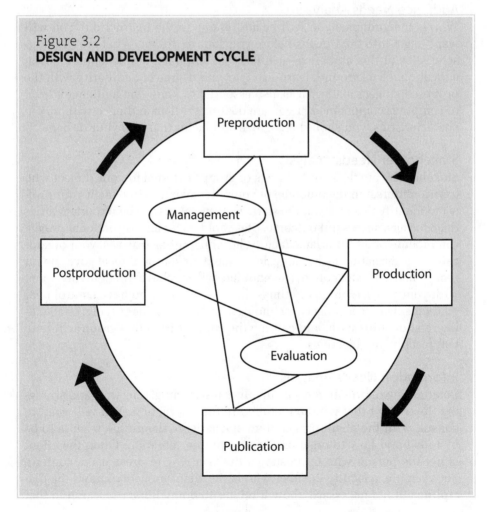

Figure 3.2
DESIGN AND DEVELOPMENT CYCLE

Client Needs Analysis

Start by interviewing your client (who may be a fellow librarian, an entire academic department, or a faculty member). You want to determine what the client hopes to accomplish with online instruction. Does the client have some specific goal in mind? What is it? For instance, will the instruction replace face-to-face lessons, or will it be a supplement to them? Is a web-based lesson really the best approach to provide the outcome the client is seeking? If so, what type of web environment will accomplish the goals best? What resources does the client have for the project? Is there a departmental budget that will pay for the project, or does the client expect it to come from your library budget?

Audience Needs Analysis

Who is the audience you will be addressing in the instruction? You will want to get into their heads before you start to design. What are the characteristics of this audience—gender, age, ethnicity, socioeconomic level, educational background, learning style, and degree of familiarity with the proposed subject matter? It is also essential to know the audience's level of computer competence. If you are dealing with an audience with mixed characteristics, you should recognize and factor that into your design.

Stakeholder Needs Analysis

Stakeholders are those individuals or groups external to your project who have an interest in the outcome of your endeavor. It will benefit your project to identify this group at the start, as its members can be important allies in ensuring a successful outcome. Stakeholders for an instructional project can include other librarians, faculty, administrators, trustees, your organization's information technology department, or state and local government representatives. Most often, stakeholders will not have direct involvement with your project, but many times they are people who have control over your organization's budgets, technology, and politics. Identifying, establishing relationships with, and gaining the support from this group will help you reach your objectives.

Information Needs Analysis

Determining information needs involves researching, selecting, and arranging the content that will be included in the instruction. You will want to consult with the client or a content specialist to determine what is to be included and how to organize it for optimum retention. Often the client is not the person who understands the best way to present the content. For example, a faculty member who is the client probably knows the discipline but not necessarily how it relates to doing library research in that discipline. Content to be included may also depend on the audience mix. For instance, if the targeted audience is made up of distance-education students, the instruction may want to emphasize online resources over print resources that require a trip to the library to use.

Resource Needs Analysis

What resources are available to support your project? You need to consider hardware and software resources. Do you have what you need to produce the instruction, or will you require additional applications or peripherals such as a scanner? What about the students' existing hardware and software? (Chapter 4 focuses in detail on hardware and software considerations.)

How much time is available to complete the project? What human resources are needed? Is there sufficient money in the budget to cover expenses? What delivery system will be used, and will your existing infrastructure support it? In the case of web-based delivery, will the instruction be delivered over a fiber-optic network or an analog phone line? The answer will shape what you decide to develop.

When you have worked through these analyses and have clearly outlined the results, you have the information you'll need to start on the next step in preproduction: design and prototyping.

Design and Prototyping

During the design and prototyping stage of the preproduction phase, important preliminary work takes place. This is the time when you will develop design ideas and instruction content and organize them into a detailed plan that sets the stage for production. This section introduces you to brainstorming for design ideas, developing scripts, and creating visual tools that will become the blueprint for your instruction.

Brainstorming

The beginning of the design stage is a good time to brainstorm. Assemble your project team (discussed later in this chapter in "Project Management"). Have each person contribute his or her ideas on what a perfect project would include. Consider both content and functionality. With content, consider the message to be communicated. Start identifying what content can be included that will help develop the skills the students will need to have. When discussing functionality, consider the level of interactivity that you will use to convey the content. When brainstorming, the sky's the limit, and no idea is too far fetched. This is particularly true in discussions of functionality. Maybe you think that some desirable interactivities are beyond the technical capabilities of your team, but this isn't the time to reject anything out of hand. It's the time to see the range of ideas and expectations that each team member brings to the project and to establish the beginning of teamwork by learning about one another. You'll find that part of the fun of doing a project like this is that you will have the opportunity to further your knowledge and expertise as you meet the challenge of learning new technologies.

One tool that can help your team reach an agreement about what a good tutorial might consist of is shopping the competition. That is, visit sites and take a look at what other libraries or educational organizations have done on similar projects. Use the various sites to trigger conversation about what each team member likes or dislikes about a particular site. It will be helpful to compile a list of criteria or questions to consider that you have identified as important to your project so that you have a basis for comparison (see figure 3.3).

A portal to library tutorial sites can be found on the Library Orientation Exchange (LOEX) tutorial page (www.emich.edu/public/loex/advanced_ search.php) or the American Library Association and Association of College and Research Libraries' Peer-Reviewed Instructional Materials Online (PRIMO) website (www.ala.org/ala/mgrps/divs/acrl/about/sections/ is/projpubs/primo/). This exercise will serve to start the design process. You will discover your team's design and organization awareness. Which team member has a good eye for design? Who on the team understands content organization? As you proceed, the skeleton of your site's architecture will start to emerge, and each team member's role will become defined.

Once you have determined the basics of what you desire from the project, the more detailed tasks of developing a script, planning the tutorial's progression through a flowchart or storyboard, and creating the interface design can begin.

Script

The script will become the nuts and bolts of the message you want to convey. It is a good idea to start with an outline that defines the main points to be made in the instruction. Often, the outline becomes apparent once the site architecture is determined. Site architecture is the design of the site, not in terms of artistic design elements, such as color or graphics, but in terms of the organization, navigation, and functional systems of the site. The script includes all aspects of the content: the wording for the text you want to include, media that illustrate the content (e.g., images, sound files, movie clips), activities to reinforce a concept, and skill checks to provide an assessment of whether users have retained what has been taught.

Figure 3.3
POTENTIAL COMPARISON CRITERIA FOR
EVALUATION OF WEB-BASED INSTRUCTION

EVALUATION CATEGORY	QUESTIONS TO ASK
Instructional design	Are the objectives clear?
	Is there provision for interactive practice?
	Is there a feedback mechanism in place?
	Are illustrations and examples incorporated into the instruction?
Subject content	Does it contain the right amount and quality of information?
	Is the material delivered in an appropriate manner for the targeted audience?
	Is the language jargon free?
	Is the content presented in concise chunks, to facilitate easy recall by students?
Audience considerations	Will the material engage the students' attention?
	Is the material covered pertinent to students' needs?
	Does the site permit student control of movement through the tutorial?
Use of media	Do the graphics, sound, and other multimedia contribute to further the instruction?
	Do multimedia components download quickly?
	Do they require use of a plug-in; if so, are instructions provided?
Visual design	Is the screen design layout clearly organized and easy to understand?
	Is the layout consistent between screens?
	Is the interface aesthetically pleasing?

(cont.)

Figure 3.3 (cont.)

EVALUATION CATEGORY	QUESTIONS TO ASK
	Is the site easily identifiable as a cohesive unit?
	Does the color scheme used contribute to the tone of the site?
Ease of use	Is it intuitive to use?
	Is it easy to navigate?
	Do pages load quickly?
Evaluation	Are there evaluation mechanisms built into the tutorial?
Accessibility	Is the tutorial accessible to disabled users?

Flowchart and Storyboard

Both a flowchart and a storyboard are tools to illustrate the step-by-step progression through the instruction. A flowchart is a visual representation of the sequence of the content of the tutorial. It shows what comes first, second, third, and so on, as well as what pages link to each other, what actions your audience will take, and what will occur when a user takes each action. It is a road map of your project. Figure 3.4 shows a very simple example of a flowchart. Symbols in a flowchart have meaning. In figure 3.4, the oblong shape indicates the beginning and end of the process, the rectangle indicates tasks, the diamonds are decision points, and the arrows show direction of flow.

The storyboard goes a step farther. It contains a sketch for each screen that includes text, information about the graphics (including placement, color, and size), design layout, color, font size and type, sound (including narration), and audience interaction. The storyboard should be detailed enough that team members know what happens on each screen, what will happen throughout the tutorial, and what each screen will look like.

Both the flowchart and storyboard are important tools of communication between the team and the client. It is the first visualization of what the project will become.

Mock-ups and Prototypes

The next step in the design process is to transform the design ideas contained in the storyboard to actual models of the site. A mock-up of the screen design illustrates how the interface will look to users. (Chapter 5 discusses the user interface design; we look more closely at testing usability in chapter 8.)

Creating a prototype of the site design is a useful tool in the early stages to determine whether the design will work before investing a great deal of time in producing the entire site. A prototype is typically a functional rendition of the site that is not necessarily fully developed but can be used for testing. One methodology for prototyping is called rapid prototyping, described earlier in this chapter, in which the instructional designers actively work with users to quickly build a series of prototypes rather than just one. In such a model, the evaluation and development activities are parallel processes in which the two groups work together to decide which features they will

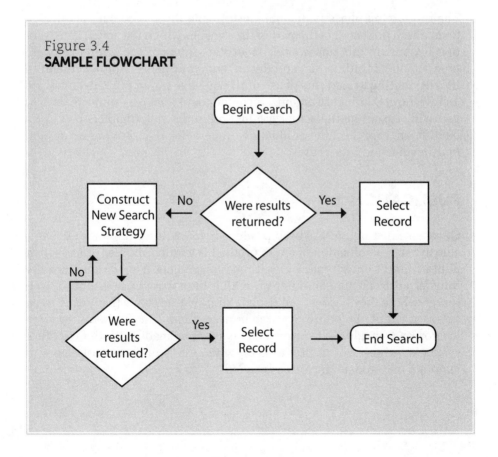

Figure 3.4
SAMPLE FLOWCHART

keep and which they will discard. It is an iterative process that has some advantages over the more traditional prototype model (Bichelmeyer 2004):

- It encourages and requires the active participation of end users in the activities of design.
- It makes an allowance for users to change their minds during the design process.
- It facilitates users' understanding of their requirements for instruction products by engaging them in the implementation of the various prototypes.
- It allows for early detection of errors.
- It can increase creativity through quick user feedback.
- It accelerates the instructional development process.

PRODUCTION

The production phase is the one most people think of when they decide to do a web project. It is the part of the cycle in which the actual construction is done. In this phase, code is written, interactivity components are programmed, multimedia is produced, and your instruction is brought to life. By waiting to start this phase until you have put in place detailed site architecture, thoroughly organized content, and a set page and site design, you will streamline the actual production of the site. Chapters 5–7 focus on different aspects of the production cycle in detail: user interface design, multimedia, and interactivity.

PUBLICATION

Once your instruction has been produced, you will want to make it available to users. Publication of a web product is a much simpler process than publication of other types of multimedia products. The various files are transferred from the computer on which they were created onto a web server, where they become published. Your instruction is then ready to be accessed simply by pointing a web browser to its URL (uniform resource locator, or web address). Arrangements must be made with the website's system administrator to provide you with sufficient access privileges to maintain and update the files as needed.

POSTPRODUCTION

The postproduction phase is as important as the planning phase. It includes such tasks as developing a marketing strategy, indexing the site, maintaining the site, and planning for the next version of the instruction.

Marketing Strategy

If your instruction is designed for use by only a specific group of students, then it may not be necessary to do more than provide a client with the URL of the site. However, if you are targeting a broader audience, it may be advisable to develop specific methods to get the word out about your project so users can find and use it. Marketing strategies can range from simple to elaborate, but often such methods as notifying appropriate mailing lists, posting an announcement on your organization's home page, or sending out a broadcast e-mail announcement are effective. With the prevalence of social networking today, viral marketing has become a popular method for spreading the word. Viral marketing is the Web 2.0 equivalent of word-of-mouth advertising. It is based on the assumption that people will share interesting content through social networking sites such as blogs, Facebook, and Twitter. Your team can explore the best means for your particular situation.

Site Maintenance

Once your instruction is published, it is important to take steps to ensure that it stays functional and current. The Web is changing constantly, and you will want to make sure that you regularly check for content updates and broken links to correct them.

Planning for the Next Version

Publishing web instruction isn't a finite project. As you proceed through the postpublication evaluation process, you will start to gather information that will form the nucleus for revisions and improvements.

TESTING AND EVALUATION

Testing and evaluation are important components during design and development, and to be useful, they should take place through the project. Testing and evaluation are the primary vehicles you have to receive essential information to help ensure that your instruction is effective. Because they are essential elements of a successful web instruction project, this subject is covered in depth in chapter 8.

PROJECT MANAGEMENT

No matter whether your project is large or small, it will require management from start to finish. A large project may call for a dedicated project manager; for a small project, one of the team members may also wear a management hat. There are many facets of a project to manage: authoring a project proposal; obtaining funding; and determining the timeline, the budget, the staff and team, resources, reports, client and stakeholder relations, and quality control.

Project Proposal

If you are part of a small organization, it might not be mandatory that you formulate a project proposal to proceed. But as the demand for digital services and increased information technology supports increases, many organizations have instituted a mandatory proposal process so that each project is carefully thought out and resources can be scheduled.

Even if this step is not required, it is a good idea to consider formalizing your proposal in writing. A succinct, well-thought-out document can be used to support your idea and sell it to stakeholders (who will appreciate a clearly outlined description that includes the project's impact, timeline, and resources requirements). If the potential funding source is from a grant, this document can serve as a basis for your grant application.

A proposal may vary in length and complexity, depending on specific circumstances, but typically it will include

- the goals of the project
- a description of activities involved
- its significance to and impact on its intended audience and the organization
- a timeline
- a budget
- required resources

Timeline

Usually time is one of the constraints on a project. For example, a university's general research and reference tutorial may need to be ready at the start of the fall term, or a professor may need a course-related tutorial two weeks before a research assignment is due. Any project is more effective if there is a detailed timeline to follow. A timeline will include the project schedule that details tasks and activities, projected completion dates, and persons assigned to each task. Project management software is available to track timelines (e.g., Microsoft Project), but a timeline can be done without investing in expensive software. A spreadsheet will work well, and a Google search will return links to free project management software.

To create a timeline, make a list of all activities involved in each phase of the project, put them in sequential order, estimate the time it will take to complete each task, and assign responsibility to each team member. You may want to set up different views of the timeline—weekly, monthly, and overall views. A good model that will work is a Gantt chart, also known as a bar chart. An example of an open-source web-based project management application can be found at Zoho Project (http://projects.zoho.com).

Budget

Managing the project budget can be a major task in a large-scale project. If you are starting with nothing, you may have to create a budget before your project is approved. Using the results from the initial resource needs analysis, you may have to consider expenditures for hardware and software. If you don't have trained staff, you may have to factor in application training to the budget. Human resources, even if you aren't paying an extra salary to someone on staff, are a major budget item, because staff hours spent on the project will most likely be one of the largest costs for which you must account.

Funding the Project

The source of funds to support your project should be identified as early as possible in the planning stages because the viability of continuing may hinge on it. If your project is small and you already have appropriate facilities, hardware, software, and trained staff, funding might not be a real issue. But if the project marks your entry into the web production arena, substantial funding may be necessary for you to be able to proceed. Communication with the administrators of your organization will provide a means to assess the situation. Is there flexibility in the current library budget that will permit funds to be available immediately, or is it necessary to ask for funding from your governing body to be included in a future budget? Does the fact that, nationally, library funding has declined significantly (American Library Association 2009) mean that you will need to research possible grant programs that can pay for your project? If you determine that a grant is the best way to approach funding the project, most application processes will extend the project implementation time because of the length of time required for application review and approval processes. The appendix at the end of this book cites various sources for locating and securing grants and funding.

Staffing and Teamwork

Forming the right team for your project and managing the resulting team dynamics may be one of the most challenging aspects of the project. As you are forming your team, keep in mind the roles that may need to be filled:

Web author—creates the web pages for the instruction

Scripting programmer—adds interactivity into the tutorial through scripting or other technologies

Instructional designer—determines the best way to present the content in an online environment to optimize retention

Content specialist—determines the content to include (may be the library's bibliographic instructor or the subject specialist for the content being presented)

Writer—writes the script and content

Editor—edits the script and content

Graphic or animation designer or videographer—understands user interface design and creates graphics and other multimedia

Systems designer—designs how the instruction will work from a technical standpoint, works with instructional designer on flowcharts and storyboard, manages authors, and selects authoring tools

Information technology specialist—provides the expertise on server and network issues

Evaluation specialist—creates evaluation plan and tools

Marketing specialist—handles the planning and execution of publicity

Project manager—oversees the process and the team

It is important to define the roles and responsibilities for each team member and to associate those roles with the tasks to be accomplished. This ensures that all participants understand the team structure and expectations.

Depending on the skills of existing library staffers, there may be a need to go outside the library to locate people with the skills to produce the instruction. Even with qualified staff, you will want to select people who will complement one another and "subordinate personal prominence to the efficiency of the whole," which is the definition of *teamwork* from *Webster's New Collegiate Dictionary*.

Resource Allocation

Most organizations don't have unlimited resources. Even if you've determined that you have the necessary resources to complete your project, you may be sharing those resources with others in your organization. For example, your content specialist may be the library's bibliographic instructor, the site designer may be the systems administrator, and the like. Most likely, your team members won't be able to devote 100 percent of their time to this project. Scheduling dedicated time that team members can commit to a particular project is important to meeting the project timelines. You also may be sharing hardware and software resources with others in your organization (and with the public), and the project manager will have to become involved in allocating those resources so they are available when team members need them.

Reports

Depending on the scope of the project, it may be necessary to submit progress reports to your client and stakeholders at crucial points throughout the process. In addition, regular reports can serve as an effective record-keeping method that will be a valuable tool for project evaluation. Reports can also be a good way to communicate the overall progress to team members. If your project is grant funded, you may be sure that there will be a reporting component required.

Client Relations

If you are working with a client, you will want the client to stay informed and satisfied with the progress of the project. Therefore, you must make time to communicate regularly. Maintaining a good relationship with the client can make a world of difference if the project gets off schedule for whatever reason. Clients are much more likely to be understanding of extenuating circumstances if they have been kept in the loop in a positive manner.

Quality Control

Overseeing the emergence of an exemplary product calls for quality checks at each step of the production. You may incorporate both formal and informal methods of evaluation if your tutorial is meeting expectations of the criteria established in the preproduction stage. These methods will be discussed in detail in chapter 8.

It should be evident by now that even though the design and development process provides a structure to follow, it is a nonlinear process with more than one way to implement each phase. There is plenty of room for variations depending on the nature of the project, the team you have assembled, the characteristics of your client, and the leadership style of the project manager. Keep in mind the main factors that will influence how you proceed: money (budget), time (scheduling), staffing (expertise), and facilities (hardware and software). Finally, remember that no matter how important it is to be systematic, it is just as imperative to provide space for creativity.

CHAPTER FOUR

SELECTING PROJECT DEVELOPMENT TOOLS

A S DISCUSSED IN the previous chapter, analyzing hardware and software needs is an important part of the preproduction stage of your web project. There are three major areas to consider: constraints that may exist depending on the hardware and software available to users, development hardware, and authoring software.

USER CONSTRAINTS

One of the main benefits of a web-based delivery system is that it can be used across platforms. A platform is the underlying hardware or software for a system, commonly called the operating system. Customarily, software application programs were developed to run on a particular platform. A developer who wanted an application to run on multiple platforms was required to write separate programs. But with the language of the Web, it doesn't matter if your students are on PC-compatible, Macintosh, or Linux platforms. However, you do have to worry about what hardware and software your audience uses to access your instruction.

So, what do you need to be concerned about? Your main concerns fall into three categories: hardware issues, browser issues, and access methods.

Hardware Issues

It is doubtful that you are in the envious situation of all of your users having late-model, identical computers. More and more, users are accessing the Web through mobile devices. Therefore, you must take into account the range of hardware they will use to access your instructional site.

Monitor Screen Size and Display Capabilities

Display capabilities can vary greatly. It is interesting to note that, as of early 2009, the majority of Internet users worldwide chose a screen resolution that is higher than 1024×768 pixels (the number of individual points of color; in this case, 1024 points horizontally and 768 vertically). But 20 percent are still using 1024×768 (W3Schools 2010). There are still some users who are viewing 800×600 pixel resolutions. As you lay out the design for your user interface, you need to take care in selecting a display size. If you design your site at a high resolution and your user's screen can display only 1024×768, that user will not be able to view the entire screen and will have to scroll both horizontally and vertically to read the contents of the screen. This is tedious for the person trying to focus on the content of a site. The display resolution should be no larger than the lowest resolution a user may have. A Google search for "screen size tester" or "screen resolution test" will return many free tools that will show how a site will display at different resolutions.

Processor Speed

The clock speed of a processor, or central processing unit (CPU), determines how fast the processor interprets and executes program instructions (commands). Since 2000, newly manufactured computers have been produced with gigahertz processors, often dual core (essentially two processors in one). A 3.6 gigahertz computer will execute 3,600 million cycles per second. Because every instruction requires a specific number of cycles, the clock speed helps determine how fast those instructions will be executed. If your users have computers with lower CPU speeds and you create a tutorial that requires a great number of commands to be issued simultaneously, users will have a hard time with the tutorial because it will respond slowly.

Random Access Memory

Random access memory (RAM) is the second part of the equation for speed, along with the processor. It is the place in the computer where data is stored during the short term for easy access. When RAM fills up, the computer must pull the data from the hard drive, which slows down processes considerably. Computers with more RAM installed will be able to run programs more quickly than those with minimal RAM. Keep in mind that your instruction isn't the only thing that is running on a computer at a given time. The operating system, web browser, and other applications use available RAM also. Graphics-intensive applications require more RAM, so keep that in mind if you are designing instruction that relies heavily on animation or video.

Sound

Although it seems self-evident, if you are planning to incorporate audio into your instruction, make sure that your audience has access to a computer with sound capabilities. In many public areas, including computer labs, the sound may be disabled so that others will not be disturbed. If part of the instruction will convey important information in audio format, you will need to decide how to deliver it in public environments (perhaps by providing access to headphones).

Browser Issues

Several different web browsers are available. Major browsers in use in 2010 are Windows Internet Explorer, Mozilla Firefox, Apple Safari, Google Chrome, and Opera. But different versions of those browsers are in the marketplace concurrently. Because users don't necessarily abandon their current browser and update to the newest version, and because latest versions incorporate new technologies that have been developed since the previous update, you may find that you have browser-compatibility issues. If you decide to incorporate a certain type of scripting to provide interaction or use some of the more recent markup language elements, in older browsers, your page may not function as you had planned. Some features that are not supported in aging browsers include Cascading Style Sheets, frames, and RSS. These are defined and discussed in later chapters. At this point, it is important to know only what browsers support the features you plan to use. There are sites like Webmonkey.com that track browser support by feature (www.webmonkey.com/2010/02/windows_browser_chart/ and www.webmonkey.com/2010/02/mac_browser_chart/). In addition, there are utilities available on the Web that you can use to test the compatibility of browsers with your pages. Browsershots.org is an example of a free open-source service that will take screen shots of your site in different browsers.

Access Method

How are your users going to access the instruction? Are they all on the local network that uses fiber-optic cable? Do they subscribe to an Internet service provider (ISP) via cable modem or a digital subscriber line (DSL)? Do any of them connect to your site via a modem over an analog phone line? If there are modem users, you will want to be able to gauge how fast your pages will load under different connect rates. Figure 4.1 shows a tool from WebSiteOptimization.com that can be used to test how fast a web page downloads at six different connection speeds. Slow load times can mean frustration for your users.

Determining the constraints your users have with their software and hardware will help you make decisions about what type of authoring systems are required for graphics, video, and audio. That, in turn, will help with decision making on selecting development hardware.

DEVELOPMENT HARDWARE

Having the appropriate development hardware to create a multimedia project will make the project move along much more smoothly. Nothing is harder than trying to create multimedia programs with substandard equipment. However, budgets can vary enormously and you may have to make concessions. What follows is a general discussion of items to consider when selecting the hardware to be used. For help in researching specific hardware and selection criteria, refer to the resources section at the end of this book.

Figure 4.1
WEB PAGE SPEED REPORT

CONNECTION RATE	DOWNLOAD TIME
14.4K	17.31 seconds
28.8K	8.85 seconds
33.6K	7.65 seconds
56K	4.75 seconds
ISDN 128K	1.73 seconds
T1 1.44Mbps	0.52 seconds

Source: WebSiteOptimization.com, www.websiteoptimization.com/services/analyze/.

Computer Selection

Before you design and produce your web-based instruction, you will need to select the computer workstations to be used. You may decide to have one central computer where the entire production will take place, or you may choose to do different portions of the production on different computers. Deciding which workstations to use must be done in conjunction with the choice of authoring software (discussed later). Software is developed according to what platform it will run on, so if you decide on an application that is available only on a Windows operating system, then you clearly need a computer that runs Windows. Similarly, each software application has minimum system requirements for it to perform properly. These include processor speed; operating system type; amount of RAM; available hard-disk space; color display capability of the video card; and availability of an optical drive, sound card, and network interface card (NIC) or modem. Normally, the software manufacturer lists both minimum requirements and recommended specifications. Don't be surprised if you discover that running a certain application on a computer with the minimum specifications results in less-than-satisfactory performance. As mentioned, any application you run will be competing with other programs for system resources. It is always a good idea to configure a computer to exceed the minimum requirements listed. The good news is that computer prices continue to plunge quickly as capacities for storage, processing speeds, and memory have increased. Powerful computers are more affordable than ever.

You will also want to investigate the input and output capabilities available on a computer before you make your selection. Most computers now come equipped with a digital video disc (DVD) burner, which will also write to compact discs (CDs). Such a drive is critical if that is the method you have chosen to back up your data or provide an alternate delivery mechanism. Most internal DVD recorder drives are designed with parallel ATA interfaces. External DVD drives either use USB 2.0 or IEEE 1394 (FireWire) connectors. The storage capacity on DVD media is approximately 4.5 gigabytes (GB), quite an increase over the CD-R capacity of 700 megabytes (MB). There are different types of DVD recording media, and it is important to understand which you need for your purposes. First, DVD-R records data once and cannot be changed. DVD-R and DVD+R are both rewritable up to a thousand times; DVD RAM is rewritable up to a hundred thousand times but is less compatible between systems than DVD-R and DVD+R.

The standard connection interface for most computer peripherals is the Universal Serial Bus (USB). Introduced in the late 1990s to standardize the wide array of PC connectors, USB 2.0, introduced in 2000, is the most common USB specification. However, USB 3.0 was released in 2008, and has a maximum transfer rate of 10 times above the 2.0 rate. As this standard becomes integrated, it will be important to make sure that equipment selected is compatible with the version of USB in the computer you are using.

Peripherals Selection

A peripheral is any external device that attaches to a computer. Although you might not know them by this term, as a computer user, you are familiar with many computer peripherals. Typically, the purpose of peripherals is to input or output data; some do both. Common input peripherals are the keyboard and the mouse. One of the most common output devices is the printer. Peripherals that serve both functions include hard disks, optical disks, and modems. Several devices that you will want to consider for a web project include monitors, video adapters, sound cards, scanners, cameras, camcorders, video cards, and removable file storage systems.

Monitor

The monitor is the most common output device, and it is not one you can choose to do without. However, as briefly described previously, there are considerations for selecting the appropriate monitor for a multimedia project.

Just a few years ago, one of the major monitor choices to make was whether to get a cathode-ray tube (CRT) or liquid crystal display (LCD) monitor. Both had their advantages and disadvantages, but the advantages of LCD have triumphed—now, this is the standard monitor available for purchase. In an LCD monitor, a tiny cell that contains a layer of liquid crystal produces each pixel. It's a more sophisticated version of the display technology you see in digital watches and is the technology that is used in laptop computers.

One of the most popular advantages that turned the tide for LCD monitors is their thin profile and light weight. Also, LCDs consume half the power of CRTs. Another benefit of the LCD is that the display-size specification is a real indicator of the viewable area. What is the downside to LCD monitors? The view angle can pose a problem. If a person sits at an odd angle to the computer screen, the picture may be hard to see and the color will be skewed. This becomes an issue if working with another person on a single monitor. Another shortcoming of the LCD in a web development environment is that its technology entails a fixed number of pixels being hardwired, which means that it has a fixed native resolution, and whatever that is, is the optimal one. Changing the resolution to see how pages display at different resolutions will be difficult to accomplish. At lower resolutions, the screen is redrawn so that the pixels are blown up to fit the screen, which results in a jagged image.

The following sections go over some of the choices to consider when selecting an LCD monitor.

Screen Size. A primary factor to consider in choosing a monitor is its size. In general, the larger the screen size, the more pixels it can display horizontally and vertically. The size is measured in the same manner as a television screen—diagonally from one corner to another. Today, screens twenty inches and larger are increasingly affordable. It goes without saying that it's best to get the largest size that you can afford when the creation of multimedia projects is your focus. The extra screen space in a larger display makes work with multiple windows at the same time much easier. Wide-screen monitors are also popular and offer the same benefit of providing more space to work.

Resolution. The higher the resolution—the number of pixels (squares) per inch—of the monitor, the sharper the image will be. It is useful to have a monitor that can display multiple resolutions so you can test your page design in the different resolutions your audience will use. In addition, LCD monitors that specify a native resolution number (e.g., 1280×1024 pixels) also support lesser resolutions (1024×768, 800×600, and 640×480).

Aspect Ratio. This figure represents the ratio of the width to the height of the screen.

Color Depth. Color depth, also called bit depth, describes the number of bits used to describe a pixel. A bit (short for binary digit) is the smallest unit of data in a computer. One bit has a value of either zero or one. Depending on the capability of the display mode and video adapter, a pixel can be described by one bit (monochrome) and up to twenty-four bits (true color). The chart in figure 4.2 shows the bit depths used to display different numbers of colors.

An important point to remember when you are relying on the colors displayed on a monitor is that different monitors display the same colors differently. It's not a good idea to get your mind set on a particular hue because it will not necessarily look the same on another display. In addition, there are only 216 colors that display consistently in web browsers on older eight-bit color monitors. In chapter 5, we will discuss issues in selecting web-safe colors to ensure the color you intend is the one your audience sees.

Dot Pitch. The dot pitch refers to the distance between the centers of two adjacent pixels. A smaller dot pitch means less granularity exists, which translates into a sharper image.

Figure 4.2
BIT DEPTH AND NUMBER OF COLORS

BIT DEPTH	NUMBER OF COLORS
1	2 (monochrome)
2	4 (CGA)
4	16 (EGA)
8	256 (VGA)
16	65,536 (high color, XGA)
24	16,777,216 (true color, SVGA)
32[a]	16,777,216 (true color + alpha channel)

[a]Special graphics mode used to achieve certain effects.

Contrast Ratio. The contrast ratio relates to the range between the brightest and darkest points a display can produce. A 500:1 ratio means the brightest white is five hundred times brighter than the darkest black.

Brightness. Brightness, also called luminance, is the amount of light that is emitted from the display.

Viewing Angle. More properly called viewing direction, the viewing angle is the maximum angle at which a display can be viewed with acceptable visual performance. This viewing range is called the viewing cone.

Response Time. The response time is the amount of time an LCD monitor takes to go from black to white and back to black. Lower numbers mean faster response time.

Video Adapter

The performance of your monitor depends partly on the video adapter (also called a video card or graphics card), which is usually installed in an expansion slot on the system board or is sometimes integrated. Its primary component is a video controller that sends data to the display and provides digital-to-analog conversion (converting strings of binary zeros and ones to output that is meaningful to humans—in this case, a picture). Video adapters contain their own memory: the computer's RAM isn't used for storing displays. Higher resolutions require more video RAM. The memory in the video adapter relates directly to the capacity of the display modes discussed in the previous section. Video adapters can offer additional functions such as video capture, television output, FireWire, or the ability to use multiple monitors. When you are working on a multimedia project, the computer you use should have the highest quality video adapter possible within budget.

Sound Card

To include audio in the project, a sound card is required. A sound card serves as both an input device (from a microphone, radio, tape deck, CD player, or CD-ROM) and output device (via speakers, headphones, or CD-R/DVD-R). It will be used in both capacities to capture audio and play it back. Sound cards are available in both analog and digital format, or with both capabilities.

Analog technology is used when inputting sound from a microphone or outputting to a speaker. The card takes normal analog (electronic transmission via signals of varying frequency) signals and converts them to digital ones (electronic technology that stores and processes data as zeros and ones) and copies it onto the hard drive or another storage device. This part of the card is called the analog-to-digital converter (ADC). To hear what's been recorded, the sound card works in reverse, converting the digital information back to analog and feeding to a speaker that generates the sound. This part of the card is known as the digital-to-analog converter (DAC).

The newer digital sound-card technology is practical for applications that need digital sound, because no conversion is required. Digital cards have provisions for digital input and output so you can transfer data directly from the source (e.g., a CD) onto your hard drive.

Sound cards come as part of the basic configuration when purchasing a new computer. A basic sound card should have a line in and a line out, but it may go beyond that and have additional input and output (I/O) connectors for things such as CD audio and video. Your sound card should support the two digital audio standards: Musical Instrument Digital Interface (MIDI), a standard for representing music electronically, and Sound Blaster, which is the de facto standard for PC sound.

You will find that most sound cards come as a chip set right on the motherboard of the computer (the part of the computer that contains the computer's basic circuitry and components). In most cases, the quality of the integrated sound is good enough for most projects. However, adding a sound card into one of the computer's expansion slots is an option for projects that require a better quality than what is built in.

In addition, don't forget to acquire a microphone and speakers so that you can input and play back the audio you create. Headphones can also be a useful tool for working on an audio digitization project.

Scanners

Scanners come in a variety of types and price ranges. A flatbed scanner is the most popular format and will serve well for most web projects. It can be used to scan photos, pictures, and pages from books. It consists of a flat surface on which you place the document or image to be scanned. When a light passes over the document, the scanner converts the light to a computer-readable format. A color scanner has three light sources, one each for red, blue, and green.

You will find two different technologies available for flatbed scanners: contact image sensor (CIS) and the traditional charged-coupled device (CCD). The CIS scanners are much smaller, sometimes only a few inches thick. This is possible because these devices gather light from red, green, and blue light-emitting diodes (LEDs) that are directed at the original document. The LEDs take up much less space than the CCD technology, which relies on a system of mirrors and lenses to project the scanned image. The CIS scanners also require less power than CCD scanners and often run from a battery or through a USB port on the computer.

The term you see most often in discussions of scanners is *resolution*. You will see scanner specifications that talk about 600×600 dpi (dots per inch) or 1200×1200 dpi. For web projects, it's not necessary to use a scanner capable of the higher resolutions. Web images display at a maximum of 72 or 96 dpi, depending on the operating system. To ensure small file size for faster downloading, you want to scan your graphics at 72 or 96 dpi. Other features to consider when choosing a scanner include mode of connectivity to the computer, maximum scan size, and scan speed. Most scanners come bundled with imaging and optical character recognition (OCR) software, so that may become a factor in choosing a particular brand or model.

Cameras

Digital cameras have become highly popular as their image quality has improved and the prices have dropped. Good-quality digital cameras are very affordable, offer convenience and flexibility that lend themselves to usefulness in web projects, and can range from compact point-and-shoot to single-lens reflex (SLR) models. Many of today's digital cameras also come with audio- and video-recording capabilities. They are also often incorporated into other devices such as cell phones and personal digital assistants (PDAs).

With a digital camera, the image is captured in a digital format that is immediately ready for transfer to a computer, and the image can then be manipulated with graphics-editing software. In a digital camera, a charge coupled device (CCD) or complementary metal-oxide semiconductor (CMOS) sensor performs the imaging. The CCD or CMOS replaces both the shutter and the film found in traditional cameras. For an in-depth discussion of digital camera technologies, refer to the HowStuffWorks article on digital cameras at electronics.howstuffworks.com/digital-camera.htm.

There are three fundamental issues to consider when selecting a digital camera: image quality, memory storage, and connectivity. In addition, there are several other features to check, such as lens type, battery life, flash capability, and file formats. Whether they are critical depends on the parameters of your project.

Image Quality. The quality of the image depends on many things, but the most marketed feature is the resolution of the CCD. Resolutions are now routinely 6-8 megapixels and even the most inexpensive cameras have sufficient pixel count for any web project. In reality, the number of megapixels is not the primary factor that ensures a quality image. Dynamic range, the range of tones the sensor is able to reproduce, is very important to quality. Other factors are the on-board image processing hardware, low light performance, and the lens (discussed later in this section).

Memory Storage. Today's digital cameras use removable storage, which comes in a variety of formats. The main advantage is that when a memory card is full, you can remove it and insert another in its place without having to stop and load the images onto a computer. A second advantage is that the cards can be inserted directly into a computer (with the correct accompanying hardware) and treated as a disk.

Types of storage systems available include built-in fixed memory, which is found in older or inexpensive cameras, and flash memory cards, which come in a variety of form factors.

The amount of storage on each system varies because different storage capacities result in different retail prices. The memory capacity of the card must be coupled with the resolution of the images being captured to determine how many images will fit on one card. In a typical example found in the listed specification of a 10-megapixel camera with a 512 MB memory card, more than 3,300 images fit on the card when the camera is set to capture good quality at 640×480 resolution, but only 117 images fit when the camera is set to its best-quality highest resolution. The higher resolution capability is very important if the desired output is a large print. For web projects, lower resolutions are preferred.

Connectivity. Once the images are on the camera, they need to be trans-ferred to a computer for editing. Some cameras provide the option of connecting directly from the camera to a computer port and into an image-download software application. However, this requires power from the camera, is a slow procedure, and can drain batteries very quickly. If you are going to download in this fashion, use the AC adapter that normally comes with the camera, and save your batteries.

Most commonly, your computer recognizes the camera's storage device as another drive. This enables you to use the features of your operating system to copy or move the files from the camera to a folder, independent of any image management software (discussed in the next section).

Different devices, known as card adapters or readers, are available that work like a bridge between the camera and the computer. You insert the memory card in the reader, which is connected to the computer, to down-load the images. The standard digital camera cable connection today is USB. A digital camera will come with the correct USB cable included. Another option is FireWire, originally developed by Apple, which is the standard referred to as IEEE (Institute of Electrical and Electronic Engineers) 1394. A major benefit of both USB and FireWire is that they are hot pluggable, which means that they can be connected and used without having to first turn off the computer.

Cameras that are integrated into other devices such as a cell phone can typically be transferred from the device via cables, Bluetooth (short-distance wireless) technology, or through its mobile networking capabilities.

Camera Features. Almost every digital camera has an LCD panel, which allows you to preview and arrange pictures without having to transfer the images to a computer. It also is the interface for adjusting camera settings such as resolution selection for basic editing, and it can serve in place of the viewfinder as well. You will want to examine how the LCD works because it is different on each model. If the LCD is the only viewfinder (and not just a supplement to the customary one), you should also consider that LCD panels are hard to see in the direct sunlight.

Check to see if the camera has a fixed- or auto-focus lens. With a fixed-focus lens everything from a few feet on will be in focus. This won't help if you need to photograph something close up. Most cameras have some kind of zoom capability, which might include either two or three predefined settings or gradual zoom action. If the ability to take close-up pictures is critical to your project, you will want to be sure that your camera includes a zoom feature. Two different types of zoom are available: optical and digital. Optical zoom is similar to the type of zoom in a regular 35 mm camera; when you zoom, the physical lens moves in and out. With a digital zoom there are no moving parts and the camera's "brain" digitally zooms in, simulating the optical zoom electronically. This process essentially crops the image and then fills in pixels to enlarge the image back to the specified size—a negative effect overall. You can accomplish the same effect using image-editing software. The most important zoom to consider, then, is the optical capacity.

Battery life is an important component of choosing a digital camera. There is a wide variation in how long a camera will last with one set of batteries. A single camera can vary depending on whether you leave the LCD in preview mode or do most of your image selection and arranging within the camera rather than after you have transferred the images to the computer. Different cameras use different modes of transfer, and some of those modes are memory hogs. If you are going to use batteries consistently, then invest in rechargeable ones, which, although more expensive up front, will save you money in the long run. There are different rechargeable battery technologies, and the more you are aware of them, the better off you will be. Nickel cadmium (NiCad) batteries are those whose performance suffers if they are not charged properly (by making sure the charge is completely drained before recharging). Nickel metal hydride (NiMH) is a more current technology that does not have memory problems. Lithium ion (LiOn) batteries are the longest lasting of the rechargeables and don't have memory problems, but they are the most expensive. Some cameras use proprietary batteries rather than standard sizes, such as AA. Whether to buy a camera with nonstandard batteries is an important consideration. Even if you use rechargeable ones, if the charge gives out at an inopportune moment, it will be much more convenient to locate regular alkaline batteries to use in the short term until you can recharge yours!

Another feature of digital cameras is the flash capability. Find out what the range is, whether there is red-eye reduction, and if you can override the flash if you choose to do so. Many cameras also have a self-timer that allows you to get yourself into a picture you're taking.

Many digital cameras are now available with the capability to capture short video clips. The type of format captured varies depending on the manufacturer. Common file formats available include Moving Pictures Expert Group (MPEG), Audio-Video Interleave (AVI), and QuickTime, which are discussed in more detail in chapter 6. If you just need a few seconds of video, using the digital camera to record can be more cost effective than purchasing a digital camcorder.

Audio capture, another option featured in many digital cameras, can be used to annotate information about the picture being taken. It also allows audio to be captured with the video clips if the clips are also a camera feature.

What image format choices does the camera offer? If you are going to use the camera for web projects, then it is very handy to have JPEG (Joint Photographic Experts Group, also discussed in detail in chapter 6) as one of the choices, because the JPEG format is supported on the Web and will save you the step of having to convert from a non-Web-supported format. Fortunately, this format is the de facto standard. If the camera captures images only in its native format, how easy is it to export it to the format you require?

Accessories. Depending on the types of images you want to create, you may also want to consider acquiring a tripod to ensure that your images are sharp. A tripod is beneficial when photographing things such as architecture. It will be essential for making a virtual reality tour, where you would be photographing a 360-degree view of a room. There are specialized accessories to help with a panoramic photographic project. Finally, although many cameras come equipped with a case and strap, don't forget to ask about these essential accessories.

Video Camcorders

Over the past few years, the barriers to widespread use of video have fallen. Digital video capability has been integrated into many digital cameras, cell phones, and laptops. Products such as Flip Video (www.theflip.com) have introduced price points that put video cameras within reach of mass consumers. Websites such as YouTube (www.youtube.com) have demonstrated the ease of creating and sharing footage.

If you are planning to incorporate video into your project, be aware that video editing is one of the most resource-hungry computer tasks. Video production requires a fast computer with plenty of RAM and hard disk space. Luckily, most personal computers today are configured with enough power and storage to handle a typical web video project.

If your project requires a higher quality than can be provided by integrated video on a multipurpose device, you might consider purchasing a dedicated camcorder. Analog camcorders have all but disappeared from the consumer market, and with good reason—digital camcorders remove the time-consuming step of converting to digital format.

Typically, digital camcorders come equipped with features such as LCD monitors and zoom lenses. These need the same considerations as discussed in the previous digital camera section. The major choice will be which digital media type to select.

MiniDV Tape. The MiniDV tape records digitally but on a digital video tape. If archiving is a concern, this may be a good option. Tapes offer good video quality but slow transfer time from camera to computer (real-time speed). Also, tapes that are recorded on repeatedly deteriorate over time. This is an older digital technology and its popularity is waning. Consider the expense of buying tapes when you are evaluating this type.

DVD Based. The DVD-based camcorders are equipped with a mini-DVD recorder that stores the video as it is captured. These discs are smaller than a regular DVD disc (3 inches and 1.4 gigabytes of storage). You want to make sure that the smaller disc will work in the DVD drive in your production computer. The price of purchasing the media over time should be a consideration for this camcorder.

Hard-Drive Storage. The hard-drive storage type of camcorder has a hard drive installed in the unit. It is a completely reusable media, just like the hard drive on a computer. These have a large storage capacity but are more susceptible to wear and tear over time because a hard drive has moving parts.

Compact Flash Memory. As with other electronics, flash memory is becoming more prevalent in digital camcorders. A flash drive can be reused unlimited times without deterioration. Because it is removable media and many computers have slots configured for flash memory, they can be very convenient when it is time to transfer the video for editing.

SD/SDHC. The capacity for storage on SD cards (Secure Digital) has increased with the advent of SDHC (Secure Digital High Capacity), which can hold up to 32 gigabytes (as of mid-2009). These removable storage memory cards are popular because they are interchangeable in many portable devices.

Video Codec

Video codec is a device or software that enables the compression and/or decompression of digital video. An algorithm, or specialized computer program, known as codec (compressor/decompressor) controls the amount of compression. Basically, a video codec is used to compress the video data to reduce file size and to decompress it for viewing. When a video is compressed with any particular codec, that same codec must be installed on the machine that will be used to view the video, because the video must be decompressed with the same codec that it was compressed with. Common codecs are M-JPEG, MPEG-1, MPEG-4, WMV (Windows Media Video), Real Video, and DV (digital video). Different codecs are more appropriate for some tasks than for others. For instance, MPEG-1, which is designed to pack a large quantity of video into a small file and is a low-loss compression technique, is used primarily with CD-ROMs but is also found on the Web. The newer MPEG-4 is a codec standard that is designed for the delivery of interactive multimedia on the Web. It includes specifications for video, audio, and interactivity. The WMV and Real Video codecs are also good choices for the Web because many computers already have these codecs installed. Some of the codecs are "lossy," meaning that frames (the individual still images in a video sequence) are dropped to decrease file size. This can result in a choppy video.

Importing a digital video into a computer for editing is just like copying files from a peripheral over a high-speed connection. The two most common high-speed digital connections that are used to transfer video to your computer are USB 2.0 and the IEEE 1394 interface, known most commonly as FireWire. You may also hear it referred to as i.LINK (Sony). Digital camcorders come equipped with these ports. If your preference is FireWire, you may need to add a card that supports IEEE 1394 if your computer doesn't come equipped with one.

Other features should be considered in making a digital camcorder selection. If the digital camcorder will be used to record from older analog camcorders, be certain additional ports are included, such as S-video. Investigate the microphone that is included. A front-mounted microphone will get better results than a top-mounted one. An external microphone is the best option; so if possible, select a model that includes a microphone jack. The size of the LCD screen can be important; a larger one makes it easier to see what's being recorded and facilitates playback. Digital camcorders are now available in high definition, and although they offer superior footage, there are drawbacks if the primary purpose of the camcorder is for web usage. They are more expensive, are not always compatible with standard video-editing applications, and often are difficult to output in high definition. Investigate the type of image stabilization: optical or electronic. With optical, the lens mechanism moves to compensate for movement. With electronic, the image captured by the lens "floats" on the CCD, and internal circuitry interprets the video. If affordable, choose optical stabilization. Check to see how the camcorder handles lighting. Many come with low-light modes that can be useful for interior filming.

Removable File Storage

You will want to take into account how you will share and store your files as your project progresses. It may be that you have access to a network file server where files can be shared with everyone on your team, but usually there will be some need to transport files between computers, make backups or archives, or store large files. As you are deciding on which type of storage to select, consider the following features:

- capacity (how much data it will store)
- media costs (for the drive and the disks)
- durability (of the storage media)
- portability (ability to be moved from one computer to another)
- speed (how fast the data transfers)
- interface (how the device connects to your computer)

An external hard drive is like the internal drive found in your computer but comes in a sealed case and connects to your computer via a USB cable. Storage capacities at more than a terabyte are now available at affordable prices.

Optical Storage. The most common medium is CD-R (CD-recordable) and CD-RW (CD-rewritable), which provide a storage capacity of more than 700 MB. The CD-R format allows you to write data to it one time, whereas CD-RW drives allow you to overwrite data previously written to disk. Storage with DVD-R and DVD-RW functions much like CD-R/CD-RW but offers up to 4.76 gigabytes of storage capacity in a single sided disc.

Media storage cards. Media storage cards, like those used in digital cameras and discussed earlier, can also be used to store all types of data in addition to images. Called flash memory, these cards provide solid-state storage, meaning that the devices have no moving parts. Cards with capacities of up to 32 gigabytes are available.

One of the most common and popular portable storage devices is the USB flash drive. They are very useful for transferring data between computers and are about the size of your thumb or a car key. Because of their size, you will also hear them referred to as key drives, jump drives, thumb drives, and pen drives. As with other types of removable storage, flash drives come in a range of capacities, ranging up to 256 gigabytes as of 2010.

AUTHORING SOFTWARE PROGRAMS

There are many different types of software applications that you may need to produce multimedia, interactive web instruction. This section presents an overview of the most common categories of authoring software. Examples of each type of tool are highlighted, but be sure to refer to the resources section in the appendix for links to comprehensive sites for researching each category. Your selection will depend on the platform you have chosen for your development hardware, the minimum system specification required, and the types of multimedia and interactivity you have decided to incorporate in your project.

Significant advances have taken place with the advent of social networking and open-source applications in the past few years. Before investing in commercial products, many of which are expensive, explore the options for developing your instruction "in the cloud" (virtualized services available over the Internet) or using freely available applications that can be as functional as commercial ones. An interesting example of developing in the cloud is available from Google, with its Google Sites service (sites. google.com).

If you prefer to purchase commercial applications, keep in mind that many software applications are available for evaluation at no charge. You can find demo versions on company websites and can test-drive them before you make a purchase decision. Also, many companies offer significant price cuts to educational institutions and students. Always check to see whether there is academic pricing if your organization qualifies as such!

Web Authoring

As Lynch and Horton (2008) note, as the Web has matured and become a mainstream tool, there are capable web-based tools and genres that have emerged to augment and even replace conventional websites. The result is that there is a move away from traditional publishing tools like Adobe Dreamweaver in favor of easier-to-use collaborative tools that don't require a high level of technical expertise to master. In the following discussion, traditional tools will be introduced, as well as some of the new possibilities for development.

HTML (Static)

There are different ways to approach authoring web pages for your project. How you decide to do it should depend on the types of interactivity you plan to use, your team members' levels of expertise, and their preference for working either directly with the source code or using a visual method.

You can write HTML without using a web editor. With the most basic text editor, Notepad (Windows) or TextEdit (Mac), you simply write the HTML markup code manually. This is probably not the most practical approach for the novice, however, because it is quite time consuming, is prone to error, and requires in-depth knowledge of HTML coding and other scripting languages. At the other end of the spectrum are simple visual editors that require no knowledge of HTML and operate like a word-processing application. An example of this is SeaMonkey, an open-source HTML editor, which is a continuation of the Mozilla suite of components (www.seamonkey-project.org). It works well for authoring very basic pages but does not include the functionality that will support the integration of higher-level features, which are discussed in later chapters. Word processors such as Microsoft Word or the open-source OpenOffice (www.open office.org) also have built-in functionality to save documents as web pages, but here again, you will sacrifice the capability to control the editing to the level that is optimal in authoring web pages.

It is best to select an application that has been developed specifically for authoring web pages. Today these applications have matured to the point at which they provide all the features necessary to build complex and advanced web pages. Prices range from free to several hundred dollars—but don't assume that the most expensive is the best. Wikipedia has a comparison of HTML editors that shows general information, operating system support, and functional features (http://en.wikipedia.org/wiki/Comparison_of_HTML_editors).

The two main types are code based and visually based (WYSIWYG, for "what you see is what you get," pronounced "wizzywig"). Both perform the same functions but are very different in how the author works to build a page.

With a code-based editor, the code is in plain view. You can see exactly which tags and attributes you are using. Unlike a plain-text editor, however, a code-based editor can automate the creation of tags and can often automate generating the higher-level features that will bring interactivity to the page. Code is generally color coded so that it is easy to distinguish from the page text. Traditionally, this type of editor has been considered the choice for power users who don't want to give up control of the code. Two examples of this type of editor are Fookes Software NoteTab (for PC, www.notetab.com) and Bare Bones Software's BBEdit (for Mac, www.barebones.com/products/bbedit/).

The visual-based editor has typically been considered more user friendly for most web authors. When using a visual or WYSIWYG interface, the author is shielded from the HTML coding and sees only how the page will display to a user. This method allows the author to concentrate on how the content should appear, but it sacrifices control of the author's ability to fine-tune the source code. Another obstacle to be aware of is that WYSIWYG code is sometimes bloated, which means that it generates unnecessary code. This generally will not make any difference in how your page displays, but it may become an issue if you need to troubleshoot or want to reformat the page. A well-known example of a WYSIWYG editor is Adobe Dreamweaver (for PC and Mac, www.adobe.com/products/dreamweaver/). Amaya (www.w3.org/Amaya/) is an open-source WYSIWYG authoring tool.

Most of each type of editor provide a bridge between the two methods. For instance, a good WYSIWYG editor will have a source inspector in which the author can view and edit the code directly. Similarly, a well-designed code-based editor will have an interface so the author can view the page layout in a browser.

Web-based HTML editors are an option as well. There are benefits to having a website editor that is available from any Internet accessible computer and is platform independent. InnovaStudio offers this type of application (www.innovastudio.com/editor.asp). Google Sites is another example.

No matter which style of editor you decide on, you will want to look for certain features that will help you achieve advanced designs and interactivity. Look for an editor that includes support for the features listed below and that can help with advanced features, which are discussed in later chapters:

- site management
- checking the integrity of source codes
- cross-browser compatibility check
- spell check
- link check
- global find and replace
- support for scripting languages such as JavaScript, Perl, and PHP
- support for standards including XHTML, XML, and XSL
- CSS (cascading style sheet) support
- support for team collaboration
- multiple document display
- design templates

Online Environments for Content Creation

If yours is a small-scale project, a simple web editor may suffice. Some offer features that help manage content to a certain extent with the inclusion of design templates and collaboration features. However, if you are embarking on a large-scale creation of web instruction modules or courses, you may want to investigate developing your instruction in one of the available networked web-based systems. A web content management (WCM) system is used to manage and control a large collection of web materials. Course management systems (CMS), also called learning management systems (CMS) or virtual learning environments (VLEs, most often in the United Kingdom), are designed to facilitate access to content and administration of courses. The potential for similar environments to match or improve on the CMS functionality has introduced Web 2.0 applications such as blogs, wikis, and Facebook into use for interactive and collaborative instruction.

Web Content Management Systems

As the name implies, a web content management system is designed to streamline the management of content on a website by permitting the separation of content from presentation. It consists of two parts: a content management application (CMA) and a content delivery application (CDA). The CMA portion allows dispersed subject specialists to manage the creation and modification of content without needing to be versed in HTML authoring. Staff members who have web design expertise can manage the CDA side of the system centrally. Typically, the systems operate through the use of templates set up centrally with defined areas that are either restricted or available for content addition or editing. Of course, features vary by system (and price!), but typical ones include format management, revision control, indexing, and search and retrieval.

As might be expected, a CMS is available in different levels, from enterprise systems that cost hundreds of thousands of dollars to open-source software such as Zope (www.zope.org).

Course Management Systems

Course management systems (CMS), as they are known in the education field, are systems that are designed to facilitate the development, delivery, and management of learning environments on the Web. Other terms for these systems include *virtual learning environment* (VLE), *learning content management system* (LCMS), and *learning support system* (LSS). In the business world, they are known as learning management systems (LMS). Many institutions are turning to these to provide a way for professors to build interactive online courses or supplement traditional classroom teaching quickly and easily. Courseware software resides not on your computer but on a server. With an institution that already has a courseware product selected and in use, it may be a simple matter to initiate a course for your library instruction. For institutions that do not have their own servers, courseware companies can host your course on their server, sometimes at no charge.

If you decide to select a course management system, there are many companies to choose from and many features available. A good tool to help compare features of many course management systems can be found at

EduTools (www.edutools.info). You should look for a system that includes the following features:

- asynchronous communication (threaded discussions and e-mail)
- synchronous communication (real-time chat and whiteboards on which users can write or draw)
- user authentication
- collaboration via group formation
- survey and testing capabilities
- content creation
- online journal
- file exchange
- grading tools
- course statistics

A framework developed for CMS and LMS is the Shareable Content Object Reference Model (SCORM), an XML-based standard designed to ensure interoperability among systems. It is used to define and access information about learning objects so they can be easily shared between different systems. This standard was developed in response to a U.S. Department of Defense initiative to promote e-learning standardization to facilitate moving course content and other related information cross-platform. Most course management systems support SCORM.

Blackboard has become the major commercial vendor in the CMS market (blackboard.com). Because of the high cost of proprietary systems, many institutions are turning to open-source solutions such as Moodle (http://moodle.org) and Sakai (http://sakaiproject.org).

Web 2.0 Options

Many course management systems are adding in Web 2.0 tools to enhance the virtual learning experience. However, sometimes instructors don't need the secure environment that a CMS provides, and so they turn directly to Web 2.0 tools to use social networking tools independently. Because, by nature, they are designed for easy access, use, and interactivity, they can offer many benefits with low barriers. In Chapter 7, ideas for incorporating interactivity are discussed in more detail.

Blogs

The term *blog* is a contraction of *weblog*. In the past several years, blogs have become mainstream tools for web-based communication. They have evolved from being simple online journals to interactive communities.

Many blogs are collaborative and support multiple user postings. Uses for blogs in education include student reflection, group collaboration, and resource sharing. They can encourage independent thought, facilitate the free flow of ideas, foster discussion, and promote debate or reflection. They can be used in place of online discussion forums or e-mail lists.

A blog is a web-based tool (the front end is a web page, the back end is database driven with an interface to update and edit content). Bloggers post discrete chunks of information called posts that are displayed in reverse chronological order and are date stamped.

Blogs can be combined with an XML-based technology that is included in most blog software: RSS (Real Simple Syndication or Rich Site Summary). Blog content is stored as XML. This code is called a feed, as in news feed. Instead of having to go to each blog of interest, you can subscribe to the content of a blog and the RSS acts as an aggregator in collecting the information and feeding it to you on request. Use of RSS is efficient for instructors who incorporate blogs into their teaching. Instead of having to go to each student's blog to review new content, you can subscribe to their RSS feed and check their aggregator regularly.

The easiest way to start a blog is to use one of many available free services. One of the best known is Blogger.com (www.blogger.com), but there are many to choose from, and you will want to find one that offers the functionality needed to make an interactive blog. Refer to the resources section in this book for several pointers to blog resources to help you get started.

Wiki

Wiki, developed in 1994–1995 by Ward Cunningham, refers to both a website and the software used to create the site. Cunningham's goal was to create a simple website on which programmers could exchange information without waiting for a webmaster to update the site. The term *wiki* comes from a Hawaiian word for fast, and a wikiwikiweb is a quick website. It is an example of social software, one that makes it easy for groups to work together in a virtual environment. Wikis emphasize a group's collective understanding rather than an individual point of view. The basic premise is that authorized users can add, edit, and delete content using nothing more than a web browser and a form (see the next section, about forms). Although this seems fraught with peril, most wiki engines have features that permit monitoring of changes and the ability to restore previous versions of a page if necessary.

Wikis come in a variety of types based on who can access them. Some are fully open to anyone. Others are gated, meaning that some pages may be restricted. There are members-only wikis and ones that have firewalls. An example of a well-known wiki is Wikipedia (wikipedia.org), a free, open-content encyclopedia.

Typical wiki features include

- page creation
- page editing
- text formatting
- linking to an external web page
- a "sandbox" for new users to experiment in (learn to use the wiki)
- a list of recent changes
- a page history
- site searching

Over the past few years, the use of wikis to both support and deliver library instruction has become more commonplace. Particularly with multisession information literacy instruction, wikis can provide a framework that emphasizes user control, radical trust, flexibility, and user autonomy. They can serve as a "bridge between common information literacy skills with which students are familiar and the skills that are considered essential in an information literacy environment" (Smith, Mitchell, and Numbers 2007, 120).

Most wiki software is open source and has been developed collaboratively. The software can be hosted locally on an existing web server, but many wikis are available in a hosted environment. Two examples of wiki software are MediaWiki (www.mediawiki.org) and PBworks (http://pbworks.com).

Facebook

The social networking site Facebook (www.facebook.com) has become almost universally used by today's college students and is so popular that as of spring 2010 it was ranked the second-highest-trafficked site worldwide on Alexa (www.alexa.com/siteinfo/facebook.com). The largest demographic on Facebook in January 2010 was thirty-five- to fifty-four-year-olds, followed by eighteen- to twenty-four-year-olds (Corbett, 2010). Developing instruction space through Facebook groups and/or Facebook pages (www.facebook.com/pages/) puts instruction in a web environment where users already spend time on a daily basis. The ability to customize the default Facebook environment with the addition of third-party applications (Facebook apps) gives even more potential.

Google Docs

Google Docs (docs.google.com) is an example of a cloud-computing document-sharing service. The web-based productivity suite of applications (word processing, spreadsheets, presentation) from Google is free and offers the ability to create and store content in a real-time collaborative environment with designed users. Library instructors are finding it useful for group projects and presentations.

Graphics Applications

If your instruction will incorporate images, some sort of graphics program will be a must for your project. You will find a wide range of choices (and price variations). As with other types of applications, graphics applications have been developed for both the professional artist and the novice. In making a decision, you will want to take into account the expertise and artistic talent of the team member who will be creating your graphics. If you have purchased a scanner or digital camera for your project, it probably had some graphics software bundled as part of the package. If so, assess whether the bundled software will meet your editing needs.

Because you will be creating graphics for display on the Web, one of the basic selection criteria should be that the application provides for the most common supported file formats: GIF (Graphics Interchange Format) and JPEG. It should also allow you to import a variety of graphic formats. These, along with other multimedia formats, are discussed in depth in chapter 6.

Graphics applications can be divided into two major categories that describe how the graphics are created and stored: image editors and illustration software. There are advantages and disadvantages to working with either bitmapped (raster) images or vector graphics, and these are discussed in chapter 6. In addition, an integration of these two types is available, called an object-based editor. Traditionally, these applications have been client-based, installed on an individual computer. However, there is a growing trend toward putting desktop image-processing applications online, so before making a decision, investigate which will serve best in your particular situation. Aviary Tools (http://aviary.com/tools/) is one good example of an online suite of imaging applications. Their comparable free online components are included in the sections that follow.

Image Editors

Image editors are programs that create raster graphics, often called bitmap images because they are created as a series of dots on a grid. Common raster file formats are BMP (bitmap), TIFF (Tagged Image File Format), GIF, and

JPEG. Bitmap image editors are the most commonly used graphics software. The industry standard is Adobe Photoshop, the high-end editor used by most professionals with a steep learning curve to go along with its powerful, complex capabilities. Many other programs are also available that can produce satisfactory graphics and that require a much lower investment of time to master. If you plan to digitize existing materials, any image editor you consider should include the ability to scan in images as well as to enhance, resize, and retouch them. However, if you need to manipulate born-digital images, there are freely available online image editors that may be acceptable for the job at hand. Aviary's image editor is called Phoenix.

Illustration Software
Illustration software includes those applications that you use to create drawings using lines and curves, known as vector graphics. Vector graphics are created through a series of mathematical statements that place lines and shapes in a two- or three-dimensional space. Common vector formats are AI (Adobe Illustrator), WMF (Windows Metafile), CDR (CorelDRAW), and SVG (Scalable Vector Graphic). Representative commercial applications include Adobe Illustrator and CorelDRAW. Aviary's online vector editor is Raven.

Object-Based Editors
A third category of graphics software, object-based editors, integrates raster and vector capabilities into one package. This category is popular for creating web graphics and animations. Object-based editors have greater flexibility because they enable you to combine images with text and line art to streamline the creation of web objects such as navigation bars, banners, buttons, and rollovers. An example of this integrated approach is Adobe Fireworks (PC and Mac, www.adobe.com/products/fireworks/).

There are issues to consider when creating graphics for the Web (see chapter 6), and you should keep these in mind when selecting a graphics program. Beneficial features that should be included to streamline the creation of web graphics include

- image optimization (to reduce the size of a graphic)
- image slicing (to enhance the download of a larger image by slicing it into several smaller images)
- color management and support for web-safe color
- batch processing of objects
- built-in templates (particularly valuable for nonartists)
- three dimensional (3-D) effects
- support for building interactivity

There are so many choices for graphics applications that the selection task can be overwhelming. Wikipedia has an article that provides links to

lists of raster and vector graphic editors at http://en.wikipedia.org/wiki/
Graphics_software.

Animation Applications

Your choice of an animation authoring application will depend on the
type of animation format you have selected. There are a variety of types of
animation, but there is no one tool that can be used to create all of them.
Just as with regular graphics, animations can be either raster or vector
objects. The various animation formats mentioned here are discussed in
depth in chapter 6.

Raster Animation Tools

One of the long-standing animations on the Web is the animated GIF. Your
graphics software may already be capable of producing animated GIFs.
For instance, Adobe Photoshop includes an animation palette. There are
stand-alone applications designed to create this type of animation also. One
example is GIF Construction Set Professional (www.mindworkshop.com/
alchemy/gifcon.html). It is possible to create some animation by scripting
to manipulate page elements. Some HTML editors (e.g., Dreamweaver) have
this functionality incorporated into their programming.

Vector Animation Tools

Similarly, your illustration software may have built-in functionality for
creating vector-based animation, so check its features before investing in
a separate program. The best-known application for creating this type of
animation is Adobe Flash (www.adobe.com/products/flash/), an industry
standard for creating animations on the Web. Its increase in popularity has
resulted in the development of third-party authoring tools that also allow
you to create Flash animations or to export a file to the SWF (Shockwave
Flash) format. Full-featured, Flash can be used to create rich interactive
content. There is a rise in open-source solutions for Flash developers;
Open Source Flash (osflash.org) is a central site for finding information on
projects and open-source application development. An example of this is
AJAX Animator (http://antimatter15.com/ajaxanimator/).

Streaming Media Tools

Another major trend in animation on the Web uses streaming media, a technology that allows users to hear or view large multimedia files without having to wait for them to download to their computers. RealNetworks (www
.realnetworks.com) was at the forefront of developing this technology; to
produce real media, you may want to select its product, RealProducer. A
basic version is available at no charge. Apple also has an authoring tool,

QuickTime Pro (www.apple.com/quicktime/pro/), which you may want to consider. Both of these programs also support Synchronized Multimedia Integration Language (SMIL), which is a protocol for synchronizing the timed playback of multiple independent media files. A good resource for the latest information on streaming technology, including authoring software, is Streaming Media (www.streamingmedia.com).

Screen Recording Animation Tools

A popular method for teaching students to use a particular application or database is to make a video screen presentation that shows the desktop activity or construct a simulation that permits students to interact as though in a live session. Available features often include support for narration, creation of callouts and hot spots, import of audio and video files, and the use of transitions. A full-featured application will support saving the presentation in the most popular file formats, including SWF, RM, WMF, and MOV. Camtasia Studio is a well-regarded commercial screen-capture application (www.techsmith.com/camtasia.asp). TechSmith also produces Jing, which is available in a free or pro version for both Windows and Mac (www.jingproject.com). CamStudio is an open-source screen-recording application (camstudio.org).

Virtual Reality Authoring Tools

If a virtual walk-through tour of your library is high on your list, you'll need to obtain specialized software to do the authoring. The industry-standard technology for this type of interaction is VR, which is short for *virtual reality*. A wide variety of software choices are available depending on what type of project you are creating and your level of expertise. An example is VRWorx (cross-platform, www.vrtoolbox.com).

Audio Software

Introducing small incidental sounds into a web project may require nothing more than the sound-recording software that your operating system includes. However, if you plan to incorporate audio into your tutorial to any extent, you will want to explore using specialized audio-editing software to record and edit sound. Audacity is a free, cross-platform, open-source sound-recording and sound-editing software (http://audacity .sourceforge.net). You can turn to RealProducer (www.realnetworks.com) to handle your streaming audio needs. There are reasonably priced editors available that are full featured, such as Adobe Soundbooth (Mac and PC, www.adobe.com/products/soundbooth/). Aviary offers a cloud solution with its audio editor, Myna (http://aviary.com/tools/myna/). You should make certain that whichever audio editor you select supports a wide range of sound files (see chapter 6 for more information on sound files).

If you already have sound files and just need to convert them to a different format, a stand-alone format converter (called batch encoder) is a more cost-effective solution than purchasing audio-editing software. Batch encoders are normally included as a part of a full-featured editing program. You can find shareware encoders for all platforms available for download from Hitsquad (www.hitsquad.com/smm/cat/FORMAT_CONVERTERS/).

Video-Editing Applications

Once you import video into your computer, you will need software to manipulate it. It's very probable that video production software will be bundled with a digital camcorder or video capture card. If this is the case, you should make that part of your purchasing decision making. Many integrated hardware and software packages are on the market, with prices ranging from less than $100 to $1,000. Well-known manufacturers such as Pinnacle Systems (www.pinnaclesys.com) have high-end products (Pinnacle Studio) as well as free solutions (VideoSpin, www.videospin .com). Adobe's Premiere (www.adobe.com/products/premiere/) is the industry standard for digital video production, but because it is designed for the professional, expect a steep learning curve. If you are new to video editing, look for software that is intuitive or that guides you through each step. As video editing and sharing has become more popular through sites such as YouTube, the range of editing choices has increased. You'll find good choices available in freeware and open source, along with the standard proprietary possibilities (http://en.wikipedia.org/wiki/List_of_video_ editing_software). Microsoft included a very nice entry-level video editor, Movie Maker, as part of Windows XP (www.microsoft.com/windowsxp/ downloads/default.mspx). In Vista and Windows 7, the program has been changed to Windows Live Movie Maker (http://download.live.com/movie maker/); however, Movie Maker is still operable in the later operating systems (OS) if you have a copy of it to install. The video-editing application included with Mac operating systems is iMovie.

The editing process involves putting video segments in the order you want and then adding transitions, text, background music, and perhaps narration. With most software, this is a drag-and-drop process, using either a timeline or a storyboard metaphor. A storyboard approach is more straightforward because each frame is represented by one thumbnail image and includes all the elements. In a timeline, each separate component (audio tracks, text, video clips, or transitions) has its own track, so the author has more control. Some software packages provide both ways to deal with editing—a good solution, so that beginners can evolve as they gain skill as editors. As with other applications, you want to make sure that your video-editing software supports the file format you have chosen (see chapter 6 for more information on video file formats).

Presentation Tools

Presentation software applications, such as Microsoft's PowerPoint, may not be your top choice to author a library instruction tutorial. Many people choose presentation software for instruction because it is easy to learn and to incorporate multimedia. The format for presentation authoring is slide creation, which lends itself to a linear progression through materials. Although most presentation software incorporates various levels of multimedia and interactivity, those features are sometimes lost when the presentation is converted to a web-viewable format or do not work identically across all browser types and versions. However, some presentation software now incorporates support for web interactivity. Some have the ability to export to Flash or PDF for delivery over the Web. Sites such as SlideShare (www.slideshare.net) provide free space to make PowerPoint presentations available over the Web. Google Docs and Zoho (www.zoho .com) offer cloud solutions for presentation creation and delivery. If you decide to use presentation software, make sure it supports the various web file formats, and be prepared to settle for interactivity that may include only the user's ability to select a link to continue.

A nonlinear approach to using presentation software is possible with a mind map. Mind maps are diagrams used to represent concepts and their connections in a visual manner. The elements are arranged by levels of importance and are grouped to show those connections. An example of a mind-mapping application is FreeMind (http://freemind.sourceforge.net). The benefit of this type of presentation is that it allows users to choose their approach to the material.

Authoring Systems

Most of the authoring tools presented so far are designed to handle one aspect of a multimedia project, such as the creation of graphics, animation, or sound. To combine these into an interactive multimedia program, some sort of programming is needed to make it all work together. However, a type of software called an authoring system has been developed so that people can develop interactive multimedia programs without having to know a programming language. This type of application allows authors to use a graphical approach to tell the program what to do by placing items in a timeline, manipulating objects on a flowchart, or organizing screens into stacks (best known from Apple's HyperCard program). Although the author looks at a graphical interface, the graphical objects are composed of underlying preset programming modules. By having preprogrammed modules, actions that might take hours to write using a programming language can be created in minutes. A few of the applications discussed under a specific category, such as Microsoft's PowerPoint, can be considered an authoring system, but usually you will hear the term used to describe more sophisticated applications like Adobe Director (www.adobe.com/products/director/). Having an authoring system greatly reduces the learning curve for nonprogrammers because it requires less technical knowledge to master. However, it is a mistake to think that most of these programs are so intuitive that you can sit down and be productive right away.

In addition to its relative user-friendliness over raw programming, one of the main advantages of an authoring system is its ability to quickly prototype an application. This feature can be very helpful for making quick mock-ups to be shown for feedback prior to producing the site in detail.

The major disadvantage of most authoring systems is the limitation that results from having an application with predetermined programming. It reduces the flexibility to go beyond what is built into the system. Many systems allow for flexibility by including external scripting functionality for the power user. Another limitation is that programs developed on proprietary authoring systems often require a specialized plug-in so they can be played on the Web. For example, Director is displayed on the Web via Adobe Shockwave Player. Finally, high-end programs like Director can be very expensive (more than $900).

Specialty Tools

Specialty tools are programs that serve to create specific components of a website. For instance, there is software that allows you to create an online quiz, and another type can capture a screen from your computer display. (Chapter 7 focuses on many specialized authoring programs used to create interactive components.) The following sections introduce a few of the common tools.

Cascading Style Sheet (CSS) Editors

Most web-editing software applications include some sort of support for working with Cascading Style Sheets (discussed in detail in chapter 5). In addition, some integrate stand-alone CSS editors into their program. However, if your web authoring program doesn't have a CSS component or isn't exactly full featured, you may find that a program focused strictly on

CSS gives you much better guidance and control in creating style sheets. The W3C website has a good section on Cascading Style Sheets, with a long list of authoring tools (www.w3.org/Style/CSS/).

Database Applications

If you decide to develop a dynamic rather than static educational instruction site, you will include a database of some sort. Potential uses for databases will be covered in more detail in chapter 7, but it is important to include consideration of a particular database application as you are determining your required development tools. Whether a database is appropriate depends on many factors, but once you decide to use a database, the next step is to choose the appropriate one for your needs. Questions to ask include the following:

- What database software (if any) is in use in your organization?
- If there is software in use, is it available to you for your project?
- How large is the database?
- What volume of traffic to the database do you expect?
- How sophisticated are your database requirements?
- Does your staff have expertise in database development?
- What will your budget support?
- What hardware requirements exist?

The needs that you determine will help you decide whether you require an enterprise-level database solution such as Oracle (www.oracle.com) or Microsoft SQL Server (www.microsoft.com/sqlserver/2008/), or a more modest solution such as Microsoft Office Access (http://office.microsoft.com/en-us/access/). Do you have the internal expertise to use an open-source solution like MySQL (www.mysql.com)? Which database is best for the scripting technologies you have decided to use?

Web Programming and Scripting Tools

If you don't have a programmer on your development team, many of the authoring tools discussed previously have integrated components to their products that permit you to write scripts without having to know a programming language. However, if you are fortunate enough to have a team member with a programming background, authoring tools are available that facilitate writing the various languages of the Web (examples include XML, Java, Perl, JavaScript, and Python, which are discussed in chapter 7). These tools allow a programmer to concentrate on the development task rather than the underlying language syntax. Much like the HTML editor, these scripting tools automate much of the process of code creation. The CNET site Download.com (download.cnet.com) is a good resource for finding links to development tools for different languages.

XML/XSLT Editors

As Extensible Markup Language (XML) and its corresponding styling language Extensible Stylesheet Language Transformation (XSLT) become more prevalent on the Web (both are discussed in detail in chapters 6 and 7), software to facilitate easy XML and XSLT authoring and validation has been developed. As can HTML, XML and XSLT can be authored by hand, but an editor is preferable to streamline coding and minimize coding errors. Web Developer's Virtual Library has a list of links to XML editors (www .wdvl.com/Software/XML/editors.html). Two popular XML editors are Altova XML Spy (www.altova.com/xmlspy.html) and SoftQuad XMetal (http://na.justsystems.com/content-xmetal/). As has happened with other technologies, major web editors include support for authoring XML.

Integrated Application Server and Authoring Tools

Another avenue to pursue if you are planning to incorporate dynamic delivery of information assembled on the fly into your instruction via a database is a web application server. An application server is a program that handles transactions between a web browser on a client computer and an institution's back-end applications that reside on a server. For example, it processes data contained or referenced in a database and delivers that content to the user's browser in HTML. Supplying many of the same functions that you can achieve with manual scripting, this tool is designed to tightly integrate several components in a single development interface. With a web application server, the developer does not have to reinvent the wheel to build a robust interaction with a database. A familiar example of an application server is Adobe's ColdFusion (www.adobe.com/products/coldfusion/).

Because application servers can be very expensive, their use may be overkill if your database access is low. Check with your information technology department. One may already be installed at your institution.

CHAPTER FIVE

DESIGNING THE USER EXPERIENCE

I T IS THROUGH the user interface, the graphical link between the student and a computer program, that every aspect of a user's possible interaction with a computer takes place. To the students who use your web instruction, the interface drives the overall experience. Without a doubt, designing and creating your library instruction user interface is one of the major challenges in the preproduction and production stages. Your goal in creating web instruction is to produce an instrument that will engage students and motivate them to actively learn in an independent environment. The successful creation of the interface requires that a wide variety of elements be brought together so that they mesh to present the instruction in the most effective manner, requiring the least explanation.

The subject of what constitutes good user interface design has been well studied and discussed. Many of the themes that are being presented here are the result of work accomplished by prominent researchers in the field of human-computer interaction, in particular the work of Ben Shneiderman (www.cs.umd.edu/~ben/) and Jakob Nielsen (www.useit.com). These pioneers have been instrumental in establishing best practices for making computers and the Internet more usable for all of us.

The purpose of this chapter is to examine the important usability factors to consider and incorporate into a winning interface. We will take a detailed look at

- user-centered design
- instructional design and content
- basic guidelines and principles for user-interface design (adapted for the Web)

- navigation
- screen layout and presentation aids
- visual design considerations
- multinational design considerations
- user accessibility
- page optimization

Not too many years ago, most web-based library instruction was created from scratch in the form of stand-alone tutorials. Although these are still very popular and allow great latitude for building a custom design for users, there are now many instruction possibilities that use predesigned containers. Examples are third-party blog or wiki-hosting sites. Although you may not have as much freedom to build a totally customized experience, there are still many decisions that can be adapted to shape your users' experience. Being familiar with user-centered design concepts will help inform the decisions you make on hosted sites.

USER-CENTERED DESIGN

From the beginning, the design process should be focused on your users or audience. You are going to be creating a teaching tool for a population that traditionally does not have a high level of comfort in the library world. To many people, the library is a mysterious place, organized with puzzling numbering schemes and a foreign language of library jargon. Acquiring a thorough understanding of the user is a must.

One of the first steps to take in the preproduction phase is the audience needs analysis, discussed in chapter 3. The results from this analysis will be the starting point for involving the user in the design process. From the analysis you should know

- who will use the instruction
- their preferred learning styles
- their previous experiences using libraries
- their prior exposure to library instruction
- their base of knowledge in the specific subject area being taught
- the level of their computer competence
- what type of hardware and software they have at their disposal
- their skill using the Web
- what their expectations are from the instruction

Involving the user doesn't stop with what you discover from the initial needs assessment. To ensure maximum usability of your program, users should be drawn in throughout the development process. How can users' preferences and opinions be gathered? Assembling a focus group as you begin the design process is one way to hear from users about what they like or don't like about website design in general, previous library instruction experiences, and various instructional methods. The one drawback to this sort of user encounter is that users can give opinions only about what they already know. If they have not experienced innovative library instruction methods or engaging interactive web instruction, they won't realize what is possible. Nevertheless, a focus group can provide a basic picture of what your audience thinks it wants.

Next you will want to develop a wire-frame prototype and have users try it out and provide feedback. A wire-frame prototype is a simple preliminary model of the site, without artwork, that identifies the main navigation and content. Adopt an iterative design process, and use testers' reactions about each updated version to make design adjustments. Several methods that work well for testing usability are discussed in depth in chapter 8.

INSTRUCTIONAL DESIGN AND CONTENT

When initiating a discussion about interface design, it's not uncommon to think primarily about screen layout and visual elements. This is important, of course, but it shouldn't be separated from the main goal of the project— to deliver instruction effectively. The instructional design of the tutorial is the place to begin.

Instructional Design

Instructional design is more than filling a page with content and throwing in a few hyperlinks. We are all used to this model of the Web: pages full of information with links that allow us to follow nonlinear paths. However, providing information isn't the same as delivering instruction. Instructional design is the systematic process of translating general principles of learning and instruction into plans for instructional materials and learning. Ritchie and Hoffman (1997) identified the following sequences that are considered essential to the instructional process:

> *Motivating the learner*: Visual and multimedia elements can contribute to the motivation factor, but incorporating such

components as problem-solving opportunities, critical-thinking exercises, and an established relevance to the learner's needs are strong stimuli.

Identifying what is to be learned: Establish clear objectives at the beginning. Let the students know what outcomes are expected.

Reminding learners of past knowledge: Many students have had some exposure to libraries in their past or to the subject being studied; offer a review to establish their existing knowledge.

Requiring active involvement: Active involvement is more than clicking on a hyperlink to move through the site. Interactive exercises that relate to a specific assignment that the students must submit let them actively engage in the learning process.

Providing guidance and feedback: Incorporate ways to let the students know if they are on the right track. Skill checks at crucial points throughout the instruction can give students a tool to assess their understanding of the material.

Testing: Testing is still the most common way for the instructor to know if students have learned what has been taught.

Providing enrichment and remediation: Offer a way for students to revisit parts of the instruction if they have a problem and to contact the instructor for help.

Chapter 3 introduced some of the major instructional design models, which may help guide your direction as you start to design the instruction.

Open versus Closed Structure

One goal of instructional design is to keep the student focused on what is being taught. The nature of the structure of the Web tends to work against this goal. The Web is an open system that can take students on a tangent with the click of a mouse. Keep this in mind as you design an instructional site. For example, you may wish to illustrate points or show examples by taking students to an external site. You want to offer this flexibility to the student but in a controlled manner. You don't want to provide links in your instruction that will take students away from your site so that they have difficulty finding their way back. Proper planning of navigation and window structure is important to keep your instruction contained.

Controlling window placement and appearance is one appropriate way to make sure that your users can return to where they left off in your tutorial. Two approaches are prevalent.

Opening a Second Browser Window

Many web users have become accustomed to having additional browser windows open to take them to a new site but leaving the original window open so they can return to it easily. It's simple to make a second window open when a user clicks on a URL: add the attribute target="_blank" to the end of the URL. For example, <a href="http://catalog.zsr.wfu.edu/" target="_blank">Online Catalog</a> takes the user to a second window. A second full-sized window will open and display the new site. For users who are comfortable moving back and forth between windows via the task bar, this can be an easy solution. However, if a user is oblivious to new windows opening (and many are), the new window can cause confusion. This method is one that Nielsen discourages in his 2007 update of the Top Ten Mistakes in Web Design (http://useit.com/alertbox/9605.html), noting that people usually don't notice what has occurred. If you decide to use this method, be certain to provide instruction on what to do so that the user knows how to return to the tutorial and doesn't end up with multiple browser windows open.

Opening Smaller Pop-Up Windows

Most web surfers are familiar with the little pop-up windows that often appear superimposed over the browser interface. Typically, they are for advertising or a survey request. In that context, they can be annoying, but when used properly, they can be an effective way to give access to external sites or additional information without having users leave the tutorial page.

Many web editor software programs can create these pop-up windows without having to know a specific script. If your software doesn't have this capability, it is easy to find window-building utilities on the Web. You copy and paste the generated script into the body of your HTML document. Doing so allows you to control how the window will appear, including whether it will have a menu or tool bar, a location field, or scroll bars, or be resizable. The size and placement of the window can be configured also.

Writing for the Web

Writing content for the Web requires a different mind-set than writing for print. Morkes and Nielsen's (1997) research has shown that reading on the Web is 25 percent slower than reading on paper, that most users scan text rather than read word for word, and web content should be 50 percent of the length of its paper equivalent (Morkes and Nielsen 1997).

How should those points influence how you write content? Morkes and Nielsen offer the following guidelines:

Be Concise. People are not as comfortable reading from a computer screen as they are reading from a print source. Reading from a screen can be tiring to their eyes. Also, although users expect to scroll down a page to read text, by keeping the text succinct, a page of information can be restricted to fit on a screen so scrolling is unnecessary.

Write for Scannability. Because people don't like to read text on a screen, they tend to scan a page to pick out key words and ideas. By planning to present content so that it is scannable, you ensure that students will have a better chance of encountering the most important points. To enhance scannability, try the following:

- Use meaningful headings that will tell the reader what content is to be covered.
- Highlight keywords via hyperlinks, color, or making the type bold.
- Incorporate bulleted lists.
- Restrict each paragraph to one idea.
- Restrict each page to one topic.
- Use graphics to illustrate key points and provide a distinctive caption.
- Include a table of contents or site map.

Use an Inverted Pyramid Style via Hyperlinks. Using a concise writing style doesn't mean that in-depth content has to be sacrificed. By using an inverted pyramid organizational style, users can start with the main points, the conclusion in essence, and use hyperlinks to continue deeper to secondary pages for more detailed information.

BASIC USER-INTERFACE DESIGN

Many of the best practices for user interface design (UID) on the Web have evolved from Ben Shneiderman's eight golden rules of interface design (Shneiderman et al. 2010). These principles apply to most interactive systems, and web designers have adapted them to relate to the web environment.

Strive for Consistency. Consistency can mean many things. There is consistency of actions, navigation, screen layout, and terminology. Providing consistency helps the user to know what to expect and to learn the interface more quickly. Consistency can also be discussed as it relates to other websites. Experienced web surfers have come to expect certain functionality from websites and recognize certain objects as having particular meanings. Straying too far from the consistency of how a typical website works may frustrate and disorient the user.

Cater to Universal Usability. Users are diverse and design should take into consideration differences in age ranges, disabilities, and technological diversity. This might mean including explanations for novices while providing shortcuts for expert users.

Offer Informative Feedback. For every action, there should be some sort of response. This may be as modest as having a third color designation for the ALINK (Active Link) in addition to ones for unvisited (LINK) and visited (VLINK) links. Some graphics are designed to give visual feedback as the cursor passes over them. More substantial feedback should be programmed when asking users to complete more complex activities, such as submitting forms, so they can be confident that they executed the action correctly.

Design Dialogs to Yield Closure. Information sequences should be grouped to have a beginning, middle, and end. Users shouldn't be left guessing whether they have reached the conclusion of a topic.

Prevent Errors. Any system should be designed so that users don't experience serious errors; if that is not possible, users should be able to "fail gently." This means that your design should anticipate potential error-causing incidents and provide corrective measures. Error correction should be worded in a straightforward, constructive, and positive manner so that users don't feel as though they have done something wrong. If a link has become outdated, provide specific directions for handling it. If higher-end technologies are being included, provide instructions for system and plug-in requirements at the start so users know what they need to use the tutorial; don't make them wait until they try to access an unconfigured file type on the introductory page. Provide links to the sites where users can download additional software.

Permit Easy Reversal of Actions. Users should be able to undo any action without dire consequence. In a web form, include a reset button. Navigation should allow users to back out of a screen and return to the previous one.

Support Internal Locus of Control. Skilled users of the Web want to feel that they are in control of their experience. Program in enough flexibility so that those users don't feel that they are being held back. One simple tool for freeing savvy web users is to provide a search engine or site map to allow them to move through the instruction more freely.

Reduce Short-Term Memory Load. Humans can process only a limited number of chunks of information in short-term memory (seven plus or minus two is the rule). Concise content, short screens, and real-world metaphors can help minimize information overload. This style of writing lends itself to the concept of chunking, or dividing material into small segments that can be more easily digested. Chunking can be directly related to the concept of learning objects, discussed in chapter 1.

NAVIGATION

Navigation in an instructional site is second only to content in importance to the success of the instructional design. In fact, navigation can be an organizational tool for designing your content delivery. Without effective navigation, users can become lost, and content may become inaccessible. This section looks at various types of navigation and related issues.

Qualities of Successful Navigation Systems

There are general principles of good navigation design that are commonly accepted as critical to success:

- Design for the user.
- Provide a variety of navigation options.
- Let users know where they are, where they've been, and where they are going.
- Provide context.
- Be consistent.
- Follow web conventions.
- Provide feedback.
- Don't surprise or mislead the user.

With a good navigation system, the site's users will always know where they are, where they can go next, and where they have been. Always highlight the current location so that it tells the user "you are here." Use a visual placement marker to highlight the present position of users. Indicators of the current location should also include such information as your organization name, just in case the user has entered your tutorial from a back door instead of at the top level.

Types of Navigation Systems

Depending on the size of the site that the navigation is designed to serve, setting it up can range from straightforward to complex. A site with breadth (many pages at the same level) and depth (multiple levels) may require more than one navigation system. Let's take a look at the types of navigation systems that might be appropriate.

Introductory Splash Screens. Although not a navigation system in its entirety, a splash page can provide an introduction to a site and sets the tone. Often it is used to highlight main sections of the instructional module, and as such, it can be considered to be a navigational aid. Splash screens should be used with care because users may find them a barrier to the content. If you decide to have a splash page, be sure to include a text link option to bypass it.

Kalbach (2007) identifies three general navigation types: structural, associative, and utility.

Structural Navigation

Structural navigation includes both global and local systems and provides access to content following the structure of the site.

Global Systems. A global system is a sitewide navigation device. It provides access to areas of your site beyond the specific module you are presenting. This type of navigation device can be useful if you have a number of instructional modules available for students or if your content is multimodular in structure with each module or topic standing as a self-contained unit.

Local Systems. If you consider your overall subject the main site, think about each individual topic or module as a subsite. Local navigation systems provide a way to maneuver through the subsite. Because users prefer to have information delivered one screen at a time and to read scannable text, it may be necessary to present one element of a particular topic on each screen. With a local navigation mechanism present, users can see what additional elements are included and can get to them efficiently.

Local navigation systems should be used in tandem with global systems. There should always be a way for users to return to other areas of the site. Most likely you will find that a combination of navigation systems gives users the best navigation experience.

Utility Systems

These systems are ones to help the user find information about the site and its functions. Examples of utility systems are site maps and indexes. Sometimes this type of information is presented in a hierarchical manner, which shows the layout of the information contained.

Associative Systems

Sometimes links can be used to create semantic relationships between two related pieces of content. Often you will find such links embedded into the text of the page. Because they are not overt navigation tools, users can easily miss them as they scan through the text. If the link is to an incidental piece of information, then this may be an acceptable solution. If you are trying to emphasize the importance of the link, however, figure out a way to bring it into prominence, perhaps by creating a bulleted list, so that it stands out for the reader.

Navigation Methods

There is no single way to create the various navigation systems. Limited only by their imaginations, web designers have produced different methods that serve the same purpose. Following are some of the most popular methods and their advantages and disadvantages.

Text

Using text links as navigation is simple to do and can be read by any browser. If you decide to go with text, keep the text length concise so that the link doesn't overlap into a second line, and devise a visual clue so that users will know they are looking at a navigation tool. Successful methods include highlighting each menu item with a small graphic or offsetting the menu by highlighting it with a different-colored background. Such visual clues set the navigation text apart from the rest of the content on the page. Tables of contents and site maps are typically text based.

Tool Bars: Image Maps, Tabs, and Icons

Many web designers build graphical navigation toolbars, which take many different shapes. (Using graphics effectively is discussed in greater detail in chapter 6.) Using graphics for navigation ensures that the system will stand apart from the text content of the page. A few popular permutations of the graphical toolbar that you may come across include image maps, tabs, and icons.

An image map is a graphic object that is subdivided into areas, each of which takes users to a different destination. The clickable areas (or hot spots) of an image map are defined by specifying coordinates in the HTML coding and attaching a URL destination to that area.

Tabs have become a popular way to separate content into different categories. They offer a real-world metaphor with which most people are familiar. They work particularly well when there are a limited number (fewer than five or seven) main category divisions. They work very well for showing where users are and where they can go.

Icons are small graphics that are meaningful representations of particular topics, functions, or actions. Users today are comfortable with icons as navigational devices because icons have become pervasive in computer and web environments to represent common actions, such as printing or returning home.

Menu Trees

A menu tree, or nested navigation, is a way, through scripting, to display a collapsible menu, that is, one that can contain several levels. When completely closed, the user sees only the top level of the site hierarchy. Clicking a link displays the next level down. To close a particular menu, the user clicks any other link, which collapses the previous branch of the tree just expanded.

Drop-Down Menus

Drop-down menus illustrate a way to supply navigation without taking up much real estate on the screen. Most users are familiar with these and know to click on them to get a list of options. Drop-down menus are fairly easy to assemble by using a script. Many script libraries (which are discussed in chapter 7) have free scripts you can adapt to use for your menu. Many web-editing programs now include this type of scripting functionality with a user-friendly interface.

Breadcrumb Trails

A breadcrumb trail shows the hierarchical structure of a site so that users know where they are in relation to the overall site. It tells users where they are in the hierarchy of the instruction. It pinpoints their location in the context of the entire site, showing the path from the top layer to the current page. Breadcrumb trail navigation is best suited for a large, complex site, and so it may have limited applicability in an online instructional setting, where guided navigation may be more appropriate. However, if you are planning an intricate instructional site, breadcrumb trails are a simple-to-construct, space-conserving way to show navigation to the user.

Arrows
Users associate an arrow on a screen with the action that will move them forward or backward one screen. Including arrows on the screen of your tutorial permits users to move sequentially and linearly through a section of the tutorial. Including arrows to proceed through a subsite supplies an extra level of navigation.

Site Maps
Site maps are used to provide a visual, ready reference of a site's structure or organization. Typically, site maps are text links that display the hierarchical order of the site's content. If they are done correctly, site maps can help users orient themselves to the information contained and can provide a level of access that permits them to choose the path of their instruction.

Search Engines
Although normally the instructional design for a tutorial is planned to proceed in a particular sequence, a search engine that locates terms on web pages can be useful in helping users who return to the tutorial to revisit a particular point or concept. They can search for something specific without having to proceed step by step through the entire instruction. This type of flexibility passes on a degree of control to the user.

Placement of Navigation Tools on the Screen

Navigation tools are incorporated into most websites today. Because most people read from left to right and from top to bottom, the left and top of the screen are the areas that are most suited for navigation. If you place your navigation tools down on the right-hand side of the screen, unless you configure the layout to adjust to the resolution that a user has chosen, there is a distinct possibility that the navigation will be hidden. For example, if a screen is designed for a 1024×768 resolution and the navigation tool is in the last 100 pixels of the screen, users who have set their computers at 800×600 will not see the navigation tool without scrolling over to the right side to bring it into view. If a designer wants to ensure that what is placed on the right of the screen shows for everyone, then the design should be set to adjust by percentage if the interface will take up the entire screen. Instead of designating a specific number of pixels for the screen by width and height, screen layout should be designated to be a percentage of the screen width and height. The use of a right-hand "column" as an information container has become common over the past several years. However, it is often used to display advertising, so if you are going to put your navigation system on the right-hand side of the screen, the design should be one that makes the purpose obvious.

Linear versus Nonlinear Navigation

Linear navigation takes users from point A to point Z in a step-by-step progression that guides them through the instruction in a structured way. Students start at the beginning and progress only as they make the correct choices to show that they have grasped the concept being taught. This may be appropriate for those with no previous exposure to the subject being covered or if you intend the tutorial to be completed in one sitting or class period. A linear approach helps ensure that students stay on task.

However, there are risks with offering only a linear progression. If the instruction is of any length, students may want to stop for a while, come back later, and pick up where they left off. If they have to enter through the first screen and work through every subsequent screen to get back to where they stopped, they'll rapidly become frustrated. What about students who want to return to the instructional module to review a particular section or concept? They will want quick, easy access to just that information. If you intend for your instruction to be accessible in this fashion, then a nonlinear navigation scheme is more appropriate.

One nonlinear approach to instructional design in web instruction is branching. With branching, the sequence of progression of the tutorial depends on the learner's response to questions and activities. Branching allows students to skip over what they already know or to be directed to remedial instruction if found to be weak in a certain subject area.

SCREEN LAYOUT AND PRESENTATION

This section discusses Cascading Style Sheets, the main tool for helping you structure the layout of your tutorial so it displays and formats optimally. In the early days of the Web, it was difficult to overcome the limitations of HTML for content presentation: HTML is a markup language, not a page-layout and formatting language. Tables were used early on as a work-around to this problem, but they were never really meant to be used for this purpose. The Cascading Style Sheets (CSS) were developed as a specification to describe the presentation including both layout and formatting, such as colors and fonts that traditionally have been embedded in HTML code tags.

Background of CSS

Cascading Style Sheets (CSS) is a style-sheet language that separates presentation (format and style) from the content and structure provided in an HTML, XHTML, or XML document. The World Wide Web Consortium (W3C), a group of more than 350 member organizations, made its first style-sheet recommendation, CSS1 (Cascading Style Sheets, Level 1), in 1996 (revised in 1999). CSS Level 1 (CSS1) addresses style using common desktop-publishing terminology. CSS Level 2, version 1 (CSS2.1) originally became a W3C Candidate Recommendation in February 2004 but was pulled back for more work in 2005 and finally returned to Candidate Recommendation status in 2007. It contains all of CSS1 and addresses layout, including content positioning, layout, automatic numbering, page breaks, and right-to-left text, and it has features for internationalization. In addition, it supports media-specific style sheets so that authors may tailor the presentation of their documents to visual browsers, aural devices, printers, Braille devices, handheld devices, and so forth. As of early 2010, CSS3 continues under development. It will contain all of CSS2.1 and extend it with new selectors, fancy borders and backgrounds, vertical text, user interaction and speech, and much more. With CSS3, the W3C is taking a modular approach so that added functionality can be implemented and tested as ready, without having to wait for all items to be completed.

How CSS Works

With CSS, a web author can control style and layout elements such as font, type size and color, margins, indentations, line spacing, and more. The CSS language provides separate style rules that are used to format HTML elements. Instead of trying to control formatting from within an HTML element, which has to be specified each time the attribute is used, CSS allows the author to specify the style once, which is then automatically applied to the HTML element each time it is used. For instance, with customary formatting in HTML (which has now been deprecated or superseded), if you wanted the headline for your page to be an Arial font that is green and in italics, you would code your headline tag like this every time you used a headline:

```
<h1>
<font face="Arial, Helvetica, sans serif" color="#009900">
<i>Headline</i>
</font>
</h1>
```

A style sheet allows for the author to specify the attributes for an element (or selector) in three ways. First is an external file (ending with the file extension .css) that resides on the web server. In this case, you enter the path to that file in the head of your document:

```
<head>
<link rel="stylesheet" href=".../tutorial.css">
</head>
```

Second is embedded in the header of the document:

```
<head>
<style type="text/css">
<!--
h1 {font-family: Arial, Helvetica, sans serif; font-size: x-large; font-style: italic; line-height: normal; font-weight: bold; color: #009900}
-->
</style>
</head>
```

Third is expressed in-line, to override the general style for one occasion:

```
<h1 style="color: #ff0000; font-family: Times, Times New Roman, serif;">A New Headline Color and Font with Inline CSS</h1>
```

The obvious benefit of using an external file to store your styles is that you have to make changes in only one document to execute sitewide modifications.

It's not necessary that you pick just one way to apply styles. Cascading Style Sheets are called that because you can use more than one style sheet on a document, with different levels of importance assigned depending on the location of the style designation. If you define different styles for the same element, the style that is closest to the HTML tag prevails. For example, the style specified in the tag takes precedence over one designated in the head of the document. The style in the head of the document is more important than the one located in the external .css file. This comes in handy when you want to make onetime adjustments to an element on a particular document or a section of a document but prefer that the original style stay in place over the rest of the site.

CSS Syntax

The CSS language is expressed in easy-to-understand scripting. As mentioned, standard desktop-publishing terminology is used, so if you understand setting up styles in that environment, it shouldn't be too difficult to learn CSS. And, as discussed in chapter 4, many development tools are available to automate the process. A specific syntax is used to construct statements that define the rules being set.

A CSS statement consists of a selector and a declaration block. The declaration block consists of a list of semicolon-separated declarations in curly braces. A declaration consists of a property, a colon (:), and a value. Take a look at this rule for a Heading 1:

```
h1 {
position: absolute;
top: +50px;
left: +50px;
color: #008080;
font-family: Verdana, Helvetica, Arial, sans-serif;
}
```

The selector is *h1* and there are five declarations in the declaration block: position, top, left, color, and font family. In each declaration, the text to the left of the colon is the property (e.g., position). The text to the right of the colon is the value (e.g., absolute). The CSS information can come from a variety of sources, which include the author (as discussed), the user (a local file controlled at the browser level, to override the author's styles), and the user agent (i.e., the browser's default presentation of HTML elements).

The main advantages of using CSS are that presentation information for an entire site can be contained in one document, allowing for swift and easy updating; that different users can have different styles to serve their particular needs (e.g., large print); that HTML code is reduced in size and complexity; and that it can be used with XML.

Browser support for CSS2.1 is increasing, but there still isn't across-the-board compliance by browser designers. If you implement style sheets for your design control, be aware that users whose browsers support different levels of CSS will be able to see the content differently. This can affect the presentation of your content, so you may want to postpone using styles until you are certain that everyone in your audience uses a browser that can handle CSS. In 2010, there is good support for CSS1 by most current browsers. Support for CSS2.1 is best in standards-compliant browsers such as Opera, Mozilla Firefox, and Apple's Safari. Some of these even provide partial support for CSS3. Detailed information about Cascading Style Sheets can be found on the W3C's website (www.w3.org/Style/CSS/).

Extensible Stylesheet Language (XSL)

An additional language for styling pages, Extensible Stylesheet Language (XSL) is used to describe how data from XML documents are presented to the user. XSL can be used only in conjunction with XML, and in fact is XML. However, CSS can be used with XML as well. This can be somewhat confusing to authors who are new to CSS and to XML/XST. Under which conditions should one be used over the other?

First, CSS is easier to learn and use. But because it is simple, it has limitations that XSL can handle. CSS is widely implemented but is only a formatting language. It attaches style properties to elements found in a source document. It cannot transform data from the source into human-readable format. It assumes that an external program handles that process. The power of XSL lies in its capability to transform XML data into HTML/CSS documents (known as XSLT, XSL Transformation)—such as ordering lists, replacing words, and replacing empty elements with text. The W3C provides a helpful chart that outlines the basic attributes of each (see figure 5.1). For detailed information on XSL/XSLT, visit the W3C website (www .w3.org/Style/XSL/).

VISUAL DESIGN CONSIDERATIONS

Visual design involves the artistic or aesthetic considerations of designing a site. A visually appealing site will attract more interest from your audience. Guidelines for designing a visually appealing site exist, of course, but because of the wide spectrum of tastes and creativity, they are open to

Figure 5.1
WHEN TO CHOOSE CSS OR XSL

	CSS	XSL
Can it be used with HTML?	Yes	No
Can it be used with XML?	Yes	Yes
Transformation language?	No	Yes
Syntax	CSS	XML

Source: W3C. Copyright © 21 September 2009 World Wide Web Consortium (Massachusetts Institute of Technology, Institut National de Recherche en Informatique et en Automatique, Keio University). All Rights Reserved. www.w3.org/Consortium/Legal/2002/copyright -documents-20021231. Available at www.w3c.org/Style/.

a much more flexible interpretation than UID guidelines are. The following sections present some of the main visual design elements to bear in mind when you are designing your instruction.

Simplicity and Clarity

No matter what other choices you make, visual simplicity should characterize your final product. You have seen websites that are so cluttered that the intended message is lost; you want to avoid that at all costs. Your goal is to get the meaning of the instructional content across to your audience as clearly as possible. If users have to wade through excessive text, links, and graphics to find the main focus of the screen, the instruction won't be successful. Include only what needs to be there, and take out the rest.

White Space

The proper use of white space can help achieve a simple, clear design. White space is the open space on a page between design elements. On a web page, white space isn't necessarily white, of course, but whatever color or texture has been designated for the background. Well-designed white space can help guide users' eyes from one screen element to the next. The space helps define the different elements on the page by acting as a cushion between them. On a computer screen, white space also provides a rest area for users' eyes. Reading from a computer screen is more visually demanding than reading from print, and white space provides users with space to absorb what is on the page before they proceed further.

Color

Color is one of the most powerful visual elements that you will have in your design. You can use color to help your design in a variety of ways. Color can accentuate, highlight, and guide the eye to essential points or links; identify recurring themes or be used to differentiate between elements; and trigger feelings and associations.

People respond immediately to color, and the scheme you choose will set the mood for the instruction. Color will elicit some sort of response even before users begin to read the content. You want to ensure that the colors you select will draw them into the learning experience.

Color Symbolism
Because colors mean different things to various populations, it is important to consider your target audiences before you decide on the color palette

for your tutorial. You should be cognizant of the different meanings of colors between cultures and of the various psychological responses that colors bring out. Figure 5.2 lists common color meanings and perceptions around the world.

People's cultural background strongly influences their response to color. For example, the color green in the United States indicates both *go* (safe) at traffic lights and environmental awareness, but in some tropical countries, it is associated with danger. In Western cultures, black is associated with death and mourning, but in Eastern cultures, white is. In the United States, white is associated with purity, but in India, red is. Understanding these differences will ensure that your instruction doesn't send the wrong message to diverse audiences on the basis of its color.

Color also evokes emotional responses (see figure 5.2). We are all familiar with the concept that red connotes warmth and that blue connotes cold. Red, orange, and yellow hues can induce excitement, aggression, and stimulation. Blues and greens can suggest security and peace.

Combining Colors

The combination of colors you choose can also have an effect on your audience. Some colors complement one another; others contrast. The use of a complementary color scheme may create a mood very different from a contrasting scheme. Deciding on the most effective color scheme is a process that can be a career in itself. However, many resources on the Web can teach you the basics of color theory so that creating an effective color scheme doesn't become an overwhelming task.

If you are like many people, you last studied color in elementary or high school. Before you start to work out your color scheme, you should reacquaint yourself with some color basics. One website you can visit to read about basic color theory is Worqx (www.worqx.com/color/).

There are three primary colors on the color wheel: red, yellow, and blue. When you combine two of the primary colors, your result is a secondary color: violet (a combination of red and blue), green (blue and yellow), or orange (red and yellow). A primary color combined with an adjacent secondary color produces an intermediate color: red orange, red violet, blue violet, blue green, yellow green, and yellow orange. These make up a basic twelve-color wheel (see figure 5.3, page 102). To complete the picture, include the neutral shades: white, black, and gray. White reflects all light and black absorbs all light. Gray is an impure white.

With just those twelve hues and the three neutral ones, you have an almost unlimited choice of colors. This is possible with variations to the basic group of tint, shade, tone, value, and intensity:

Figure 5.2
COLOR MEANINGS AND PERCEPTIONS

COLOR	PSYCHOLOGICAL RESPONSE	NOTES OF INTEREST
Red	Power, energy, warmth, passions, love, aggression, danger, excitement, desire, speed, strength	Changes meaning in the presence of other colors: with green, it becomes a symbol of Christmas; with white, it means joy in many Eastern cultures; in China, it is a symbol of celebration and luck
Blue	Peace, tranquility, calm, harmony, cold, trust, conservatism, security, technology, cleanliness, order	Used in the United States by many banks to symbolize trust; it is often considered the safest global color
Green	Nature, health, good luck, jealously, envy, renewal, environment, fertility, spring	Doesn't do well globally: problems are associated with green packaging in China and France
Yellow	Joy, happiness, imagination, hazard, illness, optimism, hope, philosophy, dishonesty, cowardice, betrayal	A sacred color to Hindus
Purple	Spirituality, mystery, royalty, transformation, cruelty, arrogance, mourning, wisdom, enlightenment	Appears very rarely in nature
Orange	Vibrancy, flamboyance, energy, balance, warmth	Signifies an inexpensive product
Brown	Simplicity, earth, reliability, comfort, endurance	Food packaging in the United States is often colored brown with success; in Colombia, brown discourages sales
Gray	Intelligence, futurism, modesty, sadness, decay, staidness, maturity, conservative	The easiest color for the eye to see
White	Purity, cleanliness, precision, innocence, sterility, death, youth, simplicity	Signifies marriage in the United States but death in India and other Eastern cultures
Black	Wealth, formality, evil, anger, remorse, power, sexuality, sophistication, death, mystery, fear, unhappiness, elegance	Signifies death and mourning in many Western cultures; in marketing, conveys elegance, wealth, and sophistication

Hue is color with no black, white, or gray added.

Tint is a hue plus white.

Shade is a hue plus black.

Tone is a hue plus gray or a hue plus a complementary color.

Value is how light or dark a color appears.

Intensity is how bright or dull it appears.

Figure 5.3 also shows a few proven approaches to take when deciding on a color scheme:

A monochromatic scheme uses one color in combination with some of its tints, tones, and shades.

A complementary color scheme begins by using two colors that are opposite each other on the color wheel and then incorporates tints, shades, and so on, to finalize the colors.

A triadic color scheme comprises three colors that are selected by drawing an equilateral triangle within the color wheel.

An analogous scheme uses two or more colors side by side on the color wheel.

For those who might be challenged when it comes to selecting colors, utilities are available to help choose a harmonious color scheme for a website. One is Color Wheel Pro (www.color-wheel-pro.com), which uses examples created in Flash that allow you to preview potential color schemes by rotating a color wheel. Once you find a scheme that works for your project, you can export the palette and use it in image-editing programs, such as Adobe Photoshop.

In selecting a color scheme, a primary consideration will be the legibility of the text against the background color. Legibility depends on many factors, but color is one of the important aspects, along with font, font size, and word style (which will be discussed shortly). When you are deciding on a color combination to increase readability, you are safest in going with a high-contrast combination. Black text on white background has high contrast, and red text on blue background has a very low contrast. Figure 5.4 (page 103) illustrates that the high contrast is more easily read (even with the grayscale used here).

Using Colors to Show Similarities and Differences

Color can be a useful tool for helping users see relationships among screen elements and to differentiate among tutorial components. For instance,

Figure 5.3
COLOR WHEEL AND COLOR SCHEMES

Monochromatic

Complementary

Analogous

Triadic

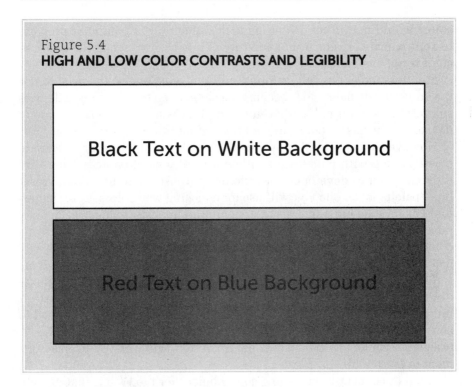

Figure 5.4
HIGH AND LOW COLOR CONTRASTS AND LEGIBILITY

Black Text on White Background

Red Text on Blue Background

color-coded titles and subtitles can help users see the levels of importance and organization of information. The proper use of color also can enhance navigation systems. The key to using color coding effectively is to use visual clues consistently throughout the site. A cautionary note, however: don't rely strictly on color to provide visual clues. You may have color-blind users or users with other visual impairments that make color coding useless to them!

Browser-Safe Colors?
In the early years of web design, the issue of how to ensure colors displayed consistently across all types of monitors was a big one. Color capability among monitors varied; most only had eight-bit video cards that would display 256 colors. There were obvious display inconsistencies between Macintosh and PCs. (For more discussion on monitor color capabilities, see chapter 4.)

To address this problem, a 216-color palette was developed using colors that appeared to display in the same way across platforms and in all browsers. Why were only 216 used instead of 256? The forty colors that were discarded were those that varied on Macs and PCs. But by restricting the number of colors to 216, designers were able to be certain that colors would not dither. Dithering is the attempt by a computer program to approximate a color from a mixture of other colors when the required color is not available.

Monitors today typically support millions of colors, so the need to use the browser-safe palette has become obsolete. Even today's mobile devices support sixteen-bit color (driven by the inclusion of cameras on many devices), so web-safe colors are not needed for those, either.

However, most graphics applications still include the browser-safe palette, along with palettes that allow for millions of choices. There are different palettes developed for different purposes. The RGB (red, green, blue) palette is the one you will use for choosing web colors. Color values for RGB are stated in numerals by assigning an intensity value to each pixel ranging from 0 (black) to 255 (white) for each of the RGB components in a color. For example, the RGB value for black is 0 0 0, white is stated as 255 255 255, and red is 255 0 0.

The HTML language uses hexadecimal numbers for color coding. Hexadecimal refers to the base-sixteen number system, which consists of sixteen unique symbols: the numbers 0 to 9 and the letters *a* to *f*. You will need to convert your colors from their RGB values to their hexadecimal values. A Google search for "RGB hexadecimal converter" will link you to an assortment of these tools.

Another concept in managing color choices for the Web is that of web-smart colors. The web-smart colors are those 4,096 colors composed of any three pairs of identical hexadecimal digits (0–9 and a–f), such as #dd1188. To see the difference between browser-safe, web-smart, and unsafe colors, visit the 4096 Color Wheel (http://ficml.org/jemimap/style/color/wheel.html). As you pass your cursor over the wheel, the hexadecimal value is displayed for all three choices. As is the case with browser-safe color palettes, the need for web-smart colors is waning. But it is useful to be aware of the choices.

How Many Colors?

Although it may be tempting to include many colors, using too many can distract and overwhelm users. You'll do best if you stick to Ben Shneiderman and colleagues' (2010) guidelines: "use color conservatively" and "limit the number of colors." Many design guides suggest limiting the number of colors to four. Like other visual-design guidelines, this is not set in stone, but it is a good basis to work from.

Link Colors

The first hyperlinks were all blue that changed to purple once they had been visited. As the art of web design evolved, many web authors began to tie their link colors in with the overall color scheme of the site. Usability experts recommend that the visited and unvisited links be variants or shades of the same color, so that they are clearly related (Nielsen, 2004).

Highlighting

Highlighting refers to various methods used to make critical information prominent to users. In web design, colors or patterns are often used to bring attention to text or objects, but they are not the only way to highlight information. Figure 5.5 shows several highlighting techniques that you may consider and lists their advantages and disadvantages. It's important to use highlighting judiciously. You want to use highlighting to bring something to the user's attention but not overpower other objects on the page. One highlighting possibility that CSS2 has made feasible is the ability to designate a background color behind an element in the page.

Backgrounds

Page backgrounds are used to create a mood for the site. A background should contribute to the purpose of the site and enhance the content. Be conscious that the background can have a positive or negative effect depending on how it is designed and used.

Backgrounds can be either a color or an image. If you decide to specify a color as your page background, select it using the color guidelines discussed earlier in this chapter.

If you prefer an image, there are some additional considerations. A background image is a GIF or JPEG file (see chapter 6) that is tiled across and down the screen by default. Because of this, you should consider the following factors:

File size: Keep the file size small because the browser will have to download it to display the image. Think in terms of pixels. A background image that is fifty pixels by fifty pixels will be small enough to download efficiently at most connection speeds.

Pattern: Select a pattern that will tile seamlessly horizontally or vertically so that it seems to be one continuous pattern.

Readability: Choose a subtle pattern that won't interfere with the readability of the content.

Image dimensions: Try not to use one large image as your background. Because backgrounds tile, if you design your image to display on a 1024×768 screen, it will tile on a large screen and not be viewable in its entirety at a smaller resolution. An image of that size will also be very large.

Figure 5.5

ADVANTAGES AND DISADVANTAGES TO HIGHLIGHTING TECHNIQUES

HIGHLIGHTING TECHNIQUE	ADVANTAGE	DISADVANTAGE	USE FOR
Color coding	Show relationships among screen elements	Some people have difficulty distinguishing colors. Use redundantly with another highlighting system.	See section on color
Blinking	Gets users' attention	Distracting, illegible, annoying	Don't use
All uppercase characters	Easily recognized as a headline	Not as easy to read as mixed case	Use for table labels and some headings
Underlining	Along with color, an indication of a hyperlink	On a Web page, underlining means a hyperlink	Use only in conjunction with a hyperlink
Oversized characters	Get attention easily	Takes up a great deal of screen space	Use for headings
Center and right alignment	Gets attention quickly	Difficult to read long blocks of text	Use for headings and accents

If you are using style sheets (and you should!), CSS2 includes a specification that increases the ways you can use backgrounds. Instead of tiling an image automatically across and down the page, CSS2 allows an author to specify whether the image should repeat or tile horizontally or vertically for one row, and it allows for placement and positioning of a single image on the page. Here are the values for repeating and their meanings:

repeat: horizontally and vertically

repeat-x: horizontally only

repeat-y: vertically only

no-repeat: display only one copy of the image

Value statements for positioning an image on the page are similar and can be seen on the W3C site (www.w3.org/TR/CSS21/colors.html#q2).

Figure 5.6 shows four implementations of a single image using background specifications in CSS2. On each screen, in addition to the image, the coding that would reside in the style sheet is displayed here to show its syntax. With a single image (see lower-left screen), variations in coding (shown on each screen) enable an author great flexibility in composing a background to create the best feel for the page.

Linking

As HTML coding sophistication has evolved, choices on how to show hyperlinks have expanded. In the early days it was straightforward—if you saw a blue, underlined block of text, you knew that that was the place to click to be taken to a different location. Now, however, links can be displayed a variety of ways. Links are shown in all the colors of the rainbow, in different fonts, and often are not underlined. Users have also become more sophisticated. Nielsen (2004) compiled a list of usability guidelines for showing textual links:

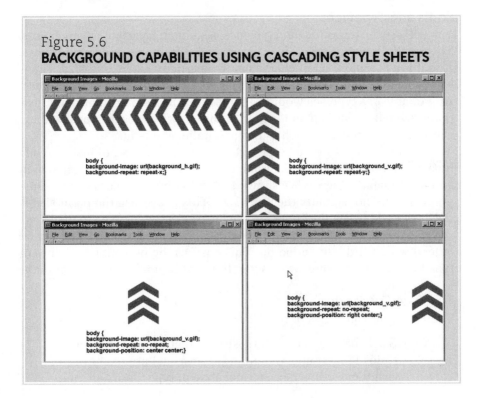

Figure 5.6
BACKGROUND CAPABILITIES USING CASCADING STYLE SHEETS

- To maximize the perceived affordance of clickability, color and underline the link text.
- If link text is colored, underlining is not always necessary. Two examples are navigation menus and other lists of links. Green and red can cause problems for color-blind users.
- Don't underline any text that isn't a link.
- Use different colors for visited and unvisited links.
- Never show text in your chosen link colors unless it's a link.
- Don't use tiny text for links and don't place links too close together. This causes usability problems for older users.

Typography

Type has always been an important component of graphic design because it contributes greatly to setting the tone or mood of a design. However, effectively controlling type on a page has traditionally been a frustrating experience. The following subsections discuss typography on the Web and some of the issues you will encounter. Let's start by reviewing some of the common terms you will hear.

Fonts and Typefaces

You will see the terms *font* and *typeface* used interchangeably many places. They really have different definitions, and it helps to understand these. A font is a complete set of characters in a particular style and size. Times New Roman in twelve points is a font. A typeface contains a series of fonts. An example of a typeface would be Times New Roman, in eight-point, ten-point, twelve-point, and so forth. In addition, within each typeface there can be many variations, such as normal, italic, and bold.

You should be aware that type sizes aren't standard: a point size in one typeface is not necessarily the same dimension as the same point size in another typeface. Figure 5.7 shows that different typefaces of the same point size are not actually the same size. This is because the point size is the distance between the bottom of the lowest descender (e.g., in the letters *j* or *y*) to the top of the highest ascender (e.g., in the letters *l* and *d* or capital letters) with a little bit added on. This ensures the prevention of lines of type touching each other when set with no additional space.

Typeface Categories

There are four categories of typefaces:

Serif: Serif characters have little strokes that decorate the letters. Times (Times) and Garamond (Garamond) are examples of serif typefaces, a more formal style of type. Serifs are helpful in providing a visual barrier to the tops and bottoms of letters, creating a horizontal emphasis that moves the eye as it travels along the line of text. For this reason, many people feel that a serif typeface is the most readable.

Sans serif: Sans-serif letterforms have no strokes and are more contemporary in style. Popular sans-serif typefaces are Arial (Arial) and Tahoma (**Tahoma**). Some experts believe that a sans-serif typeface is easier to read on a computer screen than a serif one. Because of the low resolution on many computer screens, there aren't enough pixels to give the detailed definition to the serifs on each letterform.

Monospace: In monospace typefaces, each letter takes up the same amount of space, similar to the old typewriter fonts. In other words, an i is as wide as an r. An example of a monospace typeface is Courier (`Courier`).

Decorative: The decorative category includes just about everything that doesn't fit into the other categories. Decorative type can evoke a wide range of moods and works best for titles and other accent text. These typefaces shouldn't be used in body text because they are often more difficult to read. Script (*Script*) and Bauhaus (**Bauhaus**) are good examples of decorative type.

Combining Typefaces

A combination of typefaces makes a more appealing visual design, but just as with color, it's not a good idea to overdo it. Pick two typefaces, one

Figure 5.7
COMPARISON OF TYPEFACES AT SAME POINT SIZE

This is 14-point Arial.
This is 14-point Futura Lt BT.
This is 14-point Verdana.
This is 14-point Times New Roman.
This is 14-point Garamond.

serif and one sans serif, to use. If you use the serif for your body text, then select a sans serif for the headings. And if you decide on a sans serif for your text, use a serif for its companion. Using two different serifs or two different sans serifs tends to look careless and indistinct.

Text Alignment

Text should be left aligned because it is easier to read. This doesn't mean that center and right alignment shouldn't be used, but they should be reserved to accent and highlight.

Text Case

Mixed uppercase and lowercase letters are much easier to read than are all capital letters. According to Nielsen (2000), it takes readers 10 percent longer to read a block of text that is in all capitals.

Text on the Web

When text is transported from the printed page to a computer screen and the Web, challenges arise. What holds true in print isn't necessarily so on a screen display. How to handle text on the Web also depends on whether your users have the latest versions of the browsers they use.

Font Sizing. Controlling font size on web pages has always been a challenge. Originally, font sizes were specified using the sizes 0 to 7. If no font size is specified, the default size was 3. The browser developers decided what point size 3 equaled. As of version 4.01 HTML specifications, these controls have been deprecated, which means that they have been outdated by newer concepts and have steadily become obsolete. For now, they are still interpreted, but the use of controls through CSS is recommended. Cascading Style Sheet specifications for fonts are accomplished through setting a series of font properties that include family (e.g., Helvetica, sans serif), style (e.g., normal or italic), variant (e.g., normal, small caps), weight (e.g., normal, bold, bolder, lighter), stretch (e.g., normal, wide, narrower), and size (e.g., small, medium, or large).

In regard to size, there is still plenty of room for author confusion. Figure 5.8 shows common different units of measurements used in CSS2. Some are absolute, which means that users can't adjust them (through the browser). This may be an attractive option for some designers who want to guarantee their pages display exactly as designed. Others are relative, which means that they are scaled on the basis of the font-size preference set in the user's browser. It is preferable to use a relative size to increase accessibility to users of your site; also, relative units scale better from one

Figure 5.8
COMMON FONT-SIZING OPTIONS IN CSS2

UNIT	DESCRIPTION	TYPE	NOTES	EXAMPLE
Em	unit of measurement equal to the current type size	relative	1 em in 10-point type is equal to 10 points. Works well in conjunction with percentage base sizing set in the body style. Relative to a parent element.	p { font-size: 1.2em; }
Px	stands for pixels; defines a measurement in screen pixels	absolute	consistency across browsers, but ignores user preferences	p { font-size: 18px; }
%	a percentage relative to another value	relative	based on the size of a parent element	p { font-size: 70%; }
Pt	point: a point is 1/72nd of an inch	absolute	good for print style sheets, can be inconsistent on different browsers and ignores user preferences	p { font-size: 12pt; }
Pc	pica: equivalent to 12 points; 6 picas = 1 inch	absolute		p { font-size: 10pc; }
Keyword	include xx-small, x-small, small, medium, large, x-large, xx-large	relative	relative to users' preferred medium settings in their browsers. Limited choices, only 7 sizes.	p { font-size: x-small; }

medium to another (screen to printer). Most savvy designers who want accessible sites use either the "em" or "%" measurement.

For detailed information on CSS2 specifications for fonts, visit the W3C website (www.w3.org/TR/2009/CR-CSS2-20090908/fonts.html#font -size-props). If you find this a bit more technical than you like, a helpful resource you might visit is the wiki CSS-discussion list (http://css-discuss .incutio.com/?page=UsingFontSize).

Browsers and Fonts. Use of CSS provides a way to specify any typeface for your web page. The property used to specify fonts in CSS is font family. A declaration would look like this: *h2 {font-family: Verdana, Helvetica, Arial, sans-serif;}.*

User-Controlled Font Display. No matter what text typeface you decide to use, most browsers allow users to override your choice and select their own font style and size. This may not be what you had in mind, but it is an important bit of user control that allows your audience to get to your content using their browser's preferences.

Font Availability. Whatever font you designate, if that font is not installed on the user's computer, it will not appear. For this reason, it is wise to use fonts commonly found on most computers. Common Windows fonts are Arial, Verdana, Helvetica, Times New Roman, Georgia, Courier New, and Comic Sans. Common Mac fonts include Arial, Geneva, Helvetica, Courier, and Times. Because you have no way to be sure what fonts are on users' computers, you should always specify more than one font when coding using {font-family:} in your stylesheet. If your first choice of font is one found commonly on one platform but not the other, then make sure your second choice is a font commonly found on the opposite platform. The final choice should always be either of the generic font designations, serif or sans serif, so you give the browser some indication of the kind of font you want displayed.

Platform Display Differences. Text is rendered 33 percent larger on a Windows computer than on a Macintosh. The Mac OS uses 18 pixels to render 18-point text, and Windows uses 24 pixels to do so. This is because Macintosh assumes a display at a resolution of 72 dpi, but Windows assumes 96 ppi. The result is that the same size text will appear much smaller on a Mac than on a PC.

Text and Screen. It should come as no surprise that screen resolution affects the appearance of text size. When you are selecting a typeface size, test it at different resolutions. What is legible on a 1024×768 screen may be more difficult to read at a higher resolution.

Images as Text

Because of the limitations of rendering typefaces on the Web, web designers often turn to graphics to guarantee that the style of type they have chosen displays exactly as intended. By creating a text graphic, you can introduce more personality into your design. However, the downside to this solution is that your audience will experience a longer download time for displaying the graphics (for a detailed discussion, see chapter 6). If you decide to use graphics for some of your text, be sure to include the ALT (for alternate text) attribute (also discussed in chapter 6) so that the text is accessible to those who turn off graphics or are visually impaired.

MULTINATIONAL AUDIENCE DESIGN CONSIDERATIONS

As it becomes more common to see cases where students for a specific online class can be located in highly dispersed locales, including different countries, there are issues that you should address to ensure a good learning experience to all. It is best to take a global approach to instructional design. Loring (2002) provides a useful checklist of issues to consider:

- languages that your targeted audience uses
- hardware, software, and infrastructure available
- cultural variables that could affect instruction (e.g., political, economic, social, religious)
- the role of the teacher and expected instructor-student interaction

Of course, although using the design guidelines that have been discussed in this chapter is a good idea, you will want to pay particular attention to some of the details that Loring (2002) cites:

- Use smaller chunks of information in each screen's presentation.
- Choose color schemes wisely (see the discussion on color earlier in this chapter).
- Be certain the sounds you use don't have meanings other than what you intend.
- Use images cautiously—images of people, their dress, and even animals can have different meanings in different cultures.
- Pay attention to the sequencing of images used to depict a concept, as some languages read from right to left.

When working with text, be sure to do the following:

- Use short concise sentences.
- Avoid jargon and slang.
- Position words correctly to accommodate right-to-left and vertically read languages.
- Leave room in tables and graphics for translations. The space taken up by translation will be different depending on the language.
- Be aware of expressions that have a distinct meaning when put in a certain order.

USER ACCESSIBILITY

An integral part of your design should address ensuring that it meets standards for access by disabled users. Unfortunately, as the Web has become more graphical and multimedia laden, it has become less accessible to those who have visual, auditory, motor, and cognitive impairments. If you are mindful of this need as you plan your project, it really won't be hard to design an accessible site. As part of its Web Accessibility Initiative Standard, the W3C has compiled its Web Content Accessibility Guidelines (WCGA) 2.0 (overview available at www.w3.org/WAI/intro/wcag.php). To make content more available to all users, the consortium worked to improve on its original 1.0 version of guidelines that had been structured according to priority checkpoints. Version 2.0, which became a W3C Recommendation in December 2008, is organized around four design principles of web accessibility. The goal of this change is to be able to apply more broadly to different and more advanced types of web technologies. The W3C provides a quick reference to aid web authors' success at meeting these requirements at www.w3.org/WAI/WCAG20/quickref/.

The four principles and critical guidelines with each are as follows:

Principle 1: Perceivable—Information and user interface components must be presentable to users in ways they can perceive.

- Provide text alternatives for any nontext content so it can be changed into other forms people need.

- Provide alternatives for time-based media.

- Create content that can be presented in different ways without loss of information or structure.

- Make it easier for users to see and hear content, including by separating the foreground from the background.

Principle 2: Operable—User interface components and navigation must be operable.

- Make all functionality available from a keyboard.

- Provide users enough time to read and use content.

- Do not design content in a way that is known to cause seizures.

- Provide ways to help users navigate, find content, and determine where they are.

Principle 3: Understandable—Information and the operation of user interface must be understandable.

- Make text content readable and understandable.

- Make web pages appear and operate in predictable ways.

- Help users avoid and correct mistakes.

Principle 4: Robust—Content must be robust enough that a wide variety of user agents can interpret it, including assistive technologies.

- Maximize compatibility with current and future user agents, including assistive technologies.

The W3C also maintains a page that contains information on tools that are available to help evaluate whether a site meets accessibility guidelines: www.w3.org/WAI/ER/tools/.

PAGE OPTIMIZATION

An important part of your students' experience with your instruction is whether the pages load quickly. Users become impatient if they have to wait several seconds for a page to display. Slow-loading pages hinder the focus on the learning that is, after all, your main goal. Graphics can be one of the biggest hindrances to quick-loading pages. The next chapter discusses solutions in more detail. You should be aware, however, that there are other things that can slow down a page display. Even extra spacing can contribute to a bloated page. Ways to reduce this slowness include page optimization, or the process of minimizing HTML file size to maximize page-display speed.

Visual-Based Web Editors

As discussed in chapter 4, visual-based (WYSIWYG) web editors are more user friendly than code-based ones are. You don't need to know HTML to produce professional-looking web pages. The down sides to this type of editor are that it does not always create code efficiently and often leaves unnecessary code behind during the editing process. Thus, WYSIWYG editors may be the biggest cause of code bloat.

Optimization Tips

There are many ways to streamline your website to maximize speed. Following are a few examples of some adjustments you can make. These ideas and additional tips are available in Andrew King's (2008) book on web optimization:

Properly position CSS and JavaScript: Positioning CSS in the head of your page and JavaScript in the bottom (body) enables progressive rendering.

Use CSS instead of tables for page layout: This has been covered earlier in the chapter but bears repeating!

Minimize HTTP requests: Each unique object in a web page requires a request to the server and a reply back to the client. The more objects, the more time is required to display all objects on a page.

Convert graphical text to styled text: CSS gives much more control for the ability to style text to achieve a desired look, so it isn't as necessary these days to turn to graphical text.

Resize and optimize images: This will be covered in more depth in chapter 6.

Optimize multimedia: This will be covered in more depth in chapter 6 as well.

Use CSS rules instead of inline styles: Replace the use of embedding your font and other display styles in your structure tags (i.e., <p>). Instead, create CSS rules and put those in an external style sheet.

Optimization Tools

Some software programs are designed to automate the optimization process. Most work in a similar manner by removing excess spaces, tabs, quotes, unnecessary attributes, and so forth. Some provide you with a report of what changes were made and the percentage of file reduction.

An example of a web-based optimization tool is WebSiteOptimization .com (www.websiteoptimization.com/services/analyze/).

CHAPTER SIX

MULTIMEDIA
Using Graphics, Sound, Animation, and Video

MULTIMEDIA IS THE integration of text, graphics, sound, and video or animation in a computer-based environment. Because the Web is a multimedia environment, it is easy to envision incorporating multimedia into an instructional tutorial to enhance the learning experience. This chapter examines the various media and issues surrounding their use.

MULTIMEDIA AND INSTRUCTION

When you contemplate how and when to incorporate multimedia into online instruction, there is an assortment of considerations. This section examines the benefits and limitations of multimedia, explores some of the appropriate uses of multimedia for instruction, and discusses multimedia issues that can influence its effective use.

Benefits and Limitations of Multimedia

Why is multimedia good to use in an online learning experience? Students have different learning preferences, and for that reason alone, offering information in more than one medium is beneficial. Many researchers have found advantages and disadvantages to using multimedia as a part of instruction.

Advantages

Allows representation of knowledge in a variety of ways: Students can read text to learn abstract principles and see practical application through an animation, for example (Bates and Poole 2003).

Addresses different learning styles and preferences: Multimedia provides opportunities to teach individuals and incorporate their preferred learning styles. Some students learn best through an auditory channel (lecture), but others learn best through visual channels. Multimedia can provide both.

Can provide a more active learning environment: Allows teachers to bring the real world to the learner through the combined use of two or more media such as sound, images, text, animation, and video.

Better learning and retention: Multimedia engages students and provides multiple learning methods.

Motivation: Studies show that learners consistently show positive attitudes toward multimedia (particularly interactive multimedia, which is discussed in chapter 7).

Disadvantages

Equipment requirements: The hardware and software required for multimedia development may be a burden on organizations that are limited in their abilities to install and maintain them.

Start-up costs: The initial costs for resources to support multimedia development can be prohibitive.

Complexity and lack of standardization: Much multimedia today is still proprietary. It is often difficult to configure various components so that they can work together.

Mayer's Principles of Multimedia Learning

Richard E. Mayer (2009, 5) studies the effects of multimedia on learning and has concluded that people learn better from words and pictures than from words alone. Thus, his definition of *multimedia instruction* is "presentations involving words and pictures that are intended to foster learning." From the research, he developed twelve principles for effective multimedia learning, arranged here by the theoretical function they serve:

Principles for Reducing Extraneous Processing in Multimedia Learning

Coherence principle: Students learn better when extraneous material is excluded from multimedia presentations. Learning is hurt by irrelevant words and pictures and by interesting but irrelevant sounds and music. Learning improves when unneeded words are eliminated.

Signaling principle: Students learn better with cues that highlight the organization of essential material.

Redundancy principle: Students learn better from graphics and narration than from graphics, narration, and on-screen text.

Spatial contiguity principle: Students learn better when on-screen text and graphics are physically integrated. For instance, if a block of text explains a graphic, retention increases if the text is integrated in the graphic rather than being located beside or below it.

Temporal contiguity principle: Students learn better when corresponding words and pictures are presented simultaneously.

Principles for Managing Essential Processing in Multimedia Learning

Segmenting principle: Students learn better when a multimedia lesson is presented in user-paced segments rather than as a whole unit.

Pretraining principle: Students learn better from a multimedia lesson when they know the names and characteristics of the main concepts.

Modality principle: Students learn better from graphics with narration than from animation with on-screen text.

Principles for Fostering Generative Processing

Multimedia principle: Students learn better from words and pictures than solely from words.

Personalization principle: Students learn better from conversational rather than formal words.

Voice principle: Students learn better when narration is in a friendly human voice rather than a machine-generated voice.

Image principle: Students do not necessarily learn better when the speaker's image appears on the screen.

Appropriateness

Multimedia can offer an enhanced learning experience, but only if used properly. It should be used only when it can contribute something to aid student learning, for instance, as discussed in the previous section. Using it just because it is "cool" is not a suitable reason. Some viable reasons for including multimedia are identified in the following sections.

Navigation

The importance of navigation was discussed in the previous chapter. Using images to build a navigation toolbar is a popular design approach. Images can serve to highlight the navigation scheme for the tutorial. Regular web users are accustomed to looking for navigation icons and images that will direct them through a site.

Establish a Theme or Mood

Students may become more engaged if the appropriate tone is set for particular learning. Images, audio, or animation are all possible means to create just the right setting.

Identification

Including a library logo or some other identifying graphic helps ensure that students know the origin of the instruction. If users come into your tutorial at a point other than the starting page, having identification helps to orient them to the current location.

Tell a Story

A picture, we've heard countless times, is worth a thousand words, and in many situations, an image does in fact provide information much more effectively than words do. One common use of images and illustrations is in conjunction with virtual library tours. Pictures of the different areas of the facility and floor maps help familiarize potential library users and give patrons a good way to become acquainted with how the building is organized.

Illustration

Using illustrations or screen captures is another way to convey an instructional point effectively. For instance, you can describe what students should expect to see when they conduct a search, but showing a screen-capture image of what you are describing allows students to associate the description with a representation of the screen they will see.

Demonstration or Simulation

Often, the best way to get a concept across is through demonstration or simulation. A typical type of demonstration shows how to conduct searches using particular search software.

Visualization

Visualization is a way to help students grasp difficult concepts and ideas. By including graphics, charts, diagrams, animation, and even 3-D objects, designers can help students visualize to make content more understandable. One concept that students commonly have difficulty understanding is Boolean logic. By simply incorporating a graphic of a Venn diagram, students can immediately see the meaning of the operators AND, OR, and NOT.

Multimedia Considerations

As you are deciding on what types of multimedia to integrate into your instruction, always keep your audience's best interests in mind. You will want to consider each of the following elements.

Bandwidth

Bandwidth is the amount of data that can be transmitted in a certain amount of time. Any type of multimedia requires additional bandwidth. Even when students have a good connection, nonstreaming multimedia files have to be downloaded, and this takes time. Keep the size of multimedia files as compact as possible by using file compression. This will be discussed later in this chapter. If you are incorporating files of any size, communicate that to the user. It will help prevent the frustration of long download times.

Plug-Ins

Plug-in applications are separate programs that are installed and run as part of your browser. Many of today's latest multimedia technologies require a plug-in so the media can be viewed or heard. Once installed, plug-ins permit multimedia to become integrated into the browser environment, but most people don't make the effort to download and install them until they face the need to view a page that requires one. Be kind to your students. State at the beginning of the tutorial what plug-ins are required, and provide a link to their download sites.

Integrating Web 2.0 Tools and Websites

The advent of Web 2.0 technology has opened up a world of possibilities for incorporating multimedia content that is hosted on other websites

and/or created by others. A prime example is YouTube (www.youtube
.com), where videos can be uploaded and shared, and then embedded
into your web-based instruction. There are benefits for institutions that
have the ability to create multimedia instructional components but do
not have the infrastructure to house large amounts of multimedia. There
are also opportunities to find preexisting videos that cover the content
you wish to include. There are videos about copyright, plagiarism, remix-
ing, database searching, and Boolean logic, just to mention a few. When
making a decision to incorporate content created by another party, you
must research the copyright status of the multimedia you wish to use
before using it.

Hardware and Software Requirements

It's worth mentioning again that your use of multimedia should not exceed
your audience's capacity to access it. Before you invest a great deal of time
and money in developing sophisticated multimedia elements, be certain
your users have the hardware and software capabilities to play and view
what you create. If you have a diverse user group, consider making a high-
tech and a low-tech version of your instruction.

Accessibility

Incorporating multimedia into instruction presents a particular challenge
in regard to accessibility to all potential users. By its nature, multimedia
content can shut out users. Vision-impaired users can't see graphics or
animations. They need a text alternative that can be spoken by a screen
reader. Hearing-impaired users can't hear audio narration. They need a
visual alternative to audible materials. Audio clips should have text alternatives, and video clips should be captioned. The bottom line is that you
should provide multiple representations of your multimedia content to
address the needs of users with disabilities.

As accessibility issues have come to the forefront in the past years,
developers have started to address building accessibility functionality into
their multimedia development tools and to provide instruction for doing
so on their websites. The Adobe site is a good example (www.adobe.com/
accessibility/). It includes instructions for building accessibility into Flash
and Dreamweaver, along with information about accessibility issues in
general, tools, case studies, and examples of accessible sites.

Investigate to determine the most effective way to make your multimedia
instruction accessible to all your potential users, keeping in mind that text
is the most widely accessible content there is!

TYPES OF MULTIMEDIA

The basic divisions between types of multimedia with which most of us are familiar include graphics, sound, animation, and video. However, in the world of computer multimedia, the lines of distinction often blur. For instance, animations can include text, sound, and video. Videos can include text, animation, and still images. As you explore the various types of multimedia, be on the lookout for formats that overlap other categories and have more than one function. You will also see several references to interactivity capabilities, which are discussed in greater depth in chapter 7.

Graphics or Images

When the Web was first popularized, the combination of text and images constituted multimedia on the Web. Now, however, images are almost a given on any particular web page. Nevertheless, creating graphics for the Web is different from creating them for print. The following subsections examine some of the basics of computer imaging and how to work with web graphics.

Raster (Bitmap) versus Vector Images
Computer graphics come in two different flavors: raster (also called bitmap) and vector. It is helpful to have some understanding of what each type is and to understand their differences and the benefits and drawbacks of each type.

Raster images are made up of small squares called pixels that are arranged in a grid. Each pixel is a tiny unit of color that comes together with the other pixels to form the images you see on your screen. When you create a raster image, you set the number of pixels that will be in the grid, and that determines the resolution, measured in dots or pixels per inch (dpi or ppi). When you view raster images at the size they were created, you will not see the pixels. However, if you zoom in on an image with a photo-editing application, the individual pixels appear (see figure 6.1).

Raster images are resolution dependent. If you increase the size of a raster image, the pixels are simply enlarged and the edges appear jagged. Computer screens typically display at 72 or 96 dpi. That is why an image scanned in at 300 dpi looks so large on a computer monitor. If you are creating a raster image that will be displayed only on a computer monitor (and is not intended for printing), there is no reason to create it any larger than 72 dpi.

Because they are created on a grid, raster images are rectangular in shape. Some raster formats support transparency, which designates some of the pixels to be invisible to the eye, thereby giving the illusion of a nonrectangular shape. Transparency permits one color to be specified as see-through. This capability allows the rectangular raster image to appear to be other shapes because it permits a web page's background color to show through the transparent pixels. Because they are resolution dependent, it is difficult to resize raster images without degrading the quality. Making the graphic smaller forces your imaging program to throw away pixels. Resizing the image to a larger size forces the program to create new pixels and to guess what new pixels to create.

Resizing is different from scaling. Scaling takes place when you adjust the image size by dragging the corners of it in a page-layout program. This does not permanently change the image, but it does change how it displays. If you enlarge an image via scaling, the result will be pixelated much as the example in figure 6.1. It's best to create raster images at the size you plan to use them. Because scanners and digital cameras both produce bitmap images, you can control size creation from the image-editing software. For a discussion of potential imaging programs, refer to chapter 4.

Vector images are made up of mathematically described objects. The objects can be lines, curves, and shapes, and they have attributes such as color, fill, and outline. Vector graphics are resolution independent: they are scalable and can be manipulated without losing their qualities, illustrated by the arrow in figure 6.2 that has had its size reduced and enlarged. A font is an example of a vector object.

Unlike bitmap images, vector images are not restricted to a rectangular shape, so they are much more flexible in combination with other objects. One major advantage of vector images is that their file size is small because the file really represents an equation the operating system uses to re-create the object. Another advantage is the ease with which you can edit and resize a vector image. The major disadvantage is that they are not suitable for photo-quality images. They are best suited for line drawings. Vector images are normally created using illustration software such as Adobe Illustrator.

As you will discover in the next section, most graphics on the Web today are raster images. However, nearly all illustration programs include the capability to convert a vector image to a raster image so that it can be viewed on the Web. Just be certain that the image is sized correctly before converting it. For a summary of raster and vector features and file formats, refer to figure 6.3.

Metafiles

Metafile formats are those that contain both raster and vector data. They are vector overall but contain at least one object that is a bitmap.

Traditional Web Graphic Formats

Although there are a multitude of formats that can be used to create computer graphics, browsers support only a limited number of them for display on the Web. The two standard web-image formats are GIF and JPEG, both of which are raster images. At this time, those are the only two image formats that can universally be displayed in all browsers without resorting to a plug-in. However, several newer formats have been developed for use on the Web. Their level of support and potential is discussed later in this chapter.

GIF (.gif). The Graphics Interchange Format (GIF, pronounced "jif") was defined in the late 1980s by CompuServe. It incorporates a compression scheme that keeps file sizes at minimum with no loss of data (lossless compression) while preserving sharp detail. The compression used is LZW (which stands for its inventors Lempel, Zev, and Welch), a scheme that efficiently compresses large fields of homogeneous color. Files in the GIF format have a palette limited to 256 colors (8 bits). There are two GIF standards: the initial version, 87a, and 89a, which supports transparency.

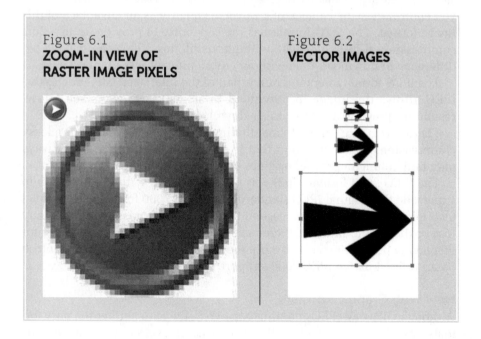

Figure 6.1
ZOOM-IN VIEW OF RASTER IMAGE PIXELS

Figure 6.2
VECTOR IMAGES

The GIF format also supports interlaced images; every eighth row in an image is displayed, then every fourth, then every second. This allows users to view emerging images as they are being downloaded to their computers, a particularly attractive technique if your audience includes those who use modems to access your instruction.

The GIF format is most useful for images that have a limited number of colors or large areas of solid colors, as with line art and cartoons. This format works nicely with logos and illustrations with type. Vector images convert well to the GIF format because of its lossless compression and ability to support transparency. You can also use the GIF format to create animated images, which will be discussed shortly.

JPEG (.jpeg, .jpg). The JPEG (pronounced "JAY-peg") acronym stands for Joint Photographic Experts Group, the committee that developed the standard in the late 1980s and early 1990s. The JPEG image format is designed to compress full-color or grayscale realistic images. The JPEG format supports 24-bit color, or more than 16 million colors. Because it provides significantly more image information than a GIF format (with its 256-color limit) does, JPEG is better suited for photographs and scanned artwork. It is, however, a lossy compression, which means that some data is discarded during the compression process. This loss may or may not be discernible to the naked eye, depending on the quality of the original and the amount of compression. The ability to specify degree of compression with JPEG, which gives you control over the balance of size versus quality, is an advantage of this image format. The JPEG format has the capability to provide up to a 20:1 compression of full-color data without visible loss. This can make a big difference in download time without any significant loss of image data.

The JPEG format offers its counterpart of the interlaced GIF. Progressive JPEG allows the image to download in stages, so viewers see a low-resolution preview until the image downloads completely.

There is one caution worth mentioning about JPEG. Because it is a lossy compression, the information that is discarded is gone forever. Always maintain an uncompressed original of the image and work from it.

The JPEG 2000 format (.jp2) was created in 2000 with the intention to supersede the original JPEG standard. The JPEG 2000 format uses wavelet technology to enable an increase of 20 percent compression without any loss or distortion. In 2010, there is still very limited browser support for displaying JPEG 2000 without a plug-in. As of this writing, only Macintosh Safari offered native JPEG 2000 support.

New Web Graphic Formats

Although GIFs and JPEGs dominate the Web, they are neither the only formats available nor necessarily the best format in every circumstance. This

Figure 6.3
COMPARISON OF RASTER AND VECTOR IMAGES

	RASTER (BITMAP) IMAGES	VECTOR IMAGES

Key points	Pixels in a grid
	Resolution dependent
	Resizing reduces quality
	Easily converted to other bitmap
	    formats
	Restricted to rectangle
	Minimal support for
	    transparency
		Mathematically described
		    lines and curves
		Resolution independent
		Scalable
		No background
		Cartoon like
		Inappropriate for
		    photorealistic images

Common file formats	.bmp: Bitmap
	.gif: Graphics Interchange
	    Format
	.jpeg, .jpg: Joint Photographic
	    Experts Group
	.png: Portable Network Graphics
	.pict (Macintosh)
	.tiff, .tif: Tag Image Bitmap File
	.psd (Adobe Photoshop)
		.ai: Abobe Illustrator
		.cdr: CorelDRAW
		.cmx: Corel Exchange
		.cgm: Computer Graphic
		    Metafile
		.dxf: Data Exchange Format
		    (Autocad)
		.svg: Scalable Vector
		    Graphics
		.wmf: Windows Metafile

Support for both raster and vector	.eps: Encapsulated Postscript .pdf: Adobe Portable Document Format .fla: Flash .swf: Small Web Format	

section takes a look at some of the image formats that have been developed for several years but are now beginning to be viable for mainstream use on the Web.

PNG (.png). The PNG (pronounced "ping") format refers to Portable Network Graphics, designed to be the successor to GIF. Interest in an alternative to GIF increased when the company that owns it announced that programs implementing GIF would require royalties. The PNG compression was developed expressly to be royalty free and contains a number of improvements over the GIF format. It was developed in 1995 and issued as a W3C recommendation in October 1996. Because it was designed for transferring images over the Internet, and because most of the major browsers and imaging programs now support the format, it is likely that you will see it used more frequently.

The PNG format supports three main image types: true color, grayscale, and palette based. Because JPEG supports only true color and grayscale, and GIF supports only palette-based color, PNG is a potential alternative to both of these formats in certain circumstances.

As with GIF, PNG is a lossless compression, but, unlike GIF, is not restricted to a 256-color palette. Because it supports up to 48-bit color, PNG can display complex color schemes with no loss of data. When rendered as to guidelines, PNG has a higher compression rate than GIF.

The PNG format also supports transparency, but again it improves on what GIF can offer. The GIF format supports transparency of one color, and PNG allows for up to 254 levels of partial transparency.

Interlacing is also incorporated into PNG. The GIF format uses one-dimensional interlacing, whereas PNG uses a two-dimensional scheme, which results in a more quickly displayed image. With only one-sixty-fourth of a PNG downloaded, a viewer sees a preview of the entire image, but at that same fraction, a viewer would see only one-eighth of a GIF image.

Should you use PNG? If your authoring software supports PNG and your audience's browsers also do, then PNG may well be a worthwhile format. For more information on this promising web format, visit the PNG home site (www.libpng.org/pub/png/).

SVG (.svg). All the web graphic formats discussed so far have been raster (bitmap). Because vector graphics have some benefits over raster images, developing a standard for supporting display of them over the Web has been a priority for some time. Currently, there are a number of proprietary vector graphic formats being used, but all require plug-ins, which prevents their widespread use as raster graphics. Because no single format is widely supported for either viewing or design and because there is little cross-platform support, in 1999, W3C took on the development of a vector graphic standard. The SVG (Scalable Vector Graphics) standard is a language for describing two-dimensional graphics in XML, along with a set of application program interfaces (APIs) on which to build graphics-based applications. The language issues instructions to describe how a figure should appear by assigning attributes to SVG elements. In other words, it is coded in plain text within an HTML document with no other files involved. The SVG format allows for three types of graphic objects: vector shapes (paths consisting of straight lines and curves), raster images (with color gradations), and text. Drawings in SVG can be dynamic and interactive. And SVG is an open standard that has development support from many organizations, including major players such as Sun Microsystems,

Adobe, Apple, and IBM. It is also well suited for display on small and mobile devices. As of March 2010, all major browsers with the exception of Internet Explorer (IE) offer some level of support for displaying SVG. Microsoft has announced that IE version 9 will support SVG display.

The SVG format has several advantages over the traditional web graphic formats:

Scalability: Because it is a vector format, SVG can be scaled to any resolution without degradation of quality.

Smaller file size: A smaller file size translates, of course, to faster download time.

Scripting and animation: The SVG format has the capability to render dynamic and interactive graphics.

Plain-text format: The SVG language is written in plain text. This makes it possible to use a variety of tools to read and modify an SVG file. It also contributes to a smaller file size.

Ability to apply styles: The SVG format can be changed with CSS, unlike bitmapped images, which cannot be changed once they have been created in anything but a graphics program. This means, for instance, that you can easily change text in objects to a different font or color.

Selectable and searchable text: The text content of an SVG graphic becomes searchable, can be indexed, and can be displayed in multiple languages. This has great benefit for disabled users.

Open standard: The SVG format is an open recommendation developed by a cross-industry consortium.

As of January 2003, SVG 1.1 had become a W3C recommendation. The format SVG Tiny 1.2, intended for use with small devices, became a W3C recommendation in December 2008. For detailed information on SVG, visit the W3C's SVG site (www.w3.org/Graphics/SVG/).

For a comparison of the four web graphics formats, refer to figure 6.4.

Icons

An icon is a small picture intended to represent a word or phrase. On the Web, icons are small graphic elements on a web page that represent a topic or additional information on another page or, once clicked, a function for the user. Icons are a common tool on commercial sites; for instance, many people know what the shopping cart icon means. Appropriate icons on an educational site can be valuable also. A good icon contains a visual image that a user can recognize more quickly than written text. Figure 6.5 illustrates some well-known web icons that have potential usefulness on instructional sites.

Figure 6.4
ADVANTAGES, DISADVANTAGES, AND USES OF WEB GRAPHIC FORMATS

	ADVANTAGES	DISADVANTAGES	USE FOR
GIF	Can be indexed to a set color palette (helps with browser-safe color determination) Lossless compression scheme Supports transparency Superior when compressing a few distinct colors Supports interlacing Supports animations	Limited to a 256-color palette	Line art Logos Cartoons Type and fonts Black-and-white images Images with large areas of solid color
JPEG	Supports 24-bit true color Preserves broad range and subtle variations in brightness and hue Can specify degree of compression Supports progressive download	Has difficulty with sharp edges (which come out blurred) Lossy compression scheme Doesn't support transparency	Full-color or gray-scale realistic images Images with lots of complex, gradient color variations
PNG	Supports 48-bit true color Cross-platform control of image brightness Two-dimensional interlacing Lossless compression, higher rate than GIF Variable transparency Supports true color, grayscale and palette	No multiple-image support for animations	Use in place of either GIF or JPEG if appropriate
SVG	Fully scalable for zooming and panning XML based W3C recommendation Compact download size Editable and searchable text Multiple levels transparency Supports scripting and animation Ability to apply CSS Open standard Plain-text format (can use a variety of tools to create it)	May require use of a plug-in to view (Internet Explorer does not support native display of SVG in its browser)	Use when implementing vector graphics that you desire scalability control over

Clip Art

Clip art is off-the-shelf artwork originally designed for use in desktop publishing and prepared in a standardized format for nonspecific use and wide distribution. With the popularization of the Web, clip-art libraries have become a common resource for artists and nonartists to incorporate art into their web pages quickly and economically. Clip art includes visual elements such as bullets, lines, and arrows, as well as subject-related illustrations on almost any topic under the sun.

Clip art is available commercially from many companies, but there are also plenty of clip-art libraries on the Web. It is a simple matter to download clip art from the Web, but it is important to know that you can't assume that all clip art is freely available for download and use. Be aware that clip art may be copyrighted and that many clip-art sites have terms and conditions for users of their art. It is your responsibility to familiarize yourself with specified rules and to comply with them.

Finding clip art online is not difficult. A Google search for "clip art library" will return plenty to choose from. A good example of a library with free content is the Open Clip Art Library (www.openclipart.org) that was started in 2004 and now has more than ten thousand public domain images from more than five hundred artists.

Image Maps

As mentioned in chapter 5, an image map is a graphic defined so that users can click on different areas to go to various destinations, retrieve a document, or run a program. These areas are called hot spots and are defined by x and y coordinates (the horizontal and vertical distance from the left-hand corner of the image). There are two types of image maps, server side and client side. The server-side map stores the map data on the server, which means a longer response time for the user, because the client browser must query the server for the map destination. With client-side maps, the map data is embedded in the HTML document and interpreted by the browser program on users' computers. Response time for users is faster with a client-side image map, so it's best to use that type.

Image maps are often used as the main menu on a visually based introductory page. A designer with a little imagination, however, is likely to see opportunities to use them throughout an educational tutorial. An image map can be quite effective to simulate the functionality of a specific interface, for example.

Image maps can be created in many web editors. Hot spots are selected by drawing one of three shapes (circle, rectangle, or polygon) and assigning a destination to that spot.

Rollover Images

A rollover (also known as a mouseover) is a JavaScript technique that allows a web author to program a page element change when a user's cursor passes over something on the page. The page element is usually a graphic, and rollovers are often used in navigation tool bars. Rollovers invite a feeling of user interactivity because changes take place in response to the user's activity.

To make rollovers, create two graphics with the same dimensions. One will load when the page first displays. The second will swap places with the first when the cursor passes over the original image. Another common use is the remote rollover, which causes a previously invisible graphic element to appear when the user passes the cursor over a certain page element. In that case, you'll prepare a third image, which doesn't necessarily have to be the same size as the first two, because it loads in a different part of the page. With a remote rollover, the third image will appear in a different location at the same time that the second image appears in place of the first. Don't hesitate to use rollovers just because you don't know how to write JavaScript. Many web editors include behind-the-scenes scripting to create rollovers. It is also easy to find free rollover scripts on the Web. One such script is the Mouseover Machine, which has become available at many sites over the past few years. The free utility creates a rollover script based on the information you enter into fields in a form at a participating site. Once the code is generated, you simply cut and paste it into your HTML document.

Figure 6.5
USEFUL WEB ICONS

⊠ Email	🖼 Blog Posting
🎞 Video Clip	🔊 RSS Feed
🔊 Audio Clip	🧩 Plug-In
🖨 Print	🔍 File Type
💬 Comment	🔲 Share It!

Image Optimization

Even though GIFs, JPEGs, and PNGs are compression formats, there are other steps you can take to ensure that your images are optimized for faster download times:

- Use only meaningful graphics; remove everything else. This tip bears repeating because it is so easy to get carried away using graphics.
- Select the most appropriate format for the type of graphic you are using. Figure 6.4 can help you decide which type is best.
- Size the images accurately.

- Keep resolution to 72 dpi. If you are not printing the image, there is no need for any higher resolution.
- Always use width and height attributes. This allows the browser to render the rest of the page while the graphic downloads.
- Make the width and height of the image the exact size that will display. Don't use the width and height attributes of the <image> tag to resize the image. If you do, either image quality will decrease or you will waste bandwidth because the full image still needs to download.
- Crop images to discard extra space around the image's subject matter.
- Reduce the number of colors (bit depth) in the image as much as possible in palette-based formats (GIF and PNG) to take out unnecessary color. If you do it carefully, the reduction will be invisible to the naked eye.
- Optimize JPEG files. The less compression, the better the image quality and the larger the file will be.
- Reuse graphics sitewide. Because browsers cache files as they download, images that are repeated will appear quickly. If the browser recognizes a file name, it will look to the cache to retrieve it rather than to the originating server.
- Store your images on the same server as your instructional site. This helps minimize the slight lag that an extra domain name server lookup entails.

Many graphics applications include the ability to optimize images for the Web. For instance, Adobe has incorporated ImageReady into Photoshop. This utility is used to prepare and optimize images for use on the Web.

If you don't have access to an optimizing application, you can access utilities available on the Web, some of which involve a fee. One free example is Image Optimizer (www.imageoptimizer.net/Pages/Home.aspx). You provide the path to an image on your computer. The utility examines the file and can optimize it to one of six different sizes.

Image Slicing and CSS Sprites

Image slicing is an older technique that combines image editing with HTML. It allows large images to be sliced into a number of pieces, which are then reassembled in an HTML table. Although the main goal of image slicing was to facilitate faster download times, in reality no bandwidth was saved, although there may have been an illusion of speed to the end user. This was a more common technique in the days before CSS-P (Cascading

Style Sheet Positioning) solved the difficulties of exact placement of objects on a web page.

With the evolution of CSS, a more efficient method is now available: CSS sprites. Typically, sprites were two dimensional images or animations that were integrated into a larger scene in video games. In the web environment, designers use the term *sprite* to refer to small images or icons that are stitched together into a single image to reduce the number of requests the browser makes to the server to download images. Through the use of CSS, different areas of the larger images can be selected to display at different points of the page. The goal of using sprites is to make a web page load faster. Dave Shea's (2004) article provides a good introduction to CSS sprites. The CSS Sprite Generator is an example of one utility available to create sprites (http://spritegen.website-performance.org).

Labeling Images

The ALT attribute provides an alternative way to reveal the content of your images to those who cannot or choose not to view graphics. The ALT attribute looks like this in HTML code:

```
<img src="intromenu.gif" width="540" height="399"
alt="Start Menu">
```

Users with visual disabilities or those who have turned off image loading in their browsers will either hear from a screen reader or see the text alternative. If this attribute is ignored or overlooked during the authoring process, the site will not be accessible to all visitors.

Audio

Today the Web is no longer primarily a visual medium; as bandwidth has increased and technology has matured, the delivery of audio over the Internet has become very common. Proper use of audio can serve many purposes on an educational site—for example, to set a mood, provide an alternate communication channel apart from the visual material, or give an audible clue for different actions within the interface. As with other multimedia, the important thing to remember is to use audio for a specific purpose and not to overdo it.

File Formats

There are two main categories of sound on the Web today: self-contained (must be downloaded to the local computer before users can hear it) and streaming audio. The following subsections explore the first category of audio file types. Streaming audio is examined in the presentation of streaming media later in the chapter.

AU (.au). The first audio file format used on the Internet, Audio File Format (AU) was intended for use on Unix computers. It is also the standard sound format for the Java platform. This format supports a 2:1 compression ratio, which gives the format a relatively small file size of about 8 kilobytes (KB) per second of audio. It is probably the closest to a nonproprietary audio standard available on the Internet, and so it can be found in quantity from sound libraries. Because the quality of AU files is not high, they work well for short clips and sound effects but should not be the first choice for a project that relies heavily on sound.

AIFF (.aiff, .aif). Apple developed the Audio Interchange File Format (AIFF) for the Macintosh platform. The AIFF format is uncompressed, so the files can be large. Its sound quality is better than that of the AU format. It is comparable to a WAV file (see the next subsection) for the Mac.

WAV (.wav). Developed by Microsoft, the Waveform Audio File Format (WAV) is the PC and Windows equivalent of Apple's AIFF. Because it is the native sound file format for the platform that has the overwhelming majority of presence on the Internet, it is common to see. However, it, too, is an uncompressed format, and just sixty seconds of WAV audio can take up more than 10 MB of disk space. The WAV format has a comparable sound quality to AIFF. Because it is uncompressed, WAV is the preferred format for saving archival versions of audio. However, because of its large size, as file sharing has increased over the Internet, its popularity has declined.

All three store recorded sound that originates as analog and is converted to digital. The next file type is quite different.

MIDI (.midi, .mid). The Musical Instrument Digital Interface (MIDI) format is a protocol adopted by the electronic music industry for controlling music synthesizer devices (both keyboards and sound cards). It doesn't represent music sounds directly (as do AU, AIFF, and WAV); instead, it transfers information that tells the synthesizer what to play to produce a musical composition. Thus, MIDI might be compared with vector graphics in that both file types consist of instructions or commands. Like a vector file, the MIDI file sizes are smaller than their counterparts because the instructions consume much less data. One drawback to the MIDI format is that it plays only instrumentals, not voices.

MPEG. Both an audio and a video compression format, MPEG is also the acronym for Motion Pictures Experts Group, and it is explained in full in the video section of this chapter.

MP3 (.mp3). MPEG-1 Audio Layer-3 is the most popular audio format on the Web today. Although it is most famous for the illegalities involved with downloading files, MP3 is in fact just an efficient audio-compression format. The compression ratio is 12:1, yet the sound quality is preserved in compression. Although it has often been assumed to be an open (nonproprietary) standard, this isn't the case, as it is a patented encoding format.

Ogg Vorbis (.ogg, .oga). The issue with MP3's proprietary format led to the development of a completely open and free audio compression, Vorbis, from the Xiph.Org Foundation. The code for the latest release is available from the Vorbis website (vorbis.com). It is frequently used in conjunction with Ogg container, a fully open multimedia bitstream format designed for efficient streaming and storage. When used together, it is known as Ogg Vorbis. Ogg Vorbis has become popular in open-source communities, but MP3 technology is extremely entrenched in the public eye. However, an increasing number of audio players support Ogg Vorbis in their products, and it is commonly used to encode freely available content.

Windows Media Audio (.wma). Microsoft's Windows Media Audio (WMA) audio format is proprietary and compressed, designed initially as a competitor to MP3 and RealAudio. It has now positioned itself as a competitor to the Advanced Audio Coding format used by Apple for iTunes. The initial reason for the development of WMA most likely was related to the patent issue with MP3, which had to be licensed to be included with the Windows operating system (OS). A WMA file is often encapsulated in an Advanced Systems Format (ASF) file. This format specifies how the metadata for the file is to be encoded. The advantages that WMA claims over MP3 include being better suited to low bitrates (especially around 8–64 kilobits per second) and producing better quality at a given bitrate than MP3. To play WMA files, you can use the Windows Media Player or other players such as Winamp. It also has a digital rights component that protects against the unauthorized reproduction of copyrighted material.

File Download versus Inline

Linking to a sound file is the simplest way to include sound in a web page. This method is the most appropriate when supplying certain types of files such as sound clips that accompany other material. Providing a link puts the control of the sound into the user's hands. When using a link, remember to include all the information about the file that is important to the audience: type of file format, file size, and estimated download time. A typical link might look like this:

<a href="boolean.ogg">Hear about Boolean Logic</a>

When the user clicks on this link, either a player or a plug-in will be invoked, depending on the browser and its configuration.

Sounds may also be embedded, that is, be put in line so that they are a part of your page and result in sound playing automatically in the background when the page loads. Since HTML version 4.01, the <object> tag embeds media in a web page. The older <embed> and <bgsound> tags were never sanctioned and should not be used. You will find that there is only spotty support for embedded sounds from browser to browser, so be prepared to test in different browsers and across platforms to ensure that the sound works as you intend.

A third option for including sound files is JavaScript, which can script having sound play when the screen loads or in response to different mouse actions.

If you decide to include background sound, do your audience a favor and give them the controls to turn the music on and off. What sounds great to one person may sound like fingernails across the blackboard to others.

Using Existing Sound Files

If you don't have the experience or expertise to create your own audio files, you'll probably want to access the many sound libraries that are available on the Web for clips. However, be careful when downloading others' sound files, and always research the copyright requirements. Copyright issues in the music industry are complicated. Several organizations deal with various aspects of music copyright, including the American Society of Composers, Authors and Publishers (ASCAP, www.ascap.com), Broadcast Music Inc. (BMI, www.bmi.com), the Recording Industry Association of America (RIAA, www.riaa.com), and the Harry Fox Agency Inc. (HFA, www.harryfox.com).

Animation

Animation can be defined as the creation of the illusion of movement. This is accomplished through subtle changes in a sequence of stationary screen elements or images. Although motion across the screen is a primary type, animation also deals with any change in an object: change in brightness, color, size, shape, or into another object altogether (metamorphosis). It can include a variety of different media: text, vector and raster graphics, audio, and video. An animation is not just a viewable object; it can also incorporate elements of interactivity for user response.

When is animation appropriate to use? Good uses, as identified by Jakob Nielsen (2000), include

- indicating transitions
- illustrating change over time
- showing multiple information objects in the same space
- enriching graphical representations
- visualizing three-dimensional structures
- attracting attention

Basic Animation Concepts

In-depth instruction about animation is beyond the scope of this book. However, it is helpful to become acquainted with a few key ideas so that, as you look at the various animation technologies, you can recognize similarities and differences in approach.

A common element of all animation is the ability to create sequential frames and then work with the timing and transition of those frames to ready them for playback. To best understand this procedure, it is worth becoming familiar with a few basic terms and concepts:

Cycling (looping): This involves creating cycles of motion that end the same way they start, allowing the reuse of the cycle as many times as needed. On the Web, cycling helps keep the file size of an animation smaller, thus conserving download time.

Key frame: The animator designates specific objects at critical points on the animation timeline, and the computer program then fills in the motion between these frames.

Sprite: This is a graphic image that can move within a larger graphic. Software that supports sprites allows the designer to create individual animated images that can be combined into a larger animation.

Tweening: Short for *in-betweening*, tweening is the calculation (made by the application software) for determining the intermediate frames between two key frames to simulate motion.

Timeline: A timeline is a scale measured either in seconds or frames that provides an editable, visual record of animation events.

The different types of animation fall into one of two main categories: prerendered and real time. Prerendered (also called frame-by-frame) animations include those that are downloaded in their entirety to the users' computers before they can be played. These typically are rendered in raster (or bitmap) format and are thus larger files. Real-time animations are often vector based, which means that the file being downloaded contains instructions only (meaning a much smaller file size) that the computer reads, interprets, and then renders all on the client side.

If you are new to the world of animation, refer to the resources in the appendix for a list of links to animation information and tutorials. In the world of computer animation, you will find that technologies often overlap. It may not be necessary to try to pigeonhole the various technologies, but be aware of the major difference between animation and video. Remember that video takes a continuous motion and breaks it down into discrete frames, and animation starts in the opposite direction with independent frames that are then put together into a series to form the illusion of movement.

Types of Web Animation

The following subsections introduce you to some of the web animation technologies available today. It is beneficial to have an overview of what each is designed to do because it is important to pick the right one for your purpose. Some of these animation technologies are easier to implement if you are a novice; others have a steep learning curve that requires an extensive investment of time.

Animated GIF (.gif). In the GIF 89a standard, a GIF image can be animated by combining several images into a single file. Animations are easy to create and are supported by most web browsers. Because the GIF 89a standard is a GIF format, it works bests with a limited number of colors and with illustration images instead of photographic ones. There are some drawbacks, namely that it tends to create large file sizes that don't compress well and that it has no sound capabilities. But for small animations, animated GIF is serviceable.

To create animated GIFs, you will need a GIF-89a-generating application. Some image-editing programs include this as part of the package, or you can download a freeware or shareware application from the Web. Begin by creating several images with identical dimensions. Make small changes in each image that will be the basis for the illusion of movement. Each of these images will become a frame in the animation. Use as few frames as possible to limit file size. Once you have opened all of your images in the GIF-generating program, you will arrange them in order, set the timing for each frame, and run the optimization utility that is part of the program. This utility handles such tasks as generating a palette for the file based on all of the frames, applying special dithering to prevent flickering, and optimizing the frames so only areas that change from frame to frame are included—each of which greatly reduces the file size.

MNG (.mng). Multiple-Image Network Graphics (pronounced "ming," MNG) has been developed as the format to handle all of the multi-image capabilities that are not supported in PNG and is the PNG counterpart to an animated GIF. MNG specifications were released in 2001. Its developers included a number of features that show promise to improve on animated GIF capabilities:

- object- or sprite-based approach to animation
- nested loops for complex animations
- integration of both PNG- and JPEG-based images
- support for transparent JPEGs
- unpatented compression either lossless (for PNG) or lossy (for JPEG)

The MNG has not gained traction and continues to suffer from limited browser support for display; its popularity is also hindered by the increased use of other formats such as Flash and SVG. For additional information, visit MNG's home page (www.libpng.org/pub/mng/).

Flash (.swf). The Adobe Flash file format (SWF) continues to be a leading web animation and interactivity format. It is created by using the authoring tool Adobe Flash software. The program is a full-featured animation authoring system that has come a long way in the years since its inception in 1996. It can be used to create rich content via a WYSIWYG interface, uses a robust scripting language called ActionScript, and has a compact file format. It has support for CSS, accessibility, and Unicode. Flash is vector based, which is one reason for its popularity. Vector-based animations are, of course, scalable and download quickly. In fact, Flash files can stream so that users don't have to wait for the entire file to download before viewing it. However, Flash is not limited to just vector graphics; it also allows the incorporation of bitmaps, MP3 and AVI audio, and interactivity. Flash animations can be exported as AVI, MOV (discussed later in this chapter), and animated GIF. Adobe's Open Screen Project (www.openscreenproject .org), an industrywide initiative to enable rich Internet content across any device, anywhere, saw the removal of proprietary restrictions on the use of SWF in third-party software development.

Director Shockwave (.swd, .dcr). Shockwave is designed to be highly interactive; it supports audio, animation, and video. Shockwave files are created in Adobe's Director authoring software. Director's (and therefore Shockwave's) strength lies in its ability to create advanced interactivity.

Which should you create—Flash or Shockwave files? Director preceded Flash and wasn't originally designed for the Web. Its main function was to create offline multimedia productions in stand-alone programs. It has a higher learning curve than does Flash and a higher price tag. However, if you are well versed in using Director, the latest versions are more web focused. If you are both creating for the Web and planning to publish to CD-ROM, you can do both with Director. If you are creating strictly for the Web, stick with Flash because it was designed as a web-authoring tool. Also, Flash is more widely available to users through their browsers. Almost all browsers have the Flash player installed. Fewer than 60 percent have the Shockwave plug-in.

3-D Graphics. Three-dimensional graphics provide the perception of depth to two-dimensional images. When they are animated, they can be viewed from different angles and distances. Animation is what makes 3-D objects appear real to users and makes them such effective visualization tools, but creating them requires both creativity and technical proficiency. Learning to produce 3-D objects and animations is not simple; even with 3-D authoring software, plan on a major commitment of time. Following is a simplistic summary of the steps involved in creating 3-D elements:

1. Most 3-D animations start with solid geometric objects that are called primitives (spheres, cubes, cylinders, and the like). When thinking about 3-D, it is helpful to understand the three dimensions of space, the x (width), y (height), and z (depth) planes. The x and y axes are the two-dimensional (2-D) coordinates, and the z axis adds the third dimension. Adding the z-axis to a 2-D object is called extrusion.

2. Combining, resizing, or re-forming the primitives can create other shapes, which is called modeling.

3. To make the shapes look realistic, you add color, textures, and light sources to the object. Other effects include reflection, transparency, and smoothness.

4. You create a 3-D space by positioning the objects, light, ground plane, and sometimes a background.

5. Animation is added via a timeline of movements and events.

6. The last step is to render the final scene, which is where you define the quality and type of the output.

X3D (.x3d, .x3dv, .xedb). X3D is the new web 3-D standard. It is the successor to Virtual Reality Modeling Language (VRML), which was developed as a screen-description language that describes the geometry and behavior of a 3-D scene or world. This language originated with the goal of creating shared virtual worlds on the Internet. The X3D format extends the capabilities of VRML, supports multiple data encodings (XML, VRML classic and binary), and has improved graphics features. The X3D specification is designed to be more flexible than VRML to accommodate the evolution of the standard. It is an open-source Web 3D Consortium project. To learn more, visit the project site (www.web3d.org), which offers a frequently-asked-questions section along with information about the specifications and available tools (viewers, authoring, and developer).

Video

Video is a multimedia format that requires careful planning to use appropriately over the Web. There are three traditional video file formats that are commonly seen online: Audio-Video Interleave (AVI), MPEG, and QuickTime (discussed in the following sections). All three of these are files that users must first download to their computers before they can view them. Because of bandwidth constraints and the fact that video files can be quite large, it is best to incorporate video in short clips that are less than a minute long. Remember to always prepare your users for the wait they will encounter in downloading by specifying the anticipated download time, the size of the file, and the playing time.

AVI (.avi)

Audio-Video Interleave (AVI) is Microsoft's proprietary format for video for Windows. Because it has been a part of Windows, the majority of computer users can view it, which accounts for some of its rise in popularity. However, although you can find plenty of AVI files on the Web, its use is declining because of its characteristically large file sizes. However, AVI does have the advantage of being most likely playable on most PCs without the need to install a viewer or plug-in. A significant disadvantage is that it will not play on a Mac. Microsoft is no longer supporting video for Windows and is replacing AVI with the Advanced Streaming Format (ASF).

QuickTime (.mov, .qt)

QuickTime, developed by Apple, is both a file format and a software architecture for multimedia development, storage, and playback. It is a technology that developers use extensively, and it enjoys widespread support.
QuickTime movies can incorporate a variety of media types, including
audio, graphics, video, text, MPEG, vector media, virtual reality, and 3-D.
More than fifty file formats can be imported and more than twenty-five can
be exported (see www.apple.com/quicktime/pro/specs.html). This flexibility in delivering multiple formats makes QuickTime versatile indeed.
Although originally developed for the Macintosh, QuickTime now supports both platforms equally well. The QuickTime plug-in is supported in
the major browsers, but QuickTime movies cannot be played in Windows
Media Player or Real Player.

QuickTime Virtual Reality

QuickTime Virtual Reality (QTVR) is an enhanced version of Apple's
QuickTime standard and adds the ability to tour through a virtual scene
or examine 3-D objects by rotating them. A virtual scene in QTVR is a
panoramic movie, created through a series of photographs taken in up to
a 360-degree range and stitched together. The result is a cylinder-shaped
image that surrounds the viewer, who can look in all directions, forward,
backward, up, and down. Each one of the stitched photos is called a node,
and when one or more nodes are connected, the viewer can move through
the scene by clicking on designated hot spots.

The second type of QTVR format is an object movie, which allows users
to simulate the action of picking up an object and turning it around to view
it. As with the panorama, this is created with a series of still photographs
that include shots of all sides, including top and bottom, of an object. The
photos are stitched together and then can be rotated to view the object from
any direction by using a mouse. Production in QTVR can be expensive
because it requires specialized equipment, training, and photography skills.
It can, however, give users a unique experience.

MPEG (.mpeg, .mpg, .mp3, .mp4)

MPEG (pronounced "EM-peg") is the acronym for the Moving Picture
Experts Group, which develops standards for digital video and audio
compression. There are various MPEG codecs. Commonly used for computer videos, MPEG-1 was created for use with CD-ROMs, video games,
and other media that require high-quality video and audio playback. It
supports up to thirty frames per second, the same as a standard television,
and a high compression ratio. This, combined with the fact of it having
been designed as a digital video capture and playback technology, meant

that it quickly became a popular method to deliver video content over the Web. Also, MPEG-1 is an audio compression standard; MP3 is part of the MPEG-1 family MPEG-1 Audio Layer 3. MPEG-4 has been developed to become a compression standard for interactive multimedia on the Web, CD distribution, videophone, and broadcast television. MPEG-4 absorbs many of the features of MPEG-1 and 2 and adds others, including support for 3-D rendering, object-oriented composite files, and digital rights management. With MPEG-4, users can interact with a scene that can be composed from real sources such as video or from synthetic ones such as vector-based objects. Authors can empower users to modify scenes by deleting, adding, or repositioning objects. The MPEG-4 format supports scalable content. QuickTime has been selected as the basis for starting development of the MPEG-4 standard (.mp4). You can find detailed information about these standards at the website that MPEG maintains (www.chiariglione.org/mpeg/).

Flash Video (.flv, .f4v)

This Flash video format is required if your video is to be included within a larger, more complex Flash environment. Files in FLV format can be embedded in a Flash SWF file or delivered either in a progressive download or from a streaming server (see the following section). The delivery method will depend on factors such as file size and frame rate. Shorter and lower frame rates may do well embedded, but streaming is the optimal delivery for long, large video clips and for broadcasting live events.

Screen-Capture Movie

Making a movie of the action that takes place over time on a computer screen is achieved with specialized software that acts like a video recorder. Most such programs also include an audio component so that narration can accompany the activity that takes place on the screen. Many of the available screen recording applications support both AVI and streaming technology. Other names you may hear to describe this type of technology include screen recording, desktop activity recording, and screen-capture video. One popular screen capture application is Camtasia, available from TechSmith (www.techsmith.com). TechSmith also offers a free product called Jing (www.jingproject.com) that is simple to learn and use.

Podcast

A podcast (coined from a combination of Apple's iPod and the word *broadcast*) is a series of digital media files (either audio or video) that are released episodically and downloaded through web syndication. What makes a podcast different from other media you access over the Internet has to do with its method of access. Specific client software applications are used to automatically download new files that have been identified and subscribed to by users via RSS feeds. Once the files have been downloaded to the user's computer, the user can access them locally and offline. An interesting monthly podcast that discusses issues in teaching information literacy is *Adventures in Library Instruction* (adlibinstruction.blogspot.com).

Podcasts have many potential applications in the classroom, including such things as presenting content, incorporating external guest lecturers, and capturing learner reflections and interviews.

Streaming Media

Streaming media has become the multimedia delivery method of choice. Audio, video, and other multimedia can be streamed live or on demand without the user waiting for a download. Streaming technology works differently from the traditional web transaction we are used to. A normal web transaction occurs when a user clicks on a link of some sort. The request for a file, whether it is HTML, audio, graphic, or video, is sent to a web server. The server takes the request and pushes out the file as quickly as possible and then disconnects. Back at the user's end, once the client (computer) receives the file that was sent, the computer is disconnected from the server, and the browser and plug-ins handle the display of the file. This works well for small files, like HTML and most graphics. However, with the larger files that are the norm for audio and video, the wait for the download is too long, and users get annoyed.

With streaming media, the server feeds data to users as they view it. So rather than a quick connect and disconnect from the server, there is a continuous connection for the duration of the delivery of the media. On the receiving side of the data feed, the computer must be able to collect the data and send it to the player as a steady stream. If the data arrives more quickly than it is played back, it is stored in a buffer until it is needed.

Even though the data is delivered in a stream and plays as it arrives, there is still a need to compress the data as it streams. A lossy compression is used to reduce file size significantly but entails degradation in image and sound. However, the main goal of developing streaming technology was to improve access, and it does accomplish that. There has continued to be a steady improvement in the quality as the technology has matured.

The basic process for creating streaming video and audio is to capture the video and/or audio, digitize and edit it, encode the digitized file with the appropriate codec, and deliver the file through a website.

To incorporate streaming media into a web page, you can either provide a text or graphic link or embed the file into the HTML document so it is displayed as part of the web page. Right now, streaming technology is primarily proprietary. The three major competitors in the streaming market are RealNetworks, QuickTime, and Windows Media.

RealMedia (.rm)

RealNetworks was a pioneer of streaming media technology. Media production is done with RealProducer (a free tool). However, some third-party applications also encode RealMedia content. RealNetworks streaming media requires a RealPlayer, which authors can embed in a web page. In 2002, RealNetworks launched its Helix initiative with Helix Universal Server. Helix is RealNetworks' open-source framework for delivering media. It uses Real Time Protocol/Real Time Streaming Protocol (RTP/RTSP) to stream files. A text file with a .ram extension is created and consists of a single line containing the URL (using rtsp:// instead of http://) to the RealMedia file on the Helix Server. The result is that your web page links to the RAM file, which then links to the media file, which then streams from the server to the client. It is a universal platform with support for live and on-demand delivery of all major file formats, including RealMedia, Flash, Windows Media, QuickTime, MPEG-4, MP3, SMIL, and more.

RealNetworks was an early supporter of SMIL, a language designed to synchronize multimedia (discussed in a following section).

QuickTime (.mov)

Apple arrived on the streaming-media scene later than either RealNetworks or Microsoft. However, QuickTime does a lot of things well, including having a wide number of supported file formats. QuickTime was deeply involved with the development of the MPEG-4 standard, which incorporates streaming technology. Content can be created using QuickTime Pro. QuickTime streaming media can be delivered via a server or in pseudo-streaming form from a regular web server. Apple's streaming server is QuickTime Streaming Server, which delivers both QuickTime (.mov) and MPEG-4 (.mp4) files in real time over the Internet via the Real Time Transport Protocol/Real Time Streaming Protocol (RTP/RTSP). It runs on Mac OS. However, through the Darwin open-source project, the Darwin Streaming Server (http://developer.apple.com/opensource/server/streaming/) is available for Linux, Windows, and Solaris, as well.

Windows Media (.asf, .wmv)

Microsoft's entry into the streaming media mix is called Advanced Systems Format (ASF), which stores audio, multibitrate video, metadata (e.g., the file's title and author), and index and script commands (e.g., URLs and closed captioning) in a single file. The ASF format does require a server component, specifically, Windows Media Services streaming server, to deliver the file. However, the tools to create, serve, and play ASF content are available at no charge from Microsoft's website. The player for ASF is Windows Media Player, and the production module is Windows Media Encoder. Windows Media supports the following file formats: WAV, WMA, WMV, ASF, AVI, MPG, and MP3.

SMIL

Synchronized Multimedia Integration Language (SMIL, or .smil, pronounced "smile") is a markup language developed by a W3C-coordinated group. SMIL is written as an XML application and, as of December 2008, version 3.0 is a W3C Recommendation. With SMIL, authors can write interactive multimedia presentations and are able to define and use separate elements and synchronize them to work together on a page. In addition to the ability to time the playing of the elements, SMIL allows the description of the layout of the presentation on a screen.

A SMIL presentation is a stand-alone document that looks similar to HTML, with the head of the document containing information about the layout of the presentation and the body a collection of components placed in a certain order. These components can have different media types, such as audio, video, image, or text, and they can appear sequentially or run concurrently.

Although the language has been developed so that it can be authored in a text editor, HTML editors are adding support for the SMIL tags so that it is no more necessary to know every SMIL tag than it is to know every HTML tag. Vendors are also developing SMIL-authoring tools. A SMIL player is required for viewing presentations, but again, players are available, and Windows Media Player, QuickTime, and RealPlayer all support SMIL. For detailed information on SMIL, including available development tools, visit the W3C site (www.w3.org/AudioVideo/).

LEVERAGING MULTIMEDIA THROUGH LEARNING OBJECTS

Developing materials for web-based instruction for a variety of learning styles may be well worth the effort, but there is no doubt that it can be a time-consuming and expensive proposition. In addition, most course development is undertaken on a local level with similar subject matter developed simultaneously at different institutions of learning. The concept of learning objects was originated to address these types of issues. A learning object is any digital resource that can be reused to support learning. Synonyms for the term include *digital learning materials, e-learning resources, content objects, chunks, modular building blocks*, and *Lego*. The idea behind the concept of learning objects is that instructional designers can break down instructional materials into small reusable components that can be used in different contexts. They are generally understood to be deliverable over the Internet on demand so that any number of people can access them at any time. Learning objects can include small objects such as digital images or photos, live data feeds, live or prerecorded video or audio snippets, small bits of text, animations, and smaller web-delivered applications like a Java calculator. Larger objects could include entire web pages that incorporate text, images, and other media (Wiley 2000). The University of Wisconsin–Milwaukee's Center for International Education expands on the characterization of what constitutes a learning object (Beck 2008). Learning objects

- are a new way of thinking about learning content—traditionally, content comes in a several-hour chunk, but learning objects are much smaller units of learning, typically ranging from two minutes to fifteen minutes.
- are self-contained—each learning object can be taken independently.
- are reusable—a single learning object can be used in multiple contexts for multiple purposes.
- can be aggregated—learning objects can be grouped into larger collections of content, including traditional course structures.
- are tagged with metadata—every learning object has descriptive information allowing it to be easily found by a search.

To leverage the use of learning objects, repositories have been created and maintained. One of the best known is MERLOT (www.merlot.org). A cooperative effort, MERLOT is the acronym for Multimedia Educational Resource for Learning and Online Teaching and is an open resource primarily geared toward higher education. Learning materials are peer reviewed; cataloged by discipline; and categorized by types including simulation, animation, tutorial, drill and practice, quiz or test, case study, collection, or reference material. All materials are freely available to anyone to use. In addition, MERLOT has a content builder that is available for educators to create basic learning objects. An example of a repository aimed at K–16 can be found at the website of Wisconsin's Interactive Dialogue with Educators from Across the State (IDEAS, http://ideas.wisconsin.edu). This site is searchable by grade level, subject, and keyword. Z. Smith Reynolds Library's Toolkit (http://zsr.wfu.edu/toolkit/) is an example of a library-centric repository, one that is designed to streamline the reuse of materials by providing coding to embed the object in other web environments like blogs, learning management systems, and social networking sites.

CHAPTER SEVEN

INTERACTIVITY

RESEARCH TELLS US that students retain more and understand more when they are involved in active learning environments. Active learning takes place when a student is more than just a spectator and becomes a participant in the instructional process. With web-based instruction, active learning is encouraged by incorporating interactivity. An early, simple definition of interactivity is a dialogue that occurs between a human being and a computer. It's easy to see that this alone can encompass a wide range of possibilities when you start to ponder what forms interactive web-based instruction might take. It can mean that the student has some level of control over the sequence, pace, and content of the instruction. On a higher level, it can mean that the student can act on information and transform it into having some personal meaning. Over the past few years, there has been an evolution of technologies developed that are collectively called Web 2.0. These are designed to facilitate interactive information sharing, social networking, and collaboration and have changed the face of how the Internet is used. Known as the read-write Web, Web 2.0 has significant implications for web-based instruction. This chapter takes an in-depth look at interactivity as it applies to web-based instruction, including

- categories of interaction
- interactivity methods
- interactivity languages and technologies
- interactivity development tools for nonprogrammers

CATEGORIES OF INTERACTION

A variety of technologies, both synchronous (same time, different place) and asynchronous (different time, different place), offer different kinds of interactivity on the Web. It is helpful to become familiar with the possibilities. The main categories of interaction can be divided into either individual interaction or social interaction.

Individual Interaction

Individual interaction takes place between a student and learning materials at a computer. It may also be expressed as student-resource interaction or student-content interaction. The level of interactivity depends heavily on how the instructional material is presented to the student on the computer screen. It encompasses such activities as the exchange of data, information, and knowledge from materials placed on the instructional site. Interaction can take place by various methods, which will be discussed in the next section. It can be a one-way delivery of content or a scripted exchange. Although often considered a lower (knowledge, comprehension) rather than a higher level of learning (analysis, synthesis, and evaluation), with the sophistication of programming possible today, don't discount this potential for interaction.

Social Interaction

The second category of interaction is social, which includes the various methods of communication that take place between various constituents, including learner to instructor, learner to learner, learner to guest lecturer, or learner to experts in the field. It can be an individual event or a group interaction. Because web instruction is a remote learning experience, it is important to provide avenues for participants to become acquainted and comfortable with the instructors and other students, particularly with classes that extend into multiple sessions. Social interaction can be accomplished both synchronously and asynchronously through avenues including e-mail, chats, discussion forums, social networks, wiki collaboration, virtual experiences, and blogs.

Learner-to-learner interactions can take many forms. There may be individual exchanges, but more often, students may be assigned to work collaboratively or participate in discussions to react to and evaluate other students' ideas and clarify thoughts and understanding. These types of interactions are increasingly recognized as important learning opportunities, ones that prepare students for a workforce in which teamwork is common.

Learner-to-instructor interactions are equally important interactions. They can provide encouragement, motivation, feedback, and responses to questions.

Web 2.0 has opened enormous potential for cooperative and collaborative opportunities between learners and instructors. These technologies leverage the ability for interaction greatly, and we will look at some of the most common ones, along with the more traditional methods to build in interactivity.

INTERACTIVITY METHODS

The decision about what level and types of interactivity to include in your instruction will be influenced by the scope and goals of your project and by the expertise of your development staff. However, there are simple, straightforward ways to incorporate interactivity into your teaching. The following subsections explore some common methods that are used to integrate interactivity: basic hyperlink interaction, communication, collaboration, forms, skills practice, interactive animations, image rollovers, and dynamic database interaction. Refer to figure 1.1 for the synchronous and asynchronous types of interaction that you can expect to see in online instruction.

Basic Hyperlink Interaction

At the most elementary level, point-and-click hypertext is a rudimentary form of interaction. With a hyperlink, the user makes a conscious choice to go in a certain direction or take an alternate path. In a tutorial, a clickable table of contents, navigation buttons, and text provide the student with a low level of self-direction. However, it is such a common function on any web page that incorporating hyperlinks alone should not be considered a sufficient interactive solution.

There are ways, however, to use simple hyperlinks creatively to establish an element of interactivity. Hyperlinks can be used to lead students down different paths depending on the link they choose.

Communication

Online communications can take different forms. With the advent of social software and sites, this capability has greatly expanded in the past few years. This section identifies types of communication, both traditional and new, that have potential usefulness in an online instruction environment. We look at both asynchronous and synchronous methods, including e-mail, discussion forums, collaboration, chat, conferencing, blogs and microblogs, wikis, and social networks.

E-mail

E-mail is one of the most straightforward methods of online communication. With a simple *mailto:* link, students can easily establish access to the instructor. E-mail is asynchronous, meaning that students can initiate communications with instructors at a time convenient to them (often after the midnight hour). If you are creating a multiple-session course, supplying e-mail links for all the class members can help promote student-to-student interaction. Keep in mind, however, that millennials do not turn to e-mail as their preferred method of communication, so it is advisable to offer additional means of communication as well.

Mailing Lists

For multisession courses, establishing an electronic mailing list is one option to facilitate widespread distribution of course information to all members of the class. The instructor can subscribe class members or permit self-subscription to the list. They can be set up as a one-way communication tool from instructor to students or as open for posting by all members.

Discussion Forum

Online discussion forums can be effective in facilitating information transfer, idea sharing, and collaboration. This method works well in a multisession course to direct class interaction. The instructor establishes a discussion topic, and participants respond to it and to one another's responses, creating what is called a discussion thread. A built-in feature in many learning management systems, a discussion board is an asynchronous form of communication. Many forums now offer the ability for participants to subscribe to a built-in feature where new posts will be automatically delivered by RSS feeds or e-mail notification.

Chat

In a chat program, two or more people are connected online and converse by typing in text that is transmitted to the other person's computer screen. Real-time communication may be appropriate or necessary in a number of situations. Students in different geographical regions may be involved in a group project and need to meet to talk with one another. Instructors may determine that it is beneficial for the class members to meet with one another in a real-time situation or want to establish online office hours so that a student can talk with them. A chat program is a simple way to make these situations possible. During the past few years, instant messaging (IM) has become almost ubiquitous among high school and college students. Savvy libraries are turning to IM as a tool to communicate with these students both for instruction reasons and research help. Chat is a synchronous mode of communication. One barrier to effective use of chat was the fact that different service providers offered separate program applications and protocols and students used different ones. However, it wasn't long before chat programs were developed that supported multiple protocols (see Trillian, www.trillian.im) which allows instructors to reach multiple IM networks at the same time. Also, browser-based instant messaging programs have been developed that can be embedded into a web page and that make the use of a client-based program unnecessary (see Meebo, www.meebo.com).

Web Conferencing
Web conferencing takes real-time communication a step farther by incorporating audio and video capability. Some conferencing software applications also incorporate other features that facilitate online collaboration. For instance, Windows Meeting Space (available in Vista) enables up to ten people to connect together and includes file transfer as well as the ability to view the same program. Webinars (live meetings or presentations conducted over the Web) have become common for delivering synchronous training to large groups. Typically a webinar involves a speaker delivering content to an audience with limited audience interaction via polling and/ or question-and-answer periods via texting. Audio may be delivered by telephone or with voice-over-Internet protocol (VoIP). Skype is an example of another type of software that makes use of VoIP to enable free video and voice calls over the Internet (www.skype.com). Web conferencing has many potential uses in education: bringing guest lecturers into the class, holding real-time online conferences, group meeting and virtual classes, and holding office hours are a few of the most common uses today.

Blogs
An overview of blogs can be found in chapter 4. Blogs have become a common tool for interactivity in education and in libraries. Although they are simple to set up, use, and understand, blogs can be a powerful tool for improving communications between learners and from learner to instructor. They are also an excellent tool for use in journaling or reflective learning.

Microblogging
Microblogging is a type of blogging that is limited in the number of characters that can be posted in a single post (typically 140). These short postings

are designed as a way for people to share updates about themselves or see updates about other people. Posts can be text or links to multimedia. Twitter (http://twitter.com) has become the best known of these services following the flood of media attention in the past year. Twitter posts are known as "tweets." In a September 2009 survey, Pew Internet reported that 19 percent of Internet users use Twitter or another status-update service, and those with wireless Internet devices are more likely to participate in microblogging. Twitter's use exploded in 2009, going from 2 million unique monthly visitors at the end of 2008 to 17 million by midyear (Fox, Zickuhr, and Smith 2009). It's not surprising that educators are starting to explore potential uses of Twitter for teaching and learning. Some of the ideas include sharing resources, forming social networks with other learners, following a notable expert and conversation in a field, soliciting feedback and questions on content presented, and sending out class updates.

Wikis

The idea of wikis (described in chapter 4) has been popularized by the enormous amount of attention given to the Wikipedia project. The notion of building an encyclopedia through the collective wisdom of many is an unusual one and has invited worldwide discussion about accuracy, potential for vandalism, and questions on authority of the contributors. However, its overwhelming success with the millions of daily users (this author included!) demonstrates the power of a wiki for collaboration and knowledge building. In library instruction, instructors can use a wiki as a course management system to hold course information, the syllabus, and other course materials. It can be used for student collaborative writing and group work. It can be a space to invite external experts to participate in a class. Wikipedia itself is a valuable tool in information literacy instruction, as it is an ideal springboard for discussions on evaluating information.

Social Bookmarking

Social bookmarking is a way that people can organize and share lists of Internet bookmarks (or favorite sites) on the Web. Unlike the bookmarks you save to your web browser, these become collections of web resources that you and others can access from any Internet connection. Selected resources can be enhanced for increased discoverability through the addition of descriptive terms. The concept of user or social tagging comes into play with social bookmarking. Terms that describe the content of the bookmarks are created and assigned (tagged) by the person adding the resource. A user tagging system is called a folksonomy (a blend of folk and taxonomy) as opposed to taxonomy—a classification system created by experts. Incorporating social tagging into your instructional design can be a powerful tool to help students understand how assigning descriptive terms to a resource or group of resources can help or hinder the ability of other users to find it in a web search. Another useful way to incorporate social bookmarking into instruction is to ask students to contribute resources and share them with the class through the addition of a course-specific tag. It can also be useful for student group work as a way to easily gather and share pertinent resources. One of the most popular social bookmarking sites is Delicious (http://delicious.com).

Image Sharing

Image-sharing sites such as Flickr (www.flickr.com) offer another option for teaching students how to contribute content to a shared environment, do descriptive tagging, organize, annotate, and discuss images and photos. Flickr also is a good site to discuss copyright and Creative Commons licensing, as that capability is available to image contributors. Visual content on the Internet offers special challenges for discoverability of the content contained, and Flickr has functionality that permits geotagging (tag by location) and describing individual components of an image.

Google Wave

Google Wave (wave.google.com) is a newly developed (as of Fall 2009) web-based application that is the result of a major rethinking of how to leverage electronic communication to a more meaningful form. E-mail is more than forty years old, and many other forms of electronic communication have emerged (as discussed in the preceding sections). In addition, many of these communications tools are now moving to the cloud rather than being run locally. Google Wave has taken these trends and developed a tool that incorporates existing tools into a new model of how communication and collaboration takes place. Wave users create online spaces called waves. In each wave, multiple messages and components (e.g., text, attachments, and widgets) can be included and can be collaboratively edited and appended. The waves are centrally stored and accessed. Although Google Wave is in preview form, it has already garnered a great deal of attention from educators as a potentially compelling platform for creating personal learning spaces (EDUCAUSE 2009).

Managing Information

With the massive amounts of information that are produced and delivered over the Internet, teaching students how to manage all the many disparate sources most effectively has become an important component of information literacy instruction. There are tools available to help students interact with and manage the flood of newly created content from the Web. Such tools are designed to handle RSS or web feeds, a format used to publish frequently updated content. These XML files are designed to deliver updated content to the user as specified through a subscription that the user requests from sites that offer RSS feeds. There are different methods with which this can be accomplished.

Aggregators

An aggregator is application software that pulls syndicated web content into a single location for easy viewing by the subscriber. An aggregator is also called an RSS reader, feed reader, or news reader. Some aggregators have podcasting capabilities that automatically download media files. Web-based readers are the most common and are hosted on remote servers. Bloglines (bloglines.com) is an example.

Web Widgets

A widget is portable chunk of code that can be embedded in a web page. A widget combines AJAX (asynchronous JavaScript + XML, described in more detail later in this chapter) coding with XML components to bring several feeds into larger programs or single interfaces. Syndicated content can be delivered through a widget and allows users to create their own personal learning environments. NetVibes (www.netvibes.com) and iGoogle (www.igoogle.com) are examples of free sites that users can use to set up widgets to manage their information. You'll find that many information providers like WorldCat are creating widgets for use on sites like iGoogle and Facebook.

Skills Practice

A proven method of promoting learning retention is to provide a method for students to practice newly learned skills. The two most common means of accomplishing this through web-based instruction are programming a simulation and establishing real-time connections to databases.

Simulations

Simulations work well in a variety of situations. A simulation has the look and feel of the resource being studied but provides a controlled experience. Simulations can be scripted to force users to make the right choice before being allowed to proceed further.

Live Access

When handled properly, incorporating the ability for students to practice real-time in a live online environment is an effective reinforcement. It is important to make sure, when planning a live interaction, that students don't become disoriented or lost, which is a possibility if you send them out of the instruction environment altogether. As mentioned in chapter 5, many designers use pop-up windows to introduce external applications or resources so that students remain in the instruction framework while accessing the live resources.

Interactive Animations

Chapter 6 explored several types of animation that included interactive capabilities, Flash and Shockwave among them. These types of multimedia can add a sophisticated, engaging level of interactivity to a tutorial. They can be used to build simulations or to create interactive activities that help teach concepts.

Virtual Experiences
One type of sophisticated animated interaction is a 3-D virtual world to simulate a library experience. With a virtual environment, members of a community can intermingle, work cooperatively, and use resources. Second Life (secondlife.com) is a well-known example of a virtual world. Second Life is a user-generated 3-D environment in which interactions take place between avatars. Educators have seen the potential for unique learning experiences in a 3-D environment through experiential learning, simulation, role-playing, scenario building, and collaboration. Not surprisingly, libraries see potential for outreach to extend traditional services. A good example of libraries in Second Life is the Alliance Virtual Library (infois land.org). Deciding to build a presence in Second Life requires a big commitment for development and so most likely would not be appropriate for short-term instruction needs.

Database Driven

Depending on the scope of your web instruction project, you may find that you want to turn to a database solution. If you are planning on tracking test scores or progress of students, a database will facilitate the collection of data and data analysis and can make that data available to students online. A database can be used to establish user accounts, build quiz pools, and authenticate access.

If you are considering a database for these functions, there are many to choose from with a wide range of prices. As with other software choices, consider platform restrictions and complexity. If building a database from scratch and programming the interaction is beyond your team's technical capabilities, keep in mind that course management software programs such as Blackboard, Sakai, and Moodle use databases to accomplish interactive functions.

LANGUAGES AND TECHNOLOGIES

Web-based interactivity is accomplished most often with web programming languages. The most common types are known as script languages and are often designed for interactive use, to connect diverse existing components to accomplish a new related task. A script consists of a sequence of instructions carried out (or interpreted) by another program rather than by the computer processor. Traditional programming languages (like C++) are compiled, which means that the instructions or commands are transformed into machine language that the processor reads. This results in a program that is executed much more quickly than one composed in a script language but is far more complex to write. In contrast, a script language is designed to encourage rapid development because it is easier to learn and faster to code. Script languages are often called glue languages because they excel at gluing separate application components together—often necessary when bringing interactivity to a web page.

Do you have to know one of these languages to integrate interactive elements into your tutorial? Of course not. (We will look at tools for non-programmers shortly.) However, it is useful to have an understanding of the different methods used to program dynamic, interactive websites. This section introduces the basic concepts of scripting (writing a program in a script language) and some of the common web programming languages, including both interpreted and compiled ones. By no means is this intended to be a comprehensive discussion on writing programs, but it is a basic introduction to web programming languages by a nonprogrammer to nonprogrammers. If you think you might want to learn to do your own web programming, resources included at the end of this book will point you in the right direction.

Some considerations should be taken into account when selecting a web programming language. There are several script languages criteria to examine before making your final choice (Ford, Wells, and Wells 1997):

Ease of use: Consider how easy it is to learn and to write. Is the syntax straightforward? This aspect can tie in closely with development.

Rapid development: By nature, script languages are faster to develop because they don't have to be compiled. If quick development is a goal, then the time saved by writing a script may be more important than issues such as performance level.

Power and performance: Scripted tasks have to be executed either on the server (server side) or on the client (client side). Both ways have advantages and disadvantages, and the choice of which method to use will depend on the task being programmed, the power necessary to execute the program, and how those requirements will affect performance. Again, you must consider the specifications of the computers your users will be using, the network connectivity, and the server capabilities. Compiled programs are usually quicker to execute, but if speed isn't the top priority, scripting advantages may outweigh this particular disadvantage.

Platform independence: You don't want to have to worry whether the application you create can function on a specific operating system. Your application should be platform independent. If that is not possible, choose a language that will work with your existing system.

Preserving intellectual property: Many script languages can be read easily by viewing the source of a web page. If code security is a concern, you may want to consider using a language that will offer some protection of your intellectual property.

Safety: Creating a safe environment for your users as well as your data and server is important. Some languages are safer than others, so this is something you should research.

Web Programming Languages

Web designers use many programming languages. As the Web has become more dynamic in nature, developers are increasingly choosing languages such as JavaScript and PHP that facilitate delivery of dynamic content (Strod 2009). Collectively, they are called dynamic programming languages. The following subsections, presented here in alphabetical order, briefly describe several languages that are used in web programming. Refer to figure 7.1 for a comparison.

ActionScript

ActionScript is the scripting language for Adobe Flash. The latest version (as of 2010) is version 3.0. It is an object-oriented programming language (i.e., programming organized around objects rather than actions) designed for website animation and to be similar to JavaScript. The code is frequently written in the Flash authoring environment and is saved along with the rest of the movie in an FLA file. However, it is possible to import ActionScript code from an external file stored on a server. In these cases, look for a .as file extension.

ActiveX

ActiveX has been Microsoft's answer to Sun Microsystems' Java technology. It is used to create a Component Object Model (COM) called an ActiveX Control, which is functionally similar to a Java applet. A control is a self-sufficient program that can run on an ActiveX network, though on a Windows or Macintosh platform only. ActiveX is being superseded by the Microsoft .NET initiative, designed for platform independence and rapid application development. .NET is a software development platform, not a programming language, but it supports more than forty languages. A note of interest and caution concerning ActiveX: embedding it into the Internet Explorer browser created a way to exploit users' computers with viruses, trojans, and spyware infections.

Java

Java isn't considered a scripting language but is included here because it is so closely associated with web interactivity. Java is an object-oriented programming language, much closer to a full-featured language than the script languages. It was developed specifically as an Internet application by Sun Microsystems with the goal of being platform independent. That has proved more difficult than desired and has not always been achieved. In addition, Sun and Microsoft went to court over Microsoft's desire to add platform-specific features. As a result, Microsoft decided to leave out Java system support in future versions of Windows. Sun and others have made Java systems available to those with Java-less versions of Windows.

Java can be used to create complete applications or to build small application modules called applets. In an HTML page, applets are handled much like an image. An <applet> tag tells the browser to transfer the compiled code to the browser and execute the code as long as the browser is Java enabled. An applet file is named with an extension of .class. Because a download to the browser is required, users' access speed capabilities should be a consideration when incorporating applets. Visit Sun's site for detailed information about Java (www.java.com).

JavaScript

JavaScript is one of the best-known script languages for web authors who want to create dynamic pages. It is commonly used to respond to user events such as mouse clicks, rollovers, page navigation, and validating

Figure 7.1
WEB PROGRAMMING LANGUAGES COMPARISON CHART

LANGUAGE	PLATFORM SUPPORT	LOCATION	TYPE	FILE EXTENSION	NOTES
ActionScript	Cross-platform	Downloads from server to client	Interpreted	.as	Developed by Macromedia specific to Flash Unicode support
ActiveX	Cross-platform: Windows/ Macintosh	Downloads from server to client	Compiled	.dll	Developed by Microsoft Being superseded by .NET platform
Java	Designed to be platform independent	Can be client side or server side	Compiled	.class (compiled) .jav, .java (source code)	Developed by Sun Microsystems Applet programs run on clients; servlets run on server Unicode support
JavaScript	Platform independent	Can be client side or server side	Interpreted	.js	Developed by Netscape Not standardized to be handled uniformly in all browsers Unicode support
Jscript	Multiplatform	Can be client side or server side	Interpreted	.js	Developed by Microsoft Microsoft's equivalent to JavaScript
Lingo	Cross-platform: Windows/ Macintosh	Downloads from server to client	Compiled	.dcr, .swd	Specific to Adobe Director Unicode support

Figure 7.1 (cont.)

(cont.)

LANGUAGE	PLATFORM SUPPORT	LOCATION	TYPE	FILE EXTENSION	NOTES
Perl	Cross-platform: Unix, Linux, Macintosh, Windows	Server side	Interpreted, but can be compiled	.pl	Created by Larry Wall Used often to write CGI scripts Open source, freely available Unicode support
PHP	Cross-platform	Server side	Interpreted	.php, .phtml, .php5	Developed strictly to serve web pages Open source, freely available Unicode support planned for 6.0
Python	Multiplatform	Server side	Interpreted but can be compiled	.py, .pyw, .pyc (compiled), .pyo	Copyrighted but freely usable and distributable Unicode support
Ruby	Multiplatform	Server side	Interpreted but can be compiled in JRuby and IronRuby implementations	.rb	Copyrighted but freely available Unicode support as of version 1.9
Tcl	Cross-platform	Server side	Interpreted	.tcl	Often used for CGI scripting Open source, available freely Full Unicode support
VBScript	Cross-platform	Can be client side or server side	Interpreted	.vbs, .vbe, .wsf, .wsc	Developed by Microsoft Subset of Visual Basic Freely available Comparable to JavaScript

form input and is a flexible way to integrate animation, sound, and other multimedia elements. Developed by Netscape, JavaScript is not a subset of Java, despite the similarity in the two names. JavaScript is an interpreted rather than a compiled language. Also, it is an open language that anyone can use without purchasing a license. A JavaScript script can be embedded right into an HTML page, which means that it usually functions totally on the client side. However, JavaScript support is not standardized among browsers, each of which uses slightly different implementations. This means that it may be necessary to write different scripts to work in different browsers. The two main ways to handle potential incompatibilities are through browser sniffing and object detection. With the proliferation of browser types and versions, sniffing has become more complex. Object detection works by testing for the existence of a property of an object and giving instructions for handling varied definitions of object.

To embed JavaScript, the code is inserted in a <script> tag in the <head> of HTML documents. If preferred, the code can also be a separate file that is called from the HTML page. These files end with the extension .js (e.g., navigationscript.js). JavaScript is a safe language, which means that it cannot access any system controls or hardware on a user's computer. Although JavaScript is best known as a client-side script, it is also available as a server-side language to accomplish such tasks as communicating with a relational database or conducting file manipulations on a server. It is handled a bit differently on a server. The script resides in an HTML document on the server, but the page is compiled into an executable file. Instead of the <script> tag, a <server> tag encloses the script. One benefit of a server-side JavaScript is that any browser can read it, not just those that are JavaScript enabled. Refer to the resources section in the appendix for more information on JavaScript.

Jscript
Microsoft has developed Jscript specifically for use in web pages. This is an interpreted, object-oriented language but not a cut-down version of a more powerful language. It adheres to the ECMAScript standard (www.ecma-international.org), the Web's standard scripting language. Jscript is designed for use in browsers and other applications that use ActiveX controls and Java applets. It comes bundled with Microsoft Internet Explorer and with Microsoft Internet Information Server (MIIS), or it can be downloaded at no charge. It has multiplatform support. As with JavaScript, to embed the script in a document, the code is inserted in a <script> tag in the <head> of HTML documents. For more information, see Microsoft's Scripting Technologies website (http://msdn.microsoft.com/en-us/library/d1et7k7c(VS.85).aspx).

Lingo

Lingo is the scripting language that drives Adobe's Director and is specific to it. You will not encounter it anywhere else.

Perl

Practical Extraction and Report Language (Perl), created by Larry Wall, is popular in the world of web development as the primary language used to create dynamic content through Common Gateway Interface (CGI) programming. Perl is not synonymous with CGI, however, and can be used for a wide variety of purposes. It was designed to be a language to extract information from text files and generate that information into reports.

Perl works with HTML, XML, and other markup languages. Its database integration interface supports third-party databases, including Oracle and MySQL. It derives from the C programming language and has its roots in the Unix environment. Because it is an interpreted language, it is portable across platforms, yet it isn't strictly an interpreted language. Perl has been described as a compiled scripting language. This means a Perl program can be handled in different ways depending on its intended purpose. Without delving into complex details, the result is a language that is easier to learn and faster to code than traditional programming languages but has more sophisticated capabilities than a strictly interpreted language. A program written in Perl will have an extension of .pl (e.g., formmail.pl). For comprehensive information visit the Perl websites (www.perl.com or www.perl.org).

PHP

Originally written in 1994 by Rasmus Lerdorf and known as Personal Home Page (PHP) and now called PHP Hypertext Processor, this interpreted language is similar to JavaScript and VBScript, runs on most major operating systems, and can interact with the major web servers and relational database systems. Unlike JavaScript, however, PHP is a server-side HTML-embedded scripting language. This means that the PHP script is embedded in a web page along with its HTML. Before the page is sent to the user who has requested it, the server interprets the code and executes the script. A web page that contains a PHP script will typically be given a name with an extension .php, .php4, or .php5 (e.g., webpage.php). Unlike most of the other languages, PHP was developed strictly to serve web pages; that is, it is not based on an existing language. The PHP script can be used to do the same sort of tasks that can be done with a CGI script, but according to its developers, its strength lies in the large number of database applications it supports. Version 5.0 of PHP included enhanced object-oriented functionality. A feature that has made it as popular as it is today (used by

20 million domains in April 2007) is the fact that it is a loose language, which means that the rules aren't as strict with variables. What this means for a new programmer is an easier learning curve. It is open source and is freely available for download (http://php.net).

Python

Guido van Rossum, the creator of Python, selected the name because he was a fan of *Monty Python's Flying Circus*. Python is similar to Perl because it, too, is an interpreted language that supports compilation. Known for its readability and portability to multiple operating systems, Python is deemed easy to learn because it is object oriented. In addition, it uses an uncluttered syntax that is designed to be highly readable, as it uses English keywords rather than punctuation, as in other languages. It runs on multiple platforms including Windows, Linux, Unix, Mac OS X, and Java. As with some of the other languages, it is available for download at no charge at a site full of comprehensive information (www.python.org).

Ruby

Ruby is an object-oriented programming language that blends parts of its creator's favorite programming languages, Perl, Smalltalk, Eiffel, Ada, and Lisp. It was designed as an interpreted language, but its JRuby and IronRuby implementations support just-in-time compilation. Yukihiro "Matz" Matsumoto created Ruby in 1995. The name *Ruby* was chosen to reflect its Perl heritage. It can be ported to many platforms including Unix, Mac OS X, Windows, and Linux. For more information on Ruby, visit the website (www.ruby-lang.org).

Tcl and Tk

The abbreviation Tcl stands for Tool Command Language (pronounced "tee cee ell" or "tickle"). It is an interpreted language and, like Perl, is used on the Web for CGI scripting, though not as extensively as Perl. It, too, is open source and is touted as being easy to learn and allowing for rapid development. It is often compared with Perl, and both have their disciples. One advantage of Tcl comes with its Tk (Tool Kit), which is a tool for creating graphical user interface (GUI, pronounced "gooey") front ends. John Ousterhout created Tcl. A good place to find thorough information is at the Tcl Developer Xchange (www.tcl.tk).

VBScript

Microsoft's Visual Basic Scripting Edition (VBScript) is a subset of the Visual Basic programming language. Like JavaScript, it is an interpreted script language. It is used in Active Server Pages (ASP) and in Windows

Scripting Host as a general-purpose scripting language. As with JavaScript and Jscript, to embed a VBScript in a document, you insert the code in a <script> tag in the <head> of an HTML document. Not surprisingly, it is a free language and enjoys cross-platform support. It is included with both Microsoft Internet Explorer and Microsoft Internet Information Server or can be downloaded from Microsoft's site. Visit Microsoft's Scripting Technologies website for further information (http://msdn.microsoft.com/en-us/library/sx7b3k7y(VS.85).aspx).

Web Server Technologies

This section presents a few important technologies often included in discussions on scripting but that aren't really classified as web programming languages. Instead, they are technologies that permit a web server to serve dynamic data.

CGI

The Common Gateway Interface (CGI) is actually a protocol for transferring information between a web server and a program. Its purpose is to provide a means to process interaction between users and the server. A CGI script is stored and executed on the web server in response to a request from a user. A typical example of a use for a CGI program is to process forms from an HTML page. The user fills in the form and clicks on the submit button. At that point, the CGI program takes control to process the submitted information. It might e-mail that data to a person, or it might write it to a spreadsheet. Although most people associate CGI with Perl, CGI is not language specific. Moreover, CGI can be written in any language, including Perl, Python, and Tcl. The main shortcoming of CGI is that it tends to be slow because each request that a user submits causes a new program to be launched. High traffic can overtax the server. Work-arounds to this problem have been developed. For instance, Apache has embedded the interpreter into its web server so that it can be executed without creating a new process each time. The big advantage of using CGI is that you are assured that all of your users will be able to use the program, unlike client-side technologies that users can turn off in the browser or that a particular browser version may not support. If you are interested in learning CGI or finding CGI scripts, check out the CGI Resource Index (cgi.resourceindex.com).

Web Application Frameworks

As the Web became a more dynamic environment, programmers looked for methods to streamline development time. Web application frameworks are designed to support the rapid development of dynamic sites and web services by integrating components such as an operating system, web server, database, and programming language, along with reusable code into a single cohesive software stack. Different programming languages (e.g., Java, Perl, PHP, Python, Ruby) can have one or more frameworks. Ruby on Rails is a good example of an open-source web application framework for the Ruby programming language.

AJAX

The AJAX framework is a web development technique, rather than a web application framework. It is shorthand for "Asynchronous JavaScript and XML" and has become popular for creating interactive web applications. It uses JavaScript to transfer and request data to and from the server. Its main goal is to make users feel that web pages are more responsive by exchanging small amounts of data in such a way that the web page does not have to reload to display each newly requested piece of data. The Ajax framework can be part of a larger web application framework, as it is with Ruby on Rails.

JSP

JavaServer Page is Sun Microsystems' server-side Java technology for creating dynamic web pages. The JSP technology is designed to be platform and server independent. Small programs called servlets (the server-side version of an applet) are specified in a web page and run on the server, which results in a modified HTML or XML page that is then sent to the requester. The JSP technology is also known as the servlet application program interface (API). The JSP pages end with an extension .jsp (e.g., journalist.jsp). One benefit of servlet technology is that once a servlet is started, it stays in the server memory and can be executed multiple times to fulfill requests. Sun Microsystems' Java technology site is the place to find additional information (http://java.sun.com/products/jsp/).

LAMP

With all the previous discussion of web programming languages and technologies, with mention made of various databases, server operating systems, and web server software, it doesn't take long to see that a combination of programs is required to deploy a dynamic website. The acronym LAMP represents a set of free software programs that are commonly used together to run dynamic sites: Linux (the operating system); Apache (the web server); MySQL (the database management system); and Perl, PHP, or Python (the scripting languages). They were not designed to work together, but because of their low cost and the fact that they are bundled with most Linux distributions, they have become a popular combination. When they are used in combination, they are a solution stack of technologies to facilitate electronic enterprise. Similar terms exist for the same software suite that is deployed on other operating systems besides Linux (e.g., WAMP for Windows, MAMP for Mac, SAMP for Solaris).

Markup Languages and Interactivity

By now, you understand that HTML and XML pages, by themselves, are static documents. Interactivity is added to them through the integration of scripts and other technologies. However, there are newer and more advanced markup languages that are associated with web interactivity: dHTML, VRML, XML/XSLT, and XHTML. The following subsections discuss what those are and how they are considered interactive.

Dynamic HTML

Dynamic HTML (dHTML) is not an actual specification. Rather, it is a collective term for a combination of new tags and options introduced in HTML 4.0 along with increased interactivity possibilities. A dHTML page is one that has the capability to affect the function of a static web page after it has been loaded into a browser. Some of the simple interactions that would be considered dHTML are rollovers and the ability to drag and drop objects from one place on a page to another. The three main technologies that are the primary components making up dHTML include client-side scripting, Document Object Model, and CSS. It is useful to note that dHTML as a concept has declined as newer methods for interactivity have emerged. This is the result of ongoing issues with interbrowser compatibility of scripts caused by varying degrees of browser support.

Client-Side Scripting. One of the best-known ways that web authors create dynamic pages is through client-side scripting. It is the part of the equation that actually makes changes in a page. Scripts are embedded in the web pages that are delivered to your client and your browser interprets the script to execute it.

DOM. The abbreviation DOM stands for Document Object Model, an application program interface (API) that allows HTML pages and XML documents to be created and modified as if they were program objects. The model encompasses the structure of a document as well as its behavior and the behavior of the objects that make up a page. All of the objects can be manipulated, and this is what makes interactivity possible. DOM is platform and language neutral; it allows programs and scripts to dynamically access and update page content, structure, and style of documents. This is accomplished by exposing DOM to scripting through browsers. Although scripting makes the actual changes, DOM is the component that allows objects to be changeable. Because, originally, there were incompatibilities in the DOM implementation among browsers, the W3C came up with standard specification. The best place to find in-depth information about DOM is at W3C's website (www.w3.org/DOM/).

CSS. Cascading Style Sheets (discussed in chapter 5) are a part of DOM, meaning that they are accessible to the scripting languages. Because CSS allows specific location placement of objects on a page (through specification of coordinates in the x, y, and z planes), a script can be used to move the object (or element), hide or show it, and otherwise change its properties (e.g., color and style).

X3D

X3D was previously known as VRML. As was mentioned in the section on animation in chapter 6, X3D is a screen-description language that describes the geometry and behavior of a 3-D world. This language is highly interactive, as it allows users to determine how to move through a scene.

XML/XSL

Extensible Markup Language (XML) is similar to HTML in that both use tags to describe the contents of a page. However, in HTML, tags and attributes have specific meanings and control how elements will appear on a page. For instance, <p> stands for paragraph, and when it is used, a space is inserted in the line above it by default. With XML, tags are used to delimit pieces of data, and the meanings of tags are completely up to the application that reads it. If <p> is used in an XML file, it can stand for whatever data is being described (e.g., price, person). An XML tag describes the data that is contained within it. The meanings of tags can be decided on an individual level or can be determined by a group who may want to share information in a consistent way. Because the markup symbols are unlimited and self-defining, the language is said to be extensible. Actually, XML is a subset of Standard Generalized Markup Language (SGML). Because XML is designed to deal with data, it isn't meant to be a replacement for HTML because it isn't meant to be read. Instead, HTML and XML serve two different purposes and, thus, can complement each other. While HTML handles presentation, XML handles content.

What is used to make the data from XML readable in an HTML document? The transformation is accomplished with the use of XSLT, which we discussed in chapter 5. The XSL family of languages has three parts:

1. *XSLT:* an XML language for transforming XML documents from one syntax to another

2. *XSL Formatting Objects (XSL-FO):* an XML language for specifying the visual formatting of an XML document

3. *XML Path Language (XPath):* a non-XML language used by XSLT to access or refer to parts of an XML document

Where does interactivity come into play? As is HTML, XML is static. It is an effective means to structure data but must be paired up with a programming or script language to extract data and to interface with different applications. Once again, W3C is the site to visit to find out all about XML (www.w3.org/XML/) and XSL (www.w3.org/Style/XSL/).

XHTML5

Extensible Hypertext Markup Language (XHTML5) is part of the HTML5 specification. It provides new elements and attributes that are more reflective of modern websites. In addition to specifying markup, HTML5 specifies scripting application programming interfaces (API). As of March 2010, HTML5 is a W3C Working Draft (www.w3.org/TR/html5/).

DEVELOPMENT TOOLS FOR NONPROGRAMMERS

The previous section showed that there are many choices for incorporating interactivity if you are a programmer or have one on your project team. However, what about everyone else who wants to build interactive instruction but doesn't have the background, programming skills, or desire to do their own scripting? I hope the previous section didn't scare you off, because these days it is easier than ever for nonprogrammers to build an interactive environment if you familiarize yourself with the vast assortment of Web 2.0 tools that are available. And, increasingly, using Web 2.0 tools offers so much option for flexibility and rapid course development that many web instructors are choosing to turn away from locally developed hard-to-modify tutorials to developing environments in which anyone who is a moderately savvy web user can become a web author! In this section, we are going to talk about a variety of existing tools available to nonprogrammers to facilitate building an interactive site. Keep in mind that this is a rapidly evolving industry, and between the time this is written and the time you are reading, many more tools will be available to help you. We thus consider broad categories of interactivity development aids, but don't limit your consideration to the examples that are mentioned. Use your Internet searching skills to ferret out new and exciting utilities.

Web Editors

As web editors have evolved, most are including additional features that permit behind-the-scenes scripting functionality, CSS support, and sometimes, ready-to-use scripting actions. As mentioned in chapter 4, it's important to choose a web editor that supports advanced features including CSS, layers, animations, JavaScript, applets, forms, and image maps. In addition, you want to investigate the major web editors to see if they have extensions that can help you create more robust interactive components for your site.

Script Libraries

One of the greatest things about the Web is how willing people are to share what they have created. There are plenty of script libraries (sometimes called script archives) where you can find prewritten scripts that will perform just about any interactive function you need. It's easy to locate one; try going to your favorite search engine or directory and type in the kind of script library or interaction you would like to find, JavaScript script library or rollover script, for example. Depending on what type of script you are getting, the retrieval process may be a simple cut-and-paste or a file download for files like a CGI program that have to be copied to your server. Often a script is ready to use as written, but you may find that you will want to customize it to your situation. Good script libraries include instructions for modification and installation procedures.

Be sure to read and follow the rules that have been established at each library. Because most of these libraries collect scripts from many authors, there may be different use conditions for different scripts tied to the authors' wishes. Typical conditions include leaving author credit information inside the script or providing a link to the script library. You will find a list of several script libraries in the appendix.

Applications and Online Services

A specialized application that can be used to develop interactive components is a useful tool. Some are offered at no charge to educational institutions.

Hot Potatoes and Quandary, from University of Victoria and Half-Baked Software, are two examples of this type of application (hotpot.uvic.ca). These downloadable applications are freeware (but not open source) as of early-2010. The Hot Potatoes program includes six applications; each one creates a different kind of interactive exercise. Quandary is an application for making web-based action mazes. If you want to track the results of student grades, hotpotatoes.net is a hosting service that can provide this for a fee.

Not all tools require you to download and install software to use them. Some sites offer services that permit you to build interactive quizzes, tests, and exercises and store them on site servers. Quia is a good example of this type of service (www.quia.com). For an annual subscription, Quia allows instructors to create games and quizzes, create classes and track quiz results, create class pages for communication with students, and maintain online schedules and a calendar. Another interesting service, FormSite. com (www.formsite.com), permits you to create forms and surveys, then store the data in a database on its server. It offers two levels of service, one free and one fee based. Other survey services such as Zoomerang (http:// zoomerang.com) and SurveyMonkey (www.surveymonkey.com) are also popular choices that offer both free and fee-based services.

NiceNet (www.nicenet.org) offers Internet Classroom Assistant, a free web-based communication tool that provides conferencing, personal messaging, document sharing, scheduling, and link and resource sharing. It is designed for use by secondary, postsecondary, distance-learning, and collaborative academic projects. NiceNet is an organization of Internet professionals who donate their time to provide services for the Internet community and aim to bring communication tools and resources to those without substantial budgets or great technical expertise.

A well-known library-specific tool is LibGuides (www.springshare .com/libguides/), a subscription-based Web 2.0 content management system that can be used to create subject and course-specific guides, can be used for library instruction and information literacy instruction, and contains social features to facilitate collaboration. Using templates, API libraries, and widgets, librarians can build multimedia-rich interfaces that can incorporate multimedia and interactivity and can integrate with popular sites such as Facebook and Twitter. The success of LibGuides has been extended to CampusGuides (or Community Guides; www.springshare.com/campus guides/) a similar product that facilitates the addition of other content collaborators beyond the library.

Course or Learning Management Systems

We examined course and learning management systems in chapter 4 and learned that they are designed to be a complete package to deliver all aspects of online education. By definition, this includes interaction for communication, information transfer, file exchange, and online surveys and quizzes. If you have access to such a system, it can provide you with an environment that permits you to concentrate on instructional design and content building without having to be a technology guru.

Web 2.0 Tools

It is worth a final reminder to consider the Web 2.0 tools that have been introduced and discussed in other sections of this book. Wikis, blogs, Facebook, and online application suites such as Google Docs and Zoho all are excellent choices for building richly interactive learning environments.

CHAPTER EIGHT

EVALUATION, TESTING, AND ASSESSMENT

EVALUATION WAS IDENTIFIED in chapter 3 as a critical part of every design model. Establishing effective methods to assess the different stages of a web-based project is the best way to make sure the project stays on track and accomplishes its established goals. However, the evaluation process is often the part of a project that falls by the wayside. Whether because of time or budget constraints or lack of knowledge on how to proceed, it's not unusual to hear of projects that are not evaluated in any fashion or that have chosen the wrong measurements altogether. This chapter introduces an overview of evaluation and testing methods that have been determined to be useful for measuring the effectiveness of software and instructional design processes as well as the effectiveness of the completed project. The goal is to provide you with some ideas about which method will best suit your project. It is beyond the scope of this book to cover research methodology and analysis, and there are many sources that address this in great depth.

WHY, WHAT, AND HOW MUCH EVALUATION?

You've assembled a knowledgeable team for your project, and your team members have good technical and design experience. You've done the analyses of your audience and have a good sense of how the project should be developed. Why, then, should you take on the extra time and expense of conducting tests and evaluations?

It's important to recognize that those most deeply involved in creating your web-based instruction have become so immersed that it is impossible to maintain objectivity. The only way to find out whether the design your team has developed functions as intended is to have it evaluated by people outside the project. What seems obvious to those closest to the project may not be understandable at all to outsiders. The goal of testing is to discover and correct usability flaws during the iterative design of the interface. External users can give you a fresh perspective.

Choices of evaluation methods can range from a costly multiphase test to a one-hour test with a few key users. Which method or methods you select will depend on several factors. Ben Shneiderman et al. (2010) identified these determinants for the selection of an evaluation plan:

Stage of design: Are you at the project's beginning, middle, or end?

Novelty of project: Is the project well defined, or is the project more exploratory in nature?

Number of expected users: Is the instruction for a class of twenty or for more than a thousand students?

Criticality of the interface: How critical is the function of the interface you are designing? For example, an interface for a medical system will warrant a more comprehensive evaluation effort than an interface for a library tutorial.

Costs of product and finances allocated for testing: How much money has been invested in producing the tutorial, and what amount has been delegated for testing?

Time available: How much time is there to conduct an evaluation? If time is limited, a lengthy evaluation may not be the answer.

Experience of the design and evaluation team: Do your team members have any experience executing similar projects, or is this their first?

What should you try to discover through evaluation? Focusing on the wrong evaluation objective will result in a waste of time and money. Once again, Shneiderman et al. (2010) has compiled a list of measurable human factors central to the evaluation of an interface:

Time to learn: How long does it take a regular user to learn to use the interface?

Speed of performance: How fast can a regular user work through a set of tasks?

Rate of errors by users: How many and what kind of errors do users make?

Retention over time: How much of the knowledge obtained in the instruction do users retain after a length of time?

Subjective satisfaction: What do users think about the learning experience that took place?

CATEGORIES OF EVALUATION

The two main types of evaluation are formative and summative. Both are important components of the evaluation story.

Formative Evaluation

A formative evaluation takes place during the development or implementation of a project. The goal is to help the development team recognize problems in the design of the instruction so that they can correct and improve those problems before the project is completed. When the results of a formative evaluation are incorporated into the design, the process becomes iterative, because each modified interface is then a candidate for a new evaluation. A variety of methods can be used for a formative evaluation, some qualitative and some quantitative. Examples are surveys, focus groups, and observations. Time is an important factor in conducting a formative evaluation, however, because results must be analyzed and then included in the modified interface quickly enough to stay on schedule.

Summative Evaluation

A summative evaluation occurs at the end of a project and is used to determine its impact. It is used to measure whether the goals of the project have been met, including whether the final design and implementation were successful, as well as whether users mastered content. A summative evaluation is often the tool decision makers and other stakeholders use to judge the project's worth. In a multimedia project, this evaluation often serves as the basis for later revisions to the program. Some common summative evaluations are observation, student achievement, and interviews.

EVALUATION METHODS

Some of the established software evaluation methods may be more appropriate for either formative or summative evaluations, and others can be used for both processes. In addition, some methods involve users, and others rely on experts.

User Evaluation Methods

The intended audience for your project should be involved in the evaluation process. This section examines two common methods of evaluation that involve the user: prototyping and usability testing.

Prototyping

Prototypes are primitive interface designs that are assembled quickly and cheap to produce. A prototype allows for user feedback at the beginning of the design process. Design issues can be discovered early before time and money have been invested in any actual production of the tutorial.

Prototyping may be at a low-, medium-, or high-fidelity level. Low-fidelity prototypes are those that are quickly constructed, such as paper sketches and storyboards that have no functionality but that demonstrate design concepts and layout. A low-fidelity prototype presentation for user feedback requires that a facilitator who knows the intended functionality demonstrate it. The users who will be part of the test should be representative of the targeted audience. In addition to having a facilitator present the test, development team members should act as observers and take notes on the participants' comments and reactions. If your budget allows, it may be useful to videotape the session for later reference.

Medium-fidelity prototypes simulate or animate some but not all of the features of the intended system. Some approaches to medium-fidelity prototypes are computer based and slide or video simulation. High-fidelity prototypes are fully functional. Both are more expensive than low-fidelity prototypes. Although most prototyping takes place in the early stages of the design process, medium- and high-fidelity prototypes make their appearances during the later stages because of the time required to produce them. Medium- and high-fidelity prototyping do not require a facilitator, but they do require an observer to record user actions.

Usability Testing

The purpose of usability testing is to assess your design and tutorial structure by having real users work through the program. This type of testing should be part of the formative evaluation so that any usability issues can be addressed and resolved.

Is it necessary to recruit a large number of users to get conclusive answers to your questions? According to Jakob Nielsen (2000), good results can be obtained from testing no more than five users. In research he conducted, Nielsen found that a single user provides almost one-third of all the data there is to know about a design's usability. With a second user, there is some overlap with what the first person found, and the second user therefore doesn't contribute as much new information as the first did. This trend continues as more users are added, but by the time the fifth user is tested, there is nothing much new to discover. Because of the iterative nature of the design process, you may choose to run a test at each stage of the redesign and involve five users for each test. The only time you really need to think about using more than five testers is when your audience straddles disparate user groups. Then you will want to include testers who are representative of each group. Be sure that the people you select to participate are typical rather than unusual users. Students who work in your library know more about how a library functions, so it is preferable to find students who are regular library users.

Testing should be held in a computer lab or wired classroom where there won't be interruptions. However, it doesn't have to be a sterile, noiseless location—in fact, it should not be—because the more normal a setting you can come up with, the closer to reality the test will be.

If the testing method you are using requires interaction between the user and a facilitator, prepare a list of questions and key points you are interested in exploring so that the facilitator has a guide that will be the same for all participants. The guideline is just that, however, because issues that you never considered may crop up during a session, and the facilitator will need to address those with other participants.

The facilitator should have an assistant who acts as an observer and records the feedback. As with prototyping sessions, a video recording can be a valuable tool if it doesn't make participants self-conscious.

The final step in a usability test is to compile the findings and assimilate the results into potential solutions. Share these with your team, form a consensus about what actions are best, and proceed with the interface modifications. Different measurement methods can be used during a test. Some will provide you with quantitative data; others will give you qualitative insight into users' thinking:

Success rate: This is a straightforward way to test usability. You simply record the percentage of users who are able to accomplish the task they were assigned.

Thinking aloud: Users are asked to verbalize their thoughts as they work their way through the tutorial.

Task performance: With this measurement, you simply time how long it takes users to perform assigned tasks.

Checklist-based testing: For budgetary reasons, you may decide that you prefer to do user testing without a facilitator or observer. A checklist-based test is cost effective and easily executed. Prepare a checklist of criteria that you want your testers to evaluate, and give them the list. Then leave the room, and let the testers work through the checklist as they interact with your program.

Subjective satisfaction: A big measurement of a design's success is how satisfied users are when they interact with it. A questionnaire can be useful in soliciting user satisfaction.

Usability Inspections

Users can provide important evaluation information. However, bringing in experts to review your interface design can be instrumental to design improvement during an iterative process. The term expert can refer to interface design authorities or to staff members who know the content and the tasks that will be included in the tutorial. As with user testing, usability inspections (also called expert reviews) should involve more than one person because no single inspection will uncover every design flaw. Arrange for three to five experts to participate in the review process. Expert reviews can occur at any point in the design phase and are useful because they usually can be done quickly and cheaply. The reviews can be scheduled to take place at various stages of the design process when the development team is ready for feedback. Depending on the scope of the project, feedback from the experts can be a formal report or an informal discussion with the team. There are several different methods of expert review you can choose.

Heuristic Evaluation
Developed by Jakob Nielsen (Nielsen and Molich, 1990), heuristic evaluation is one of the most popular types of usability inspection. Evaluators are given a short list of design-usability principles (heuristics), such as Shneiderman's eight golden rules (see chapter 5) or Keith Instone's usability heuristics for the Web (http://instone.org/heuristics/). The experts inspect the interface on their own and determine its conformance with the list. They usually go through the interface at least twice; the first time to become acquainted with the system and the second to focus on the specific principles. After all of the evaluators have completed their solitary inspections, they meet and aggregate their findings. Additional in-depth information about conducting heuristic evaluations is available at Nielsen's site (www .useit.com/papers/heuristic/).

Guidelines Review

If your organization has established specific guidelines to which your web documents must conform, then you may want to perform a guidelines review. In this type of evaluation, the interface is checked for adherence to any organizational interface design requirements.

Pluralistic Walk-Through

In a pluralistic walk-through, the users, developers, and usability experts meet in a group setting and work through task scenarios to evaluate how usable a system in fact is. A benefit of this type of evaluation is that the participants will be a diverse group, contributing different levels of skills and points of view. Normally, this type of session includes a facilitator who coordinates the discussion and participant input.

Consistency Inspection

The purpose of a consistency inspection is to ensure consistency across multiple products from the same development effort. In the case of library instruction tutorials, if you are developing two or more tutorials on various topics, having the same look and functionality across all of them will benefit the students who use them. Consistency can be checked in regard to such factors as color, screen layout, terminology, and navigation format.

Cognitive Walk-Through

A cognitive walk-through involves experts playing the role of users walking through the program interface to accomplish specific tasks. Often, users prefer to learn by exploring a new interface rather than by reading formal instructions. By putting themselves in the users' shoes, the inspectors can break down different tasks into specific steps and identify sequences that are likely to cause difficulty. To prepare for a cognitive walk-through, team members decide which tasks should be tested and then compile a list that breaks down each task into a sequence. Experts should have some knowledge of the targeted audience profile so they understand the goals. Those goals should be defined and listed. During the evaluation phase, the information gathered in the preparatory stage is analyzed and predictions are made about the degree of difficulty users are likely to encounter as they try to reach their goals.

Formal Usability Inspection

A formal usability inspection is the most structured type. Adapted from software inspection methodology, it formalizes the discovery and recording of usability problems. It is undertaken by a team of several people, each of whom, in addition to inspecting the design, has a specific role: moderator, designer, recorder, and inspector. These roles are played during a formal meeting held after the design has been inspected. During the meeting, the moderator walks the team through each scenario or task, and the inspectors report each defect found at that particular stage. The recorder logs each reported defect. The final step is to assign the identified defects to be fixed to the appropriate development person. Because this method is detailed, it clearly takes longer to prepare and requires more people to carry out than some of the other methods do.

Inquiry Methods

In addition to user evaluations and usability inspections, asking users questions and soliciting their feedback can yield much valuable information. You can discover what they like or dislike, what their needs and expectations are, and how well they comprehend the program. Several avenues for collecting information from users are especially useful.

Questionnaires

A questionnaire is a written list of questions distributed to and completed and returned by one or more users. Although the term is often used interchangeably with the word *survey*, a questionnaire is in fact an instrument that can be used to conduct a survey. A survey, however, can also be conducted in person, over the telephone, or via an online survey form. Keep in mind when using a questionnaire that you are putting the burden on your users to complete it and return it to you. You are asking them to expend more effort on their part than with some other feedback methods.

Interviews

Interviews are direct person-to-person interaction with users. User opinions can be solicited and follow-up questions posed to clarify any issues that arise during the interview. Methods include structured sessions with specific predetermined agendas and unstructured informal exchanges. It is always a good idea to record the interview so that the subject isn't distracted by the interviewer's note taking.

Focus Groups and Group Discussions

Focus groups and group discussions can be used to gather users' impressions both before design and after implementation. To run a focus group, you gather together six to eight people with a moderator, who keeps the group on task. The moderator may demonstrate a prototype and then solicit response from the group. The main problem with focus groups as an information-gathering mechanism is that what is being collected are opinions about how participants think the program will or should work rather than data about how they would really interact if they were to sit in front of the screen and work through the program. Focus groups can be beneficial for exploring what users want from a program. What users want, however, may not be what they need.

Field Observation
Unlike observation in a usability test, field observation takes place in the users' environment. The purpose of this type of observation is to see users in action at their normal place of work or study. One component is to interview users about their work or study habits and how they would normally use the instruction.

Online Feedback
As a part of the summative evaluation process, consider providing a vehicle for users to give you feedback from within the instruction. This method can be beneficial because you receive impressions and opinions during or soon after users have worked through the instruction.

ASSESSING CONTENT MASTERY

Up to this point, we have discussed how to evaluate the effectiveness of the web instruction you are creating. Measuring the usability of the interface is an important part of ensuring the success of your project.

However, the most vital goal of an online instruction project is for learning to occur. Remember that Shneiderman identified "retention over time" as one of the factors central to the evaluation of an interface.

It is just as important to build assessment methods into your instruction to determine whether this is occurring. Many people use the terms *evaluation* and *assessment* interchangeably, but the words refer to two different activities. Evaluation is the process of judging the effectiveness and worth of the educational programs and products (e.g., web-based tutorials). Assessment is the activity of measuring student learning.

The tools to accomplish this are varied, and some methods are discussed in chapter 7. Some tools are traditional ones used to gauge retention, such as quizzes and tests. Assessment tools can be either formative or summative. They can be formal or informal. Optimally, they will be aligned with the design of the course and follow best practices for effective assessment: "learner-centered, teacher-directed, mutually beneficial, formative, context-specific, ongoing and rooted in good practice" (Palloff and Pratt 2009, 109).

Reeves (2000) discusses the need for alternative assessment approaches in an online environment and proposes three major directions that can provide more meaningful measurements:

1. *Cognitive*: Students' higher-order thinking abilities, attitudes, and communication skills are measured. Reeves mentions concept mapping, a strategy that permits students to represent the structure of their knowledge visually. Concept-mapping software could be used with this method.

2. *Performance*: Learners demonstrate their capabilities by creating a product or engaging in an activity—applying their new abilities in a realistic context.

3. *Portfolio*: The students' work is accumulated and stored over time to be reviewed to show evolution of learning and the interim steps taken to complete a course of study.

As you plan evaluation procedures, build in assessment methods to measure if and to what extent students have mastered the content. Even if your institution or the class instructor doesn't require a grade, an assessment system can help determine how effective your online instruction has been. This can be a critical factor in decision making for future online instruction projects.

APPENDIX
List of Resources

ACCESSIBILITY

Henry, Shawn Lawton, and Liam McGee. *Accessibility.* www.w3.org/
standards/webdesign/accessibility/.
The W3C's Accessibility site covers the whys, whats, and hows of accessibility.

ANIMATION

White, Tony. 2006. *Animation from Pencils to Pixels: Classical
Techniques for Digital Animators.* Burlington, MA: Oxford.
Contains lessons covering traditional to computer animation techniques.

ASSESSMENT

Kapoun, Jim. 2004. Assessing Library Instruction Assessment Activities.
Library Philosophy and Practice (1), http://unllib.unl.edu/LPP/
kapoun2.htm.
A survey of library instruction assessment tools and surveys, and part of
the continuing assessment of library instruction at Minnesota State University, Mankato. The survey included what types of questions were asked
and how they were delivered to the students. A group of 320 peer libraries
with instruction programs from across the nation was surveyed. The results
were analyzed to look for common themes and ideas.

Reeves, Thomas. 2000. Alternative Assessment Approaches for Online Learning Environments in Higher Education. *Journal of Educational Computing Research* 23 (1): 101–111.
Describes need for alternative assessment approaches in online learning environments in higher education. Alternative options discussed include cognitive, performance, and portfolio assessment.

AUDIO

Schroeder, Dave. 2007. *Digital Audio Principles.* Ojai, CA: Lynda.com.
Explains the basics of digital audio production techniques and covers the essential hardware and software. Also discusses sound theory, frequency response, the range of human hearing, and dynamic range.

BEST PRACTICES

Bianco, Cecile. 2005. Online Tutorials: Tips from the Literature. *Library Philosophy and Practice* (1), www.webpages.uidaho.edu/~mbolin/bianco2.htm.
Presents fourteen best practices for constructing online tutorials.

Blummer, Barbara A., and Olga Kritskaya. 2009. Best Practices for Creating an Online Tutorial: A Literature Review. *Journal of Web Librarianship* 3 (3): 199–216.
Traces the creation of online library instructional tutorials in academic libraries. Also illustrates the incorporation of multimedia learning theories and assessment strategies in those tutorials.

Tancheva, Kornelia. 2003. Online Tutorials for Library Instruction: An Ongoing Project under Constant Revision. In *ACRL Eleventh National Conference*, Charlotte, NC. www.ala.org/ala/mgrps/divs/acrl/events/pdf/tancheva.PDF.
A study of more than forty existing library tutorials and online library research aids that examines the experience of creating an interactive tutorial. Goals included building on Nancy Dewald's study of twenty online tutorials. Additional goal was to determine to what extent an online library instruction tutorial addresses the principles of learning theories in distributed environments, as well as the accepted principles of effective library instruction. Compiled features for the ideal online tutorial. Includes a significant bibliography of case studies and research literature.

York, Amy C., and Jason M. Vance. 2009. **Taking Library Instruction into the Online Classroom: Best Practices for Embedded Librarians.** *Journal of Library Administration* 49 (1–2): 197–209.

The proliferation of online courses has led librarians to adapt their instructional techniques and follow teaching faculty and students into the online environment. Moving beyond web pages and online research guides, librarians are becoming instructional partners in online course management systems. Through an online survey of librarians and a literature review, the authors examine best practices for such "embedded" librarians.

BLENDED LEARNING (HYBRID, DISTRIBUTED)

Bonk, Curtis, Jay Graham, and Charles Ray. 2006. *The Handbook of Blended Learning: Global Perspectives, Local Designs.* San Francisco: Pfeiffer.

This work documents global perspectives related to blended learning, including models at the institutional level for designed blended learning environments.

CASCADING STYLE SHEETS

Carlson, Lisa. *Cascading Style Sheets.* Duluth: University of Minnesota, Duluth. www.d.umn.edu/itss/support/Training/Online/webdesign/css.html.

An extensive collection of links to CSS tutorials and articles on CSS specific topics.

CASE STUDIES

Kimok, Debra, and Holly Heller-Ross. 2008. **Visual Tutorials for Point-of-Need Instruction in Online Courses.** *Journal of Library Administration* 48 (3): 527–543.

Discusses a method of incorporating demonstrations into online information and technology literacy courses and experimentations with this method in other library services, such as electronic reference services, one-shot course-related instruction, subject research guides. Addresses potential of outreach to faculty for their own professional development and as a way to incorporate information and technology literacy in their courses.

Lillard, Linda L., Scott Norwood, Kate Wise, Jan Brooks, and Royce Kitts. 2009. Embedded Librarians: MLS Students as Apprentice Librarians in Online Courses. *Journal of Library Administration* 49 (1): 11–22.

Examines a project where Master of Library Science (MLS) students at one university served as apprentice embedded librarians in nursing courses at another university. Includes results of surveys of nursing students at the end of the class and reflections of the MLS students. Explores the premise of the development of relationships in the provision of library services for distance learners.

Mitchell, Erik T., and Susan Sharpless Smith. 2009. Bringing Information Literacy into the Social Sphere: A Case Study Using Social Software to Teach Information Literacy at WFU. *Journal of Web Librarianship* 3 (3): 183–197.

Presents an approach to teaching information literacy in an academic course from a sociotechnical perspective, designed to incorporate the use of Facebook to engage students from their current skill sets.

Rao, Srivalli, Agnes Cameron, and Susan Gaskin-Noel. 2009. Embedding General Education Competencies into an Online Information Literacy Course. *Journal of Library Administration* 49 (1): 59–73.

Presents an overview of an online information literacy course and describes how the course was redesigned to embed and assess the five general education competencies (critical thinking, information literacy, critical reading, quantitative reasoning, and writing).

Shepley, Susan E. 2009. Building a Virtual Campus: Librarians as Collaborators in Online Course Development and Learning. *Journal of Library Administration* 49 (1): 89–95.

Discusses the evolution of Saskatchewan Institute of Applied Science and Technology (SIAST) Libraries' relationship with the college's online course development unit, Virtual Campus, and presents a model of the collaboration that has taken place. Describes how that relationship has affected the role of SIAST's librarians and improved communication with and services for off-campus students and faculty.

Smith, Susan Sharpless, Erik Mitchell, and Carolina Numbers. 2007. Building Library 2.0 into Information Literacy: A Case Study. In *Library 2.0 Initiatives in Academic Libraries*, edited by L. B.

Cohen. Chicago: Association of College and Research Libraries. 114–132.
Describes a pilot program designed to use Library 2.0 concepts to engage students in a collaborative environment through current information issues, collaborative social software, and information management applications.

CLIP ART

Open Clip Art Library. http://openclipart.org/media/view/media/home/.
This project aims to create an archive of user-contributed clip art that can be freely used. All graphics submitted to the project should be placed into the public domain according to the statement by the Creative Commons. If you'd like to help out, please join the mailing list and review the archives.

COLOR

Ford, Janet Lynn. *Color Worqx.* www.worqx.com/color/.
A color theory tutorial.

COURSE MANAGEMENT SYSTEMS (CMS)

EduTools. *Course Management Systems.* www.edutools.info/static. jsp?pj=4&page=HOME.
This site can be used to compare different course management systems to assist in the decision-making process.

DEVELOPMENT TOOLS

Anderson, Dave, Neil White, FlyFisher, Lee Armstrong, and Chris Hogan. *PC Technology Guide.* www.pctechguide.com.
A resource for PC computer technology guides and explanations.

Ard, Scott. *CNET.com.* www.cnet.com.
Provides information, tools, and advice on what to buy and how to get the most out of your technology.

Macworld. www.macworld.com.
Includes product information, news, help for forums users, and reviews relating to Macintosh hardware and software.

DISTANCE EDUCATION

Rogers, Patricia, Gary Berg, Judith Boettcher, Carole Howard, Lorraine Justice, and Karen Schenk. 2009. *Encyclopedia of Distance Learning.* **2nd ed. 4 vols. Hershey, PA: Information Science Reference.**
This multiple volume publication contains articles and essays on the topics relating to distance learning programs.

EVALUATION AND TESTING

Rubin, Jeffrey, and Chisnell Dana. 2008. *Handbook of Usability Testing: How to Plan, Design, and Conduct Effective Tests.* **Indianapolis, IN: Wiley Pub.**
Contains step-by-step guidelines for testing products for usability.

GRANTS AND FUND-RAISING

American Library Association. *Library Fundraising: A Selected Annotated Bibliography/ALA Fact Sheet #24,* **www.ala.org/ala/aboutala/offices/library/libraryfactsheet/alalibraryfactsheet24.cfm#libfundraising.**
In recent years, many libraries have turned to nontraditional sources of funding to ensure their ability to continue to provide necessary services. This fact sheet is designed to serve a variety of interests and funding goals.

Gerding, Stephanie, and Pam MacKellar. *Funding Sources for Libraries* **(handout), librarygrants.blogspot.com with a link from the November 19, 2009, entry to www.pamelamackellar.com/Resources.doc.**
A handout from the November 2009 webinar "Winning Grants for Libraries 101," this Word document includes government, private, community, corporate, professional association, and local sources, as well as information about newsletters, bulletins, and alert services. The authors maintain a blog on grants for libraries at http://librarygrants.blogspot.com.

INFORMATION LITERACY

Adolphus, M. 2009. **Using the Web to Teach Information Literacy.** *Online* 33 (4): 21–25.
Discusses the range of options now available using collaborative Web 2.0 methods for librarians to provide rich and meaningful learning experiences.

Association of College and Research Libraries. *Information Literacy Competency Standards for Higher Education.* **www.ala.org/ala/mgrps/divs/acrl/standards/informationliteracycompetency.cfm.**
Provides a framework for assessing the information literate individual. The standards outline the process by which faculty, librarians, and others can pinpoint specific indicators that identify students as information literate.

———. *Characteristics of Programs of Information Literacy That Illustrate Best Practices: A Guideline.* **American Library Association. www.ala.org/ala/mgrps/divs/acrl/standards/characteristics.cfm.**
Intended to help those who are interested in developing, assessing, and improving information literacy programs.

Center for Digital Literacy at Syracuse University. 2006. *SOS for Information Literacy.* **http://informationliteracy.org.**
Web-based multimedia resource that includes lesson plans, handouts, presentations, videos, and other resources to enhance the teaching of information literacy. Includes materials for instruction at the elementary, secondary, and higher education levels.

Mabrito, Mark, and Rebecca Medley. 2008. Why Professor Johnny Can't Read: Understanding the Net Generation's Texts. *Innovate: Journal of Online Education* (6), **http://innovateonline.info/pdf/vol4_issue6/Why_Professor_Johnny_Can't_Read-_Understanding_the_Net_Generation's_Texts.pdf.**
"Explores the nature of N-Gen texts as a reflection of the cognitive differences between N-Gen students and their older instructors, discusses the unique challenges this group of learners may present for instructors who do not share their technological immersion, and suggests the means by which such challenges may be overcome."

Rader, Hannelore B. 2002. Information Literacy 1973–2002: A Selected Literature Review. *Library Trends* **51 (2): 242–259.**
Review of the literature over thirty years. Draws conclusions on user instruction in different library types, includes notable websites and examples of model programs. The bibliography is annotated.

Reece, Gwendolyn J. 2005. Critical Thinking and Cognitive Transfer: Implications for the Development of Online Information Literacy Tutorials. *Research Strategies* **20 (4): 482–493.**
Surveys the literature on critical thinking and draws pedagogical requirements for fostering the development and use of higher-order thinking skills. These requirements are considered in relation to the development of computer-assisted instructional tools, such as web-based information literacy tutorials. Discusses needs for further collaboration.

Shapiro, Jeremy J., and Shelley K. Hughes. 1996. Information as a Liberal Art: Enlightenment Proposals for a New Curriculum. *Educom Review* **(2), http://net.educause.edu/apps/er/review/reviewArticles/31231.html.**
Presents a metaliteracy model of multiple literacies that should be taught: tool, resource, social-structural, research, publishing, emerging technology, and critical.

Sheffield, Sheila Webber. *Information Literacy Weblog.* **information-literacy.blogspot.com.**
A blog authored by a faculty member in the Department of Information Studies, University of Sheffield, United Kingdom, with a goal to discuss news and reports about information literacy around the world.

INSTRUCTIONAL DESIGN

Bell, Steven J., and John D. Shank. 2007. *Academic Librarianship by Design: A Blended Librarian's Guide to the Tools and Techniques.* **Chicago: American Library Association.**
Discusses the importance of why enhanced capabilities in instructional design and technology, the "blended librarian skill set," is so critical.

Dick, Walter, and Lou Carey. 2009. *The Systematic Design of Instruction.* **7th ed. Upper Saddle River, NJ: Merrill/Pearson.**
Introduces readers to the fundamentals of instructional design and helps them learn concepts and procedures for designing, developing, and evalu-

ating instruction for all delivery formats. This edition covers the impact of critical new technologies and the Internet.

Morrison, Gary R., Steven M. Ross, and Jerrold E. Kemp. 2004.
    ***Designing Effective Instruction.* 4th ed. Hoboken, NJ: John Wiley and Sons.**
Provides procedures and rationales for designing instruction. Presents a ten-element model that combines both behavioral and cognitive philosophies for designing both traditional and nontraditional interactive learning programs.

Smith, Patricia L., and Tillman J. Ragan. 2005. *Instructional Design.* Hoboken, NJ: John Wiley and Sons.
Presents documented research and theory-based treatment of instructional design prescriptions and practice. The third edition reflects the latest changes in ways of thinking about learning environments and consequent changes in interest and terminology. It examines new web-based instruction and web-based learning environments, as well as web-based learning management systems.

LEARNING OBJECTS

Beck, Robert J. *Learning Objects.* www4.uwm.edu/cie/learning_objects .cfm.
A website designed to introduce the subject of learning objects. It includes links to collections of learning objects and to organizations associated with learning objects.

Chung, Hyun-Duck, and Kim Duckett. 2009. Narrating the "Back Story" through E-learning Resources in Libraries. *In the Library with the Lead Pipe*, http://inthelibrarywiththeleadpipe.org/2009/narrating- the-back-story-through-e-learning-resources-in-libraries/.
Discusses the use of e-learning resources in libraries that help teach the "back story," or content that helps explain why the information landscape is organized the way it is rather than focusing on how to use a tool or follow a process.

MERLOT (Multimedia Educational Resources for Learning and Online Teaching). www.merlot.org.
MERLOT is a user-centered, searchable collection of peer reviewed and selected higher education, online learning materials, cataloged by registered members and a set of faculty development support services. The

goal of MERLOT is to be a premiere online community where faculty, staff, and students from around the world share their learning materials and pedagogy.

Wiley, David A. 2000. Connecting Learning Objects to Instructional Design Theory: A Definition, a Metaphor, and a Taxonomy. In *Instructional Use of Learning Objects: Online Version,* **edited by D. A. Wiley. http://reusability.org/read/chapters/wiley.doc.**
Contains a review of the literature as groundwork for a working definition of the term *learning object,* as well as a taxonomy of learning object types to present a foundation for continued research in learning objects and related instructional design theories.

LEARNING STYLES

Gardner, Howard. 1999. *Intelligence Reframed: Multiple Intelligences for the 21st Century.* **New York: Basic Books.**
Puts forth a theory of multiple intelligences. Gardner proposes that each person has a different biological composition made up of nine different intelligences: linguistic, mathematical-logical, musical, spatial, bodily-kinesthetic, interpersonal, intrapersonal, naturalist, and existential.

Gramling, Jennifer. 2004. Learning Styles. In *Education and Technology: an Encyclopedia,* **edited by A. Kovalchick and D. Kara, 418–420. Santa Barbara, CA: ABC-CLIO.**
Connects Gardner's multiple intelligences with online teaching strategies.

LIBRARIAN PROFESSIONAL DEVELOPMENT RESOURCES

Bell, Steven J., and John Shank. *Blended Librarian.* **www.blended librarian.org.**
A site designed to provide basic information about blended librarianship and information about the Blended Librarians Online Learning Community.

LOEX Clearinghouse for Library Instruction. www.emich.edu/public/ loex/.
The self-supporting, nonprofit educational clearinghouse LOEX provides information on all aspects of instruction and information literacy to libraries and librarians who are institutional members. Contains a historical

archive of library instruction materials, including both print and nonprint resources donated by member libraries and librarians. Includes a website that points to examples of work in the field of library instruction and information literacy.

LIBRARY INSTRUCTION

Association of College and Research Libraries Instruction Section. *Information Literacy Instruction List.* **www.lita.org/ala/mgrps/ divs/acrl/about/sections/is/ilil.cfm.**
The Information Literacy Instruction Discussion List (ILI-L) was created in May 2002 to foster a thriving exchange on instruction and information literacy among librarians from a variety of settings and backgrounds.

University of Texas Libraries. *Tips and Techniques for Library Instruction.* **www.lib.utexas.edu/services/instruction/tips/.**
A series that discusses teaching fundamentals such as learning and teaching styles, class planning, effective use of teaching tools, incorporation of active learning, presentation skills, and evaluation of teaching and student learning.

LIBRARY INSTRUCTION ON THE WEB

Association of College and Research Libraries Instruction Section. *PRIMO: Peer-Reviewed Instructional Materials Online.* **www.ala .org/ala/mgrps/divs/acrl/about/sections/is/projpubs/primo/index .cfm.**
The site is a project of the ACRL Instruction Section. Its goal is to promote and share peer-reviewed instructional materials created by librarians to teach people about discovering, accessing, and evaluating information in networked environments.

MARKUP LANGUAGES

W3C. All Standards and Drafts. www.w3.org/TR/.
Provides access to official information on HTML, SMIL, XHTML, XML, and XSLT.

MULTIMEDIA

Leeder, Kim. 2009. Learning to Teach through Video. *In the Library with the Leadpipe*, **http://inthelibrarywiththeleadpipe.org/2009/learning-to-teach-through-video/.**
A blog article that discusses instructional strategies and pedagogy in the use of video.

Mayer, Richard E. 2009. *Multimedia Learning.* **2nd ed. New York: Cambridge University Press.**
Examines whether people learn more deeply when ideas are expressed in words and pictures rather than in words alone. Reviews twelve principles of instructional design and presents Mayer's cognitive theory of multimedia learning.

Mayer, Richard E., and Roxana Moreno. 2003. Nine Ways to Reduce Cognitive Load in Multimedia Learning. *Educational Psychologist* **38: 43–52.**
Concludes that cognitive load is a central consideration in the design of multimedia instruction.

Shea, Dave. 2004. CSS Sprites: Image Slicing's Kiss of Death. *A List Apart: For People Who Make Websites,* **www.alistapart.com/articles/sprites/.**
Provides an introduction to sprites as a replacement for image slicing.

MULTINATIONAL DESIGN ISSUES

Loring, Linda. 2002. Six Steps to Preparing Instruction for a Worldwide Audience. *Journal of Interactive Instruction Development* **14 (3): 24–29.**
Discusses six steps to follow to develop instruction for a multinational audience: address administrative issues, begin globally, consider cultural variables, design for worldwide use, express yourself clearly, and free training of rigid rules. Includes an annotated bibliography.

NAVIGATION

Kalbach, James. 2007. *Designing Web Navigation.* **Beijing: Sebastopol.**
Discusses web navigation in relation to human information behavior and the mechanics, types, and options for creating various navigation systems.

ONLINE LEARNING RESOURCES

Dringus, Laurie P. 2008. Editor's Choice 2008: Selected Online Learning Resources. *Internet and Higher Education* 11 (3–4): 211–216.
This article is an annual compilation of useful resources that pertain to the field of online learning and uses of the Internet for instructional delivery. Resources are organized into several categories, including texts, journals, and websites.

OPTIMIZATION

King, Andrew B. 2008. *Website Optimization*. Farnham, UK: O'Reilly.
A guide to tips, techniques, standards, and methods of website optimization.

PEDAGOGY

Association of College and Research Libraries Instruction Section Instructional Technologies Committee. 2007. *Tips for Developing Effective Web-Based Library Instruction.* www.ala.org/ala/mgrps/divs/acrl/about/sections/is/projpubs/classroomcontrolsys/tips.cfm.
Offers tips on the pedagogy of web instruction and includes selected additional resources.

Cook, Douglas, and Ryan Sittler, eds. 2008. *Practical Pedagogy for Library Instructors: 17 Innovative Strategies to Improve Student Learning.* Chicago: Association of College and Research Libraries.
Gathers seventeen case studies that use unique instructional methodologies framed by sound pedagogical theory. "As the mission of academic libraries has moved away from maintaining collections toward educating users in research methodologies, new approaches to teaching are required. Many librarians come from disciplines other than education and therefore need to upgrade their skills in the area of instruction. Cases included cover the broad spectrum of education from behavioral to cognitive to constructivist. Each chapter is grounded in the educational and library literature and explores the potential of using pedagogical approaches which closely match instructional aims."

RESEARCH LITERATURE

Aharony, Noa. 2009. The Use of a Wiki as an Instructional Tool: A
    Qualitative Investigation. *Journal of Web Librarianship* 3 (1):
    35–53.
A content analysis conducted on comments directed at a class of students
on a course wiki. The results of the current research revealed the major part
of the interaction on the wiki centered on content-related comments and
contained both collaboration among the students and use of deep levels
of cognition.

Zhang, Li. 2006. Effectively Incorporating Instructional Media into
    Web-Based Information Literacy. *Electronic Library* 24: 294.
Explores and discusses in detail the application of instructional media
features in developing web-based library instruction in order to strengthen
students' online learning experience.

RSS FEEDS

Dolan, Frankie, and David Rothman. *LIBWorm: Librarianship RSS
    Search and Current Awareness.* www.libworm.com.
LibWorm is intended to be a search engine, a professional development
tool, and a current awareness tool for people who work in libraries or care
about libraries.

Teeter, Robert. 2010. *RSS: What It Is, Where to Get It, How to Make It,
    How to Use It.* www.interleaves.org/~rteeter/rss.html.
Provides a good, basic introduction to RSS feeders and their potential uses.

SCRIPT LANGUAGES AND WEB
INTERACTION TECHNOLOGIES

ActionScript.org. www.actionscript.org.
Contains tutorials, forums, articles, and other information relating to
ActionScript.

Goodman, Danny, and Michael Morrison. 2007. *JavaScript Bible.* 6th
    ed. Indianapolis, IN: Wiley Pub.
An update to the well-regarded print resource on using JavaScript.

Java. **www.java.com/en/.**
Sun's website for information pertaining to Java.

JavaScript. **http://en.wikibooks.org/wiki/Programming:JavaScript.**
From Wikibooks, the open-content textbooks collection, a guide to writing in JavaScript.

Perl Directory. **Perl Foundation. www.perl.org.**
Designed to be the central directory to all things Perl. Contains Perl programming resources including documentation, history, articles. Perl can be downloaded from this site.

PHP: Hypertext Preprocessor. **http://php.net.**
Offers tutorials, events pertaining to the PHP community, documentation, and a wide assortment of other PHP information.

Python Programming Language. **www.python.org.**
The official website for Python.

Ruby: A Programmer's Best Friend. **www.ruby-lang.org/en/.**
Ruby's official site, with in-depth information on the language.

Strod, Eran. 2009. *Dynamic Programming Languages on the Rise in Open Source.* **devX.com, www.devx.com/opensource/ Article/43102.**
Discusses how, in open-source projects, static languages such as C, C++, and Java are losing ground to dynamic programming languages such as JavaScript and PHP.

Tcl Developer Xchange. **www.tcl.tk.**
Primary resource for information about Tcl.

SCRIPT LIBRARIES

Lennartz, Sven. 2006. *AJAX, DHTML and JavaScript Libraries.* **www .smashingmagazine.com/2006/11/15/ajax-dhtml-and-javascript -libraries/.**
An extensive annotated list with links to more than sixty AJAX, JavaScript, and dHTML libraries.

TECHNOLOGIES

**Gartner Inc. 2008, July. *Hype Cycle for Emerging Technologies, 2008.*
    www.gartner.com/DisplayDocument?doc_cd=159496&ref=g_
    homelink.**
For the 2008 report, "technologies and trends at or approaching the Hype
Cycle peak include green IT, cloud computing and social networking
platforms. Corporate use of virtual worlds and Web 2.0 are slipping into
the Trough of Disillusionment, while SOA begins its ascent of the Slope
of Enlightenment."

**Gartner Inc. 2009. *Hype Cycle for Cloud Computing, 2009.* www
    .gartner.com/DisplayDocument?doc_cd=169747.**
This report provides a good overview on cloud computing and the various
issues involved with it.

TECHNOLOGY IN EDUCATION

**Bates, Tony, and Gary Poole. 2003. *Effective Teaching with Technology
    in Higher Education: Foundations for Success.* Jossey-Bass Higher
    and Adult Education Series. Hoboken, NJ: Jossey-Bass.**
Includes chapters on the role of media in education, a framework for
selecting and using technology, planning for teaching with technology,
approaches to the design of technology-based learning, and change and
stability in teaching with technology.

**Bonk, Curtis Jay. 2009. *The World Is Open: How Web Technology Is
    Revolutionizing Education.* San Francisco, CA: Jossey-Bass.**
"Explores ten key trends that together make up the 'WE-ALL-LEARN'
framework for understanding the potential of technology's impact on learning in the 21st century."

**Gibbons, Susan. 2007. *The Academic Library and the Net Gen
    Student: Making the Connections.* Chicago: American Library
    Association.**
Based on work-practice studies of students and faculty, the guide discusses
the potential futures of using Web 2.0 technologies in the academic library.
Its goal is to help academic librarians better understand the role of technology in the social and academic lives of undergraduates.

Oblinger, Diana G., Carole A. Barone, and Brian L. Hawkins. 2001. *Distributed Education and Its Challenges: An Overview.* Washington, DC: American Council on Education. www.acenet.edu/bookstore/pdf/distributed-learning/distributed-learning-01.pdf. "This overview paper identifies significant issues associated with distributed education and suggests a series of questions to help institutional leaders establish and validate their options."

Siemens, George, and Peter Tittenberger. 2009. *Handbook of Emerging Technologies for Learning.* http://ltc.umanitoba.ca/wikis/etl/index.php/Handbook_of_Emerging_Technologies_for_Learning. Designed as a resource for educators planning to incorporate technologies in their teaching and learning activities.

Smith, Shannon S., Gail Salaway, and Judith Borreson Caruso. 2009. *The ECAR Study of Undergraduate Students and Information Technology, 2009.* Research Study, Vol. 6. www.educause.edu/ecar/. This study seeks to shed light on how technology affects the college experience. It asks students about the technology they own and how they use it in and out of their academic world. They are also asked about their perceived skill level with these technologies. The focus for the report is Internet-capable handheld devices.

Williams, Joe M., and Susan P. Goodwin. 2007. *Teaching with Technology: An Academic Librarian's Guide.* Chandos Information Professional Series. Oxford, U.K.: Chandos. Introduces readers to the current technology topics and issues facing today's academic instruction and reference librarians. Provides overviews of cutting-edge technologies, offers insight into current educational uses and applications of new tools, and discusses common problems and pitfalls librarians may encounter when incorporating current technologies into their instruction services.

USABILITY

Krug, Steve. 2006. *Don't Make Me Think! A Common Sense Approach to Web Usability.* Berkeley, CA: New Riders. A primer on the dos and don'ts of good web design. The second edition adds three new chapters that "explain why people really leave websites, how to make sites usable and accessible, and the art of surviving executive design whims."

Nielsen, Jakob. 2000. *Designing Web Usability*. Indianapolis, IN: New Riders.
Definitive guide to web usability from one of the world's foremost authorities.

Nielsen, Jakob, and Loranger Hoa. 2006. *Prioritizing Web Usability*. Berkeley, CA: New Riders.
An updated companion to Nielsen's 2000 book.

USER INTERFACE DESIGN

Shneiderman, Ben, Catherine Plaisant, Maxine Cohen, and Steven Jacobs. 2010. *Designing the User Interface: Strategies for Effective Human-Computer Interaction*. 5th ed. Boston: Addison-Wesley.
Now in its fifth edition, this classic text presents a broad survey of how to develop high-quality user interfaces for interactive systems.

VIDEO

Rubin, Michael. 2009. *The Little Digital Video Book: A Friendly Introduction to Home Video*. 2nd ed. Berkeley, CA: Peachpit Press.
This guide teaches "users the basics of shooting, organizing, and editing their own footage, with short examples so they can practice the techniques as they read through the book." Includes the basics of digital video.

WEB 2.0 TECHNOLOGIES

EDUCAUSE. 2009. 7 Things You Should Know About . . . Google Wave. http://net.educause.edu/ir/library/pdf/ELI7055.pdf.
An overview of Google's new service Google Wave, with a discussion of what it is, who is using it, how it works, why it is significant, what its downsides are, where it's going, and how it might be used for teaching and learning.

Fox, Susannah, Kathryn Zickuhr, and Aaron Smith. 2009. *Twitter and Status Updating, Fall 2009*. Pew Internet and American Life Project, www.pewinternet.org/~/media/Files/Reports/2009/PIP_Twitter_Fall_2009_web.pdf.
Reports on a survey of the use of Twitter by Internet users.

Programmable Web: Mashup Dashboard. **www.programmableweb .com/mashups/.**
This site links to thousands of web mashups.

Sodt, Jill M., and Terri Pedersen Summey. 2009. Beyond the Library's Walls: Using Library 2.0 Tools to Reach Out to All Users. *Journal of Library Administration* **49 (1): 97–109.**
Discusses how Library 2.0 takes the tools of Web 2.0 and moves them into a library setting with libraries that are user centered with the goal of creating a vital and evolving organization designed to meet the needs of the current information culture.

WEB DESIGN

Lynch, Patrick J., and Sarah Horton. 2008. *Web Style Guide: Basic Design Principles for Creating Web Sites.* **3rd ed. New Haven, CT: Yale University Press.**
"Explains established design principles and how they apply in web design projects in which information design, interface design, and efficient search and navigation are of primary concern."

Porter, Joshua. 2008. *Designing for the Social Web: Voices That Matter.* **Berkeley, CA: New Riders.**
In this discussion of designing for the social web, the author addresses reasons people participate online and the psychology behind doing so, how people use a web application over time, how to get people to sign up for the first time, how to analyze effectiveness, and how to grow a social web application over time.

Stevens, Krista, ed. *A List Apart: For People Who Make Websites.* **www.alistapart.com.**
Explores the design, development, and meaning of web content, with a special focus on web standards and best practices. Includes articles on usability, testing, project management, typography, and code.

WEB-BASED INSTRUCTION

Driscoll, Margaret. 2002. *Web-Based Training: Creating E-Learning Experiences.* **San Francisco: Jossey-Bass/Pfeiffer.**
Includes chapters on the strategic advantages of web-based training, best practices, principles of adult education, and instructional design. Covers

needs analysis, designing interactions, and implementing and evaluating programs.

Dupuis, Elizabeth A., ed. 2003. *Developing Web-Based Instruction: Planning, Designing, Managing, and Evaluating for Results.* **New Library Series. New York: Neal-Schuman Publishers.**
Fourteen authors examine the entire process of creating web-based library instruction. Emphasis is on instructional design and educational technologies chosen in terms of instructional goals. Divided into three main categories: planning and management, evaluation and assessment, and design and development.

Khan, Badrul H., ed. 1997. *Web-Based Instruction.* **Englewood Cliffs, NJ: Educational Technology Publications.**
A classic title on web-based instruction, addresses design, development, delivery, management, and evaluation aspects of web-based instruction. Includes an introduction to the subject, a discussion of critical issues, and case studies.

WIKIS

Aharony, Noa. 2009. The Use of a Wiki as an Instructional Tool: A Qualitative Investigation. *Journal of Web Librarianship* **3 (1): 35–53.**
A content analysis of comments directed at a class of students on a course wiki. The results of the current research revealed the major part of the interaction on the wiki centered on content-related comments and contained both collaboration among students and use of deep levels of cognition.

GLOSSARY

Note: Definitions adopted from a variety of sources, including Wikipedia (en.wiki pedia.com) and Google (using the "define" function; www.google.com).

accessibility. the ability of everyone, especially people with impaired vision and other disabilities, to view or hear web page content

animated GIF. the combination of several GIF images into a single file to create an animation

animation. the creation of the illusion of movement

application programming interface (API). a set of routines that an application uses to request and carry out lower-level services

application server. a program that handles transactions between a web browser on a client computer and an institution's back-end (behind the scenes, usually on the server) applications or databases that reside on a server

assessment. the activity of measuring student learning

asynchronous. literally, "not at the same time"—a course in which the instruction is delivered at one time and the work can be done at another

audio. as used in this book, sound that has been digitized for storage and replay on a computer

bandwidth. the amount of data that can be transmitted in a certain amount of time

bibliographic instruction. See library instruction

binary files. digitized data that contains both text and nontextual information, in contrast to ASCII files, which contain only characters (plain text); include sound files, graphics files, and programming; frequently called binaries

bit (binary digit). a single digit number in base 2, in other words, either a 1 or 0; the smallest unit of computerized data

bitmap graphics. See raster graphics

bitrate. average number of bits that one second of video or audio data will transmit

blended learning. a combination of learning methods, usually referring to a combination of online and face-to-face; also known as hybrid and distributed

blog. See weblog

Bluetooth. an open wireless protocol for exchanging data over short distances from fixed and mobile devices

branching. an instructional technique, usually programmed text, in which the learner's response to one step determines the next step of instruction

breadcrumb trail. the part of the navigation that shows you where you are, similar to the fairy tale Hansel and Gretel; often found near the top of web pages; defines both current location and primary pages above current page

browser. See web browser

byte. the unit of data storage and transmission in computers; usually considered the code for a single character

Cascading Style Sheets (CSS). a coding method that allows the separation of presentation from the content and structure of a document

CGI (Common Gateway Interface). a protocol for transferring information between a web server and a program or processing the interaction between a user and the server

chat. a program in which two or more people are connected online and type in text that is transmitted to the other's computer screen

chunk. synonym for learning object

chunking. the division of online material into small segments

clip art. generic graphics that can be copied (clipped) and used again

cloud computing. virtualized resources provided as a service over the Internet

codec (compressor/decompressor). any technology for compressing and decompressing data

compiled language. programming in which the instructions or commands are transformed into machine language that the processor reads

content management system (CMS). designed to streamline website content management by separating content from presentation

course management system (CMS). designed to facilitate the development, delivery, and management of online learning environments; known in the business world as a learning management system (LMS)

database. a collection of organized information in which a computer can easily display and select different fields of data

deprecated. an HTML element or attribute that has been outdated by newer constructs

design and development cycle. the systematic process that incorporates planning, development, production, and evaluation of a software product from start to finish

digital. the representation of information in the language used by computers, as a series of 0s and 1s, or binary digits

discussion forum. an online platform to facilitate and manage online text discussions over a period of time among members of a group or class

distance learning. a term for all learning that takes place at locations remote from the point of instruction

distributed learning. a method of instructional delivery that includes a mix of web-based instruction, media delivery, and face-to-face classroom time

dithering. the process of juxtaposing pixels of two colors to create the illusion that a third color is present

Document Object Model (DOM). a programming interface that allows HTML pages and XML documents to be created and modified as if they were program objects; makes the elements of those documents available to a program as data structures, and supplies methods that may be invoked to perform common operations on the document's structure and data; both platform- and language-neutral; a W3C standard

download/upload. transferring files between computers or other devices

dpi (dots per inch). the number of dots that can be placed horizontally and vertically; also known as printer resolution

dynamic HTML (dHTML). marketing term applied to a mixture of standards including HTML, style sheets, the Document Object Model (DOM1), and scripting but not defined by W3C specification

element. the basic structural unit of an HTML document, indicated by start and stop tags, arranged hierarchically to define the overall document structure; can be empty; those with content also often called containers

evaluation. the process of judging the effectiveness and worth of educational programs and products

file format. a particular way to encode information for storage in a computer file

file sharing. refers to the sharing of computer data or space on a network

Flash. an animation authoring system by Adobe

flowchart. a visual representation of the sequence of the content of a web-instruction site

font. a complete set of characters in a particular style and size (e.g., twelve-point Times New Roman)

formative evaluation. an evaluation process that takes place during the development or implementation of a project

freeware. software that is free to use indefinitely

GIF (Graphics Interchange Format). a compression scheme that keeps graphics file size at a minimum with no loss of data

graphics. anything visually displayed on a computer that is not text

hard disk. a storage device that holds large amounts of data

highlighting. various methods used to make critical information prominent on a web page to users

HTML (Hypertext Markup Language). coding used to create hypertext documents, primarily for use on the Web

hybrid learning. See distributed learning

hyperlink. an image or portion of text on a web page linked to another place on the same or a different page, either on the same or on another site

icon. a graphical representation of a concept, in Internet terms the small images on a web interface that, when clicked, perform a function

image map. an image containing one or more regions (hot spots) with assigned hyperlinks to other locations

image optimization. techniques used to reduce the file size of images to enable faster download time

image slicing. the cutting of a large image into several smaller segments for efficiency in online display

information literacy. the ability to locate, evaluate, and use information effectively

instant messaging (IM). a combination of e-mail and chat room in which a user corresponds with others online by clicking on a name or names in a list and typing a message, which pops up in a window on the recipient's screen; others can join the conversation, much like a telephone conference call

instructional design. systematic process of translating general principles of learning and instruction into plans for instructional materials and learning

intellectual property. general term for intangible property rights that are a result of intellectual effort

interactivity. a dialogue between a human being and a computer

Internet. a global network of networks connecting millions of computers

interpreted language. a script language that consists of a sequence of instructions that another program carries out rather than the computer processor

iterative. a repetitive procedure that makes incremental corrections and changes in response to results of formative evaluation processes

JavaScript. a cross-platform scripting language used to integrate interactive actions on a web page or site

JPEG (Joint Photographic Experts Group). an image format to compress the size of realistic images such as photographs

learning management system (LMS). See course management system

learning object. any digital resource that can be reused to support learning

learning style. an individual's preferred manner(s) in which to think, process information, and demonstrate learning

library instruction. instruction designed to teach library users how to use and locate library resources more efficiently

lossy compression. a method in which compressing a file and then decompressing it retrieves a file that may be different from the original but close enough to be useful; used frequently on the Internet and especially in streaming media and telephony applications

markup language. a system (e.g., HTML, XML) for marking or tagging a document that indicates its logical structure (e.g., paragraphs) and gives instructions for its layout on the page for electronic transmission and display

mashup. digital media that comprises pieces drawn from preexisting sources to create a new derivative work or in web development, an application that combines data or functionality from multiple sources to create a new service

media. the physical material on which information is recorded and stored

microblogging. a type of blogging in which posts are limited in length and users share short status updates among other users

mock-up. a preliminary drawing or model providing a visual impression of a proposed website

modem (modulator-demodulator). a device or program that enables a computer to transmit data over analog telephone lines

monitor. the part of a computer that contains the screen where messages to and from the central processing unit (CPU) are displayed

MPEG (Moving Picture Experts Group). a standard for a digital video and audio compression

multimedia. the combination of text, still graphics, animation, audio, and video in a single technology such as a computer

navigation. the means by which a user can negotiate the content of a page or site

needs analysis. data collection and analysis to document the purpose and need for a given project

network interface card (NIC). a board that provides network communication capabilities to and from a computer

object. a self-contained bundle of data and code

object-oriented programming. programming that features self-sufficient modules containing all the information needed to manipulate a given data structure

open source. any software whose code is available for users to use and modify freely

optimization. the process used to minimize the size of web page or website code or graphics to maximize speed of download to the user

pedagogy. the art of teaching

peripheral. any hardware device connected to a computer, such as monitor, keyboard, printer, scanner, mouse, and the like

Perl (Practical Extraction and Report Language). the programming language most frequently used for writing CGI scripts

phishing. term coined by hackers who imitate legitimate companies in e-mails to entice people to share passwords or credit card numbers

PHP (PHP Hypertext Processor). an interpreted scripting language similar to JavaScript

plug-in. programs installed separately but run as part of a browser to allow a user to view or hear specific multimedia

PNG (Portable Network Graphics). an image compression designed to succeed GIF

podcast. a series of digital media files (either audio or video) that are released episodically and downloaded through web syndication

protocol. any set of standardized rules for exchanging information among computers, with different protocols used for different kinds of communication

prototyping. a process in which versions of an interface are created to aid in designing the final product

QTVR (QuickTime Virtual Reality). a program used to create a walk-through 360-degree panoramic virtual scene

QuickTime. by Apple, a file format and software for multimedia development, storage, and feedback

random access memory (RAM). the area in the computer where data are stored during the short term for easy access

raster graphics. computer graphics in which the image is made up of tiny dots, called pixels; also called bitmapped graphics

remix culture. a society that encourages the creation of new derivative works by making changes or improvements to works held under copyright

resolution. the number of pixels per square inch on a computer-generated display

rich content. web-based multimedia materials that are dynamic, interactive, or (preferably) both

rollover image. a JavaScript technique that allows one image to replace another on a web page when a user's cursor passes over a page element

RSS (Rich Site Summary or Real Simple Syndication). an XML format for distributing content on the Web

SCORM (Shareable Content Object Reference Model). XML-based standard designed to ensure interoperability among systems and used to define and access information about learning objects so they can be easily shared between different systems

script language. one of several interpreted programming languages used to control the behavior of web pages in response to user activities

search engine. a program that searches documents for specified keywords and returns a list of the documents or web pages where the keywords were found

shareware. copyrighted software available for downloading and use on a free, limited-trial basis

site map. a visual model of a website's content that allows users to navigate through the site to find the information they are looking for

SMIL (Synchronized Multimedia Integration Language). markup language that allows for integrating a set of independent multimedia objects into a synchronized multimedia

software. a program, or set of instructions, that tells the computer what to do

social networking. Web services that focus on building communities of people who share interests and/or activities

spam. unwanted, unsolicited junk e-mail

spyware. a technology that surreptitiously collects information about a person without his or her knowledge

storyboard. a sketch of each screen of an instructional module to be designed and developed, including text, graphic information, design layout, color, sounds, and audience interaction

streaming media. audio or video sent in compressed form over the Internet and displayed to the viewer as it arrives rather than after it has finished downloading; plug-ins are required for playback and available for most browsers

summative evaluation. the evaluation that occurs at the end of a project and is used to determine the impact of the project

SVG (Scaleable Vector Graphics). a language for describing two-dimensional graphics in XML

synchronous. communication carried out with all parties present at the same time but not necessarily in the same physical location

syntax. the formal rules that determine how keywords or commands and their components must be combined in the source code of a computer program or in shell commands

tab. an image in a navigation system that mimics the tabs on file folders

3-D graphics. graphics that provide the perception of depth

typeface. a series of fonts

Unicode. character encoding standard developed to provide a universal way of encoding characters of any language, regardless of the computer system, or platform, being used

URL (uniform resource locator). unique address of a document or a resource on the Internet in the form protocol://server domain name/pathname

usability. the extent to which intended users can meet their goals using a website or system

usability testing. testing a website to see how easy it is for humans to interact with

user agent. any software that interprets HTML documents, including graphical browsers, text-only browsers, nonvisual browsers (e.g., audio, Braille), and other systems and programs

user-centered design. a design approach in which the emphasis is on the user

user interface. the point of communication and interaction between computer and human

user interface design. the overall process of designing how a user will be able to interact with a system or site

vector graphics. digital images created and defined by a sequence of commands or mathematical statements that place lines and shapes in a two-dimensional or three-dimensional space

VLE (Virtual Learning Environment). typically, an Internet based system designed to support teaching and learning in an educational setting, more commonly used in the United Kingdom

VRML (Virtual Reality Markup Language). a standard file format for representing 3-D interactive vector graphics, designed particularly with the World Wide Web in mind and superseded by X3D

W3C (World Wide Web Consortium). international industry consortium founded in October 1994 to develop common protocols that promote the evolution of the World Wide Web and ensure its interoperability

Web 2.0. refers to the second generation of web technology that facilitates user-created content, information sharing, and collaboration; the read-write Web

web-based instruction. teaching and learning supported by the attributes and resources of the Internet

web browser. software installed on a computer that lets the user view material designed for the Web

weblog (blog). a shared online journal where people can post entries on various subjects depending on the subject focus of the blog

WebQuest. inquiry-based activity that involves students in using web-based resources and tools to transform their learning into meaningful understandings and real-world projects

white space. the open areas on a web page between design elements

wi-fi. short for wireless fidelity, used commonly when referring to the IEEE 802.11 wireless networking specification

wiki. a cooperative website where anyone can edit anything on any page

World Wide Web. the collection of all the resources accessible on the Internet mainly by HTTP

WYSIWYG (what you see is what you get). visually based website editing software

X3D (Extensible 3-D Graphics). a screen-description language that describes the geometry and behavior of a 3-D scene or world; the successor to VRML

XML (Extensible Markup Language). a text-markup language for interchange of structured data; a subset of SGML

XSL (Extensible Stylesheet Language). a language for creating a style sheet that describes how data sent over the Web using XML are to be presented to the user

XSLT (XSL Transformation). a language for transforming XML documents into other XML documents

WORKS CITED

American Library Association. 2009. *The State of America's Libraries Report 2009.* www.ala.org/ala/newspresscenter/mediapresscenter/presskits/2009stateofamericaslibraries/2009statehome.cfm.

American Library Association Office for Research and Statistics. 2007. *Serving Non-English Speakers in U.S. Public Libraries: 2007 Analysis of Demographics, Services and Programs.* www.ala.org/ala/aboutala/offices/olos/nonenglishspeakers/docs/Linguistic_Isolation_Report-2007.pdf.

Association of College and Research Libraries. (approved 2003) *Characteristics of Programs of Information Literacy That Illustrate Best Practices: A Guideline.* American Library Association. www.ala.org/ala/mgrps/divs/acrl/standards/characteristics.cfm.

———. 2000. *Information Literacy Competency Standards for Higher Education.* Available from www.ala.org/ala/mgrps/divs/acrl/standards/informationliteracycompetency.cfm.

Association of College and Research Libraries Instruction Section Instructional Technologies Committee. *Tips for Developing Effective Web-Based Library Instruction.* www.ala.org/ala/mgrps/divs/acrl/about/sections/is/projpubs/classroomcontrolsys/tips.cfm.

Bannan-Ritland, Brenda. 2004. Web-Based Instruction. In *Education and Technology: An Encyclopedia,* edited by A. Kovalchick and K. Dawson, 638–643. Santa Barbara, CA: ABC-CLIO.

Bates, Tony, and Gary Poole. 2003. *Effective Teaching with Technology in Higher Education: Foundations for Success.* Jossey-Bass Higher and Adult Education Series. Hoboken, NJ: Jossey-Bass.

Beck, Kent, Mike Beedle, Arie van Bennekum, Alistair Cockburn, Ward Cunningham, Martin Fowler, James Grenning, et al. 2001. *Manifesto for Agile Software Development.* http://agilemanifesto.org/.

Beck, Robert J. 2008. Learning Objects. www4.uwm.edu/cie/learning_objects.cfm.

Bertot, John Carol, Charles Mcclure, Carla Wright, Elise Jensen, and Susan Thomas. 2008. *Public Libraries and the Internet 2008: Study Results and Findings.* www.ii.fsu.edu/projectFiles/plinternet/2008/Everything.pdf.

Bichelmeyer, Barbara. 2004. Rapid Prototyping. In *Education and Technology: An Encyclopedia,* edited by A. Kovalchick and K. Dawson. Santa Barbara, CA: ABC-CLIO.

Corbett, Peter. 2010. Facebook Demographics and Statistics Report 2010—145% Growth in 1 Year. IStrategyLabs.com. www.istrategylabs.com/2010/01/facebook-demographics-and-statistics-report-2010-145-growth-in-1-year/.

DeBell, Matthew, and Chris Chapman. 2006. *Computer and Internet Use by Students in 2003: Statistical Analysis Report.* National Center for Education Statistics, nces.ed.gov/pubs2006/2006065.pdf.

Dick, Walter, and Lou Carey. 2009. *The Systematic Design of Instruction.* 7th ed. Upper Saddle River, NJ: Merrill/Pearson.

Dodge, Bernie. 2007. "WebQuest Page at San Diego State University." www.webquest.org.

Driscoll, Margaret. 2002. *Web-Based Training: Creating E-Learning Experiences.* San Francisco: Jossey-Bass/Pfeiffer.

EDUCAUSE. 2009. 7 Things You Should Know About . . . Google Wave. net.educause.edu/ir/library/pdf/ELI7055.pdf.

Ford, Steve, David Wells, and Nancy Wells. 1997. *Web Programming Languages.* www.objs.com/survey/lang.htm.

Fox, Susannah, Kathryn Zickuhr, and Aaron Smith. 2009. *Twitter and Status Updating, Fall 2009.* Pew Internet and American Life Project, www.pewinternet.org/~/media/Files/Reports/2009/PIP_Twitter_Fall_2009_web.pdf.

Gardner, Howard. 1999. *Intelligence Reframed: Multiple Intelligences for the 21st Century.* New York: Basic Books.

Gartner Inc. 2009. *Hype Cycle for Cloud Computing, 2009.* www.gartner.com/DisplayDocument?doc_cd=169747.

Haverkamp, Laura J., and Kelly Coffey. 1999. *Instruction Issues in Special Libraries.* www.libsci.sc.edu/bob/class/clis724/SpecialLibrariesHandbook/instruction.htm.

Kalbach, James. 2007. *Designing Web Navigation.* Beijing: Sebastopol.

Khan, Badrul H. 1997. *Web-Based Instruction.* Englewood Cliffs, NJ: Educational Technology Publications.

King, Andrew B. 2008. *Website Optimization.* Farnham, U.K.: O'Reilly.

Kolb, David A. 1984. *Experiential Learning: Experience as the Source of Learning and Development.* Englewood Cliffs, NJ: Prentice-Hall.

Loring, Linda. 2002. Six Steps to Preparing Instruction for a Worldwide Audience. *Journal of Interactive Instruction Development* 14 (3): 24–29.

Lynch, Patrick J., and Sarah Horton. 2008. *Web Style Guide: Basic Design Principles for Creating Web Sites.* 3rd ed. New Haven, CT: Yale University Press.

Mabrito, Mark, and Rebecca Medley. 2008. Why Professor Johnny Can't Read: Understanding the Net Generation's Texts. *Innovate: Journal of Online Education* (6), innovateonline.info/pdf/vol4_issue6/

Why_Professor_Johnny_Can't_Read-_Understanding_the_Net_
Generation's_Texts.pdf.

Mayer, Richard E. 2009. *Multimedia Learning.* 2nd ed. New York:
Cambridge University Press.

Mitchell, Erik T., and Susan Sharpless Smith. 2009. Bringing Information
Literacy into the Social Sphere: A Case Study Using Social
Software to Teach Information Literacy at WFU. *Journal of Web
Librarianship* 3 (3): 183–197.

Morkes, John, and Jakob Nielsen. 1997. *Concise, SCANNABLE, and
Objective: How to Write for the Web.* www.useit.com/papers/
webwriting/writing.html.

Morrison, Gary R., Steven M. Ross, and Jerrold E. Kemp. 2004. *Designing
Effective Instruction.* 4th ed. Hoboken, NJ: John Wiley and Sons.

Nielsen, Jakob. 2000. *Designing Web Usability.* Indianapolis, IN: New
Riders.

———. 2004. *Guidelines for Visualizing Links.* www.useit.com/
alertbox/20040510.html.

———. 2000. *Why You Only Need to Test with 5 Users.* www.useit.com/
alertbox/20000319.html.

Nielsen, Jakob, and Rolf Molich. 1990. "Heuristic Evaluation of User
Interfaces." Paper presented at SIGCHI conference on human
factors in computing systems: Empowering people, Seattle, WA.

Oblinger, Diana G., Carole A. Barone, and Brian L. Hawkins. 2001.
Distributed Education and Its Challenges: An Overview. Washington,
DC: American Council on Education. www.acenet.edu/bookstore/
pdf/distributed-learning/distributed-learning-01.pdf.

Palloff, Rena M., and Keith Pratt. 2009. Assessment, Academic Integrity,
and Community Online. In *Encyclopedia of Distance Learning,*
edited by P. Rogers, G. Berg, J. Boettcher, C. Howard, L. Justice, and
K. Schenk, 108–114. Hershey, PA: Information Science Reference.

Pew Internet. 2009. *Generational Difference in Online Activities.* www
.pewinternet.org/Infographics/Generational-differences-in-online
-activities.aspx.

Pew Internet and American Life Project. 2009. Trend Data. www
.pewinternet.org/Trend-Data/Online-Activites-Total.aspx (*sic*
"Activites").

Rader, Hannelore B. 2002. Information Literacy 1973–2002: A Selected
Literature Review. *Library Trends* 51 (2): 242–259.

Reeves, Thomas. 2000. Alternative Assessment Approaches for
Online Learning Environments in Higher Education. *Journal of
Educational Computing Research* 23 (1): 101–111.

Reeves, Tom, and Patricia Reeves. 1997. Effective Dimensions on
Interactive Learning on the World Wide Web. In *Web-Based
Instruction,* edited by B. H. Khan, 59–66. Englewood Cliffs, NJ:
Educational Technology Publications.

Ritchie, Donn C., and Bob Hoffman. 1997. Incorporating Instructional
Design Principles with the World Wide Web. In *Web-Based
Instruction,* edited by B. H. Khan, 135–148. Englewood Cliffs, NJ:
Educational Technology Publications.

Russell, Thomas L. 1999. *The No Significant Difference Phenomenon: As
Reported in 355 Research Reports, Summaries and Papers.* Raleigh:
North Carolina State University.

Shapiro, Jeremy J., and Shelley K. Hughes. 1996. Information as a
Liberal Art: Enlightenment Proposals for a New Curriculum.
Educom Review (2), http://net.educause.edu/apps/er/review/
reviewArticles/31231.html.

Shea, Dave. 2004. *CSS Sprites: Image Slicing's Kiss of Death. A List
Apart: For People Who Make Websites.* www.alistapart.com/
articles/sprites/.

Shneiderman, Ben, Catherine Plaisant, Maxine Cohen, and Steven
Jacobs. 2010. *Designing the User Interface: Strategies for Effective
Human-Computer Interaction.* 5th ed. Boston: Addison-Wesley.

Siemens, George, and Peter Tittenberger. 2009. *Handbook of Emerging Technologies for Learning.* ltc.umanitoba.ca/wikis/etl/index.php/ Handbook_of_Emerging_Technologies_for_Learning.

Smith, Shannon S., Gail Salaway, and Judith Borreson Caruso. 2009. The ECAR Study of Undergraduate Students and Information Technology, 2009. *Research Study,* Vol. 6, www.educause.edu/ ecar/.

Smith, Susan Sharpless, Erik Mitchell, and Carolina Numbers. 2007. Building Library 2.0 into Information Literacy: A Case Study. In *Library 2.0 Initiatives in Academic Libraries,* edited by L. B. Cohen, 114–132. Chicago: Association of College and Research Libraries.

Strod, Eran. 2009. *Dynamic Programming Languages on the Rise in Open Source.* devX.com, www.devx.com/opensource/Article/43102.

Wiley, David A. 2000. Connecting Learning Objects to Instructional Design Theory: A Definition, a Metaphor, and a Taxonomy. In *Instructional Use of Learning Objects: Online Version,* edited by D. A. Wiley. http://reusability.org/read/chapters/wiley.doc.

W3Schools. 2010. *Browser Display Statistics.* www.w3schools.com/ browsers/browsers_display.asp.

Zvacek, Susan M. 2004. Distance Education. In *Education and Technology: An Encyclopedia,* edited by A. Kovalchick and K. Dawson, 219–230. Santa Barbara, CA: ABC-CLIO.

INDEX

You may also be interested in

Reflective Teaching, Effective Learning: Instructional Literacy for Library Educators: This much-needed book introduces accessible concepts in instructional design (ID) and instructional technology (IT) that will help librarians at any level of experience.

Teaching Information Literacy: 50 Standards-Based Exercises for College Students, Second Edition: These 50 lessons can be used as a full semester course or as a single focused seminar or workshop, and show how to engage with electronic and print information resources alike.

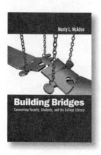

Building Bridges: Connecting Faculty, Students, and the College Library: Packed with useful tips and techniques, this handy guide offers advice on working with both students and instructors to develop successful assignments that integrate your library's resources.

No Shelf Required: E-Books in Libraries: Editor Sue Polanka brings together a variety of professionals to share their expertise about e-books with librarians and publishers.

Order today at www.alastore.ala.org or 866-746-7252!